FREER

A Legacy of Art

With appreciation for your support
as a Contributing Member of the
Smithsonian National Associate Program

Thomas Lawton ■ Linda Merrill

FREER
A Legacy of Art

Freer Gallery of Art, Smithsonian Institution

in association with
Harry N. Abrams, Inc., Publishers

Published in 1993 by the Freer Gallery of Art,
Smithsonian Institution, Washington, D.C.,
and Harry N. Abrams, Incorporated, New
York, a Times Mirror Company. No part of
the contents of this book may be reproduced
without the written permission of the
publishers.

Edited by Jane McAllister
Designed by Carol Beehler
Typset in Monotype Bembo
by William Halfpap using Apple Macintosh
Printed and bound in Japan

Cover: Detail, Maruyama Ōkyo (1733–1795),
Geese Flying over a Beach, Japan, Edo period.
Four-fold screen; ink on paper (154.8 x 349.6
cm). Freer Gallery of Art, 98.143. For full
image, see figure 68.

Frontispiece: Charles Lang Freer, 1909.
Photograph by Alvin Langdon Coburn
(1882–1966). Charles Lang Freer Papers of the
Freer Gallery of Art and Arthur M. Sackler
Gallery Archives.

Endleaves: Freer Gallery of Art courtyard,
1992.

Library of Congress Cataloguing-in-
Publication Data
Lawton, Thomas, 1931–
Freer : a legacy of art / Thomas Lawton,
Linda Merrill.
p.   cm.
Includes bibliographical references (p.   ) and
index.
ISBN 0-8109-3315-2 (cloth : alk. paper)
1. Freer, Charles Lang, 1854–1919.
2. Art patrons—United States—Biography.
3. Freer Gallery of Art.
I. Merrill, Linda, 1959– .
II. Title.   N857.5.L39 1993   92–19399
709'.2—dc20   CIP

Photographic credits
Unless indicated below, all vintage
photographs and photographs of works of art
are from the Freer Gallery. The authors wish
to thank the museums, archives, libraries, and
private collectors who supplied photographs
and/or granted permission for works in their
collections to be reproduced. Every effort has
been made to seek permission for illustrations
taken from published sources in copyright.

The following photographs are reproduced
by permission: figs. 6 and 11, Copyright ©
1991 The Detroit Institute of Arts, Michigan;
fig. 7, Grand Rapids Public Library,
Michigan; fig. 10, Burton Historical
Collection, Detroit Public Library, Michigan;
fig. 14, The Detroit Club, Michigan; fig. 32,
Hunterian Art Gallery, University of Glasgow,
Scotland; fig. 44, Aperture, New York; fig.

61, Courtesy of Library of Congress,
Washington, D.C.; fig. 67, Courtesy of
Peabody Museum of Salem, Massachusetts;
fig. 83, The Metropolitan Museum of Art,
New York; fig. 97, University of Wisconsin
Press, Madison; fig. 99, Courtesy of
Massachusetts Historical Society, Boston; fig.
105, National Museum of American Art,
Smithsonian Institution, Washington, D.C.;
fig. 138, George Eastman House,
International Museum of Photography,
Rochester, New York, reprinted with the
permission of Joanna T. Steichen; fig. 159,
Wenwu Publishing Company, Beijing; and
Notes, p. 264, Palace Museum, Beijing.

Photographs provided by the Freer Gallery
were taken by John Tsantes and Jeffrey
Crespi. Other photographers not cited in the
captions are John Henderson Studios, Detroit,
fig. 14; S. Matsubara, fig. 45; P. Dittrich, fig.
49; M. Suzuki, fig. 101; Richard Cheek,
Belmont, Massachusetts, fig. 174; and
National Photo, fig. 184.

Contents

Foreword

THIS VOLUME CELEBRATES the reopening of the Freer Gallery of Art after a period of extensive renovation. Over the past several years, the museum's traditional tranquility has been disturbed by the noise and confusion of construction. The interior courtyard was entirely removed, leaving a gaping hole at the center of the building as new space for collection storage was carved out underneath; the Peacock Room, James McNeill Whistler's legendary dining-room decoration, was partially dismantled while being thoroughly restored; and the collections, some twenty-seven thousand works of Asian and American art, were put away in temporary quarters to await reinstallation in refurbished exhibition galleries.

In the course of the construction project, the museum staff was confronted with the literal foundations of the building. Simultaneously, the historical research that guided the renovations revealed the philosophical underpinnings that support the museum. The founder, an industrialist from Detroit named Charles Lang Freer, apparently intended his Gallery to last forever. His magnanimous gift to the nation was presented with precise specifications to ensure that his vision would prevail. A man devoted to every aspect of the museum that would bear his name, Charles Freer is the focus of this book, which is the first publication to examine closely his philosophy of art and the growth of his extraordinary collections.

Freer assembled his holdings of Asian and contemporary American art around the turn of the century. He began conventionally, as a bachelor buying European etchings, but became an internationally recognized figure in the world of art. By establishing a museum in Washington, he hoped to provide a congenial environment in which visitors to the capital could view and compare the objects in his collection. As though to signify his status as a collector working in the tradition of the Medici, he commissioned the architect Charles A. Platt to design the museum after the style of the Italian Renaissance: his ambition, he said, was "to unite modern work with masterpieces of certain periods of high civilization harmonious in spiritual suggestion." The resulting Freer Gallery on the National Mall in Washington was the first museum building in the Smithsonian Institution devoted exclusively to the fine arts.

Freer perceived no incongruity in bringing together, in an Italianate building, pieces of Japanese pottery, sculptures from Buddhist caves in China, and nineteenth-century American paintings: he believed they were harmonious in aesthetic quality. Fascinated by works of diverse origin that were nonetheless related in color or surface texture, Freer detected visual similarities between some Japanese ceramics, for instance, and certain American seascape paintings. His collections were to be placed in aesthetically pleasing arrangements and thoughtful juxtapositions, always framed and unified by architecture of European character, because Freer perceived in these varied traditions the results of a common artistic impulse.

The scholar Ernest Fenollosa, Freer's trusted friend and adviser, expressed the same attitude in his *Epochs of Chinese and Japanese Art,* published in 1913: "We are approaching the time when the art work of all the world of man may be looked upon as one, as infinite variations in a single kind of mental and social effort." In an interview printed that year in the *New York Sun,* Freer stated that "all art worthy of consideration is universal." The ecumenical approach to art was not confined to orientalists alone. In the prospectus for *The Blue Rider Almanac,* the journal of the artistic movement that flourished in Germany around the same time, the painter Franz Marc wrote, "Out of an awareness of this secret connection of all new artistic production, we developed the idea of the Blaue Reiter. . . . It reveals subtle connections with Gothic and primitive art, with Africa and the vast Orient." Cross-cultural contact extended to contemporary music as well: English composer Gustav Holst used his own translations from Sanskrit in "Choral Hymns from the Rig Veda" (1908–12), and the American composer Ernest Bloch said he was inspired by oriental themes to write his Suite for Viola and Piano (1919). As it happened, that piece would be performed in the auditorium of the Freer Gallery of Art during its inaugural year.

Freer's wish to reveal commonalities across cultures continues to inform the presentation of works of art in the Gallery. In its exhibition and acquisition programs, the museum observes the founder's mandate to promote "high ideals of beauty." Yet as an institution, the Freer Gallery is by no means the same as it was when it opened seventy years ago. Freer's bequest comprised some nine thousand objects—works of art Freer himself had collected, which displayed qualities consistent with his own aesthetic taste. That assemblage was never meant to be a comprehensive survey of artistic traditions, and many of the collections now recognized as among the greatest strengths of the Freer Gallery's holdings—Chinese porcelain, for example—were largely absent from the original gift. Although Freer maintained that his American collection was incapable of being further improved, he came to believe that the other collections might be strengthened by future additions. Shortly before his death, therefore, he added a codicil to his will allowing the acquisition of "important art objects of a high standard of aesthetic quality and excellence, related to the collection as it now exists." Consequently, through gifts and museum purchases, the Freer Gallery holdings have nearly tripled in size and expanded into areas that Freer himself had not explored.

The founder could not have foreseen such tremendous growth, nor could he have imagined the advances in technical research that would radically improve our understanding of works of art. These very changes necessitated the recent renovation, which created a new two-story structure below the original building for the storage and study of the vastly expanded collections, and a new facility for the conservation and technical examination of works of art. The museum's Department of Conservation and Scientific Research now cooperates with several international organizations in the technical research and conservation treatment of works of Asian art.

Research in the history of art was a vitally important element of Freer's conception of the museum, which would be designed "with special regard for the convenience of students and others desirous of an opportunity for uninterrupted study of the objects in the collection." He was himself largely self-taught, having pursued an education in art through the books he began collecting in the early 1880s. Freer eventually obtained virtually every work on Asian art published in English during his lifetime. He also acquired all existing books on Whistler and the other American artists represented in his collection, with many of the editions inscribed by the authors; and he retained most of his exhibition and sales catalogues, some of which have his own comments and reflections noted in the margins. As part of his bequest, Freer presented his art books to the nation to form the nucleus of the Freer Gallery's research library. Through an active acquisition program, the library has grown to more than fifty thousand volumes and four hundred current periodical titles, making it one of this country's finest libraries specializing in Asian art and an invaluable resource, as well, for students of turn-of-the-century American painting.

Trained as a businessman to maintain careful records, Freer kept copies of correspondence and other materials relevant to his art holdings. These papers,

Architectural rendering of the refurbished Freer Gallery of Art by Michael Lawrence, 1990. Skylights provide natural light to the galleries, which surround the restored central courtyard. Two lower levels house new areas for research, art storage, and expanded conservation facilities. A stairwell and underground gallery, shown at the right of the drawing, connect the Freer Gallery to the Arthur M. Sackler Gallery. Freer Gallery of Art Building Records.

which were bequeathed with his art library, are filled with information that can be used to document the objects in the collection. They include letters to and from dealers and collectors of Asian and American art and many of Freer's artist friends; vouchers recording the particulars of his purchases; inventories detailing the contents of his collection at several stages of development; press-cutting books containing newspaper articles about the contemporary art world and Freer's unprecedented gift to the nation; and a remarkable group of vintage photographs that includes portraits of Freer by Edward Steichen and Alvin Langdon Coburn as well as important images by the major photographers working in Asia. Indeed, this publication is largely based on the rich resources now contained in the Freer Gallery of Art and Arthur M. Sackler Gallery Archives, which provide researchers an unparalleled opportunity for following the formation of a collection.

The valuable research materials at the Freer Gallery have inspired countless scholarly studies of works in the collection, many of which are listed in the Selected Bibliography in this volume. Publication is essential to the dissemination of information about the collections, since Freer Gallery objects may never be exhibited outside the museum. This restriction was imposed by the founder, who wanted his collections to be always available to museum visitors and who feared the damage that travel might entail. Moreover, because Freer perceived his holdings as a harmonious composition that might be disturbed by the integration of other works, he stipulated that objects from the Freer collection were the only works that could be shown in the building. Perhaps the most symbolic change that has come about as a result of the recent renovation, therefore, is the connection of the Freer Gallery of Art with the Arthur M. Sackler Gallery, which opened in 1987, by an underground exhibition hall. Together, the Galleries form the national museums of Asian art at the Smithsonian Institution. Although works from the Freer collection may never be shown in Sackler exhibition galleries, objects from the two museums can now be displayed in close proximity, allowing further comparisons of the sort that Freer himself enjoyed.

Charles Freer held the belief that a masterpiece required neither explanation nor cultural context to communicate its message: its importance lay in its aesthetic integrity, not in the evidence it might incidentally provide about religious, social, political, or economic issues. Fenollosa articulated Freer's attitude with his definition of art as a "glimpse of ultimate truth embodied in an earthly symbol." Through careful comparisons, possible only through quiet contemplation, the student of art might catch sight of that ultimate truth, which Freer believed would elevate the human spirit. It is my hope that this volume will encourage a greater appreciation of Freer's incomparable legacy of art. ■

Acknowledgments

THE STORY OF Charles Lang Freer, a self-made millionaire who became an internationally recognized connoisseur of Asian and American art, could fill several volumes and occupy the lives of many historians. Freer's building of his collection over four decades was a process that involved countless contemporary artists, art historians, art dealers, and art collectors around the world. For this general introduction to Freer's life as a collector we necessarily left out as much as we included, and every omission was made with regret. We hope, however, that this study of a few of Freer's friends, advisers, acquisitions, and adventures will stimulate further scholarship and encourage a broader appreciation of the aesthetic philosophy that underlies the Freer Gallery of Art.

Several scholars have preceded us on this path, and we gratefully acknowledge their contributions to our understanding of Freer and his collection. Helen Nebeker Tomlinson's imposing dissertation, "Charles Lang Freer: Pioneer Collector of Oriental Art," has proved an invaluable source of information, as have other essays on aspects of Freer's collecting by Thomas Brunk, Nichols Clark, David Curry, Susan Hobbs, and Kathleen Pyne. Dr. Hobbs also helped us clear up confusion about Freer's birthdate. We have benefited, as well, from the scholarship of previous and present Freer Gallery directors and curators, whose extensive research on the Freer collections is reflected in the bibliography.

Thomas Lawton is indebted to Professor Yamaguchi Seiichi of Saitama University, whose study of the relationship between Ernest Fenollosa and Freer assisted his research; to Professor Murakata Akiko, whose pioneering article on Matsuki Bunkyō remains the most detailed analysis of a remarkable career; and to Glenn Lowry, Susan Nemazee, and Jessica Hallett, who provided unlimited access to their manuscript, "Biographical Dictionary of Late Nineteenth- and Early Twentieth-Century Collectors of Islamic Art in Paris." Hin-cheung Lovell read an early version of the Asian chapters and offered suggestions that substantially improved the clarity and readability of every sentence.

Linda Merrill is grateful to the friends and colleagues who lent their expertise to reading portions of the manuscript, particularly Keith N. Morgan, who raised challenging questions about Charles Platt and the architecture of the Freer Gallery; Nigel Thorp, who took particular interest in Freer's friendship with James McNeill Whistler; Margaret Edson, who gave valued advice on matters of tone and interpretation; and Lillian B. Miller, who greatly improved several chapters with her insightful comments and unerring editorial judgment.

A number of individuals helped us obtain photographs to reproduce as illustrations. We thank especially Chris Steele of the Massachusetts Historical Society; Kathy Flynn of the Peabody Museum of Salem, Massachusetts; Mark E. Grzybowski of the Detroit Club; and Sue Kohler of the Commission of Fine Arts in Washington, D.C. We are grateful to the Phillips Library of the Peabody Museum for permission to quote a passage from Fenollosa's letter to Edward Sylvester Morse of 27 September 1884, and to the University of Glasgow, Scotland, for permission to quote from Whistler's correspondence.

We would like to express our gratitude to the many Freer Gallery staff members who eased the process of preparing the text for publication. Foremost among them is Colleen Hennessey, who gave us unstinting assistance with the rich documentation housed in the Freer archives, responded promptly to our queries, helped eliminate our quandaries, and listened sympathetically as we formulated ideas about Freer and his contemporaries. In the library, Lily Kecskes, Kathryn Phillips, and Reiko Yoshimura handled a barrage of requests for reference materials with courtesy and goodwill. John Tsantes and Jeffrey Crespi applied their considerable talents to producing the beautiful photographs that appear in these pages.

Finally, we thank the museum's publications department for seeing this book through production with its customary skill and efficiency. Karen Sagstetter, who recognized the need for a general publication on Charles Freer and his collections, proposed the project to Margaret Kaplan at Harry N. Abrams, Inc., who responded with insight and enthusiasm; Mary Cleary graciously handled a number of crucial editorial details; Jane McAllister showed rare dedication in bringing coherence to a manuscript written by two authors; and Carol Beehler captured with her elegant design Freer's high ideals of beauty. ∎

Note to the Reader
Unless otherwise indicated, all works illustrated are in the collection of the Freer Gallery of Art. Dimensions of objects are given in centimeters, with height preceding width. Vintage photographs and primary source materials are in the Charles Lang Freer Papers, Freer Gallery of Art and Arthur M. Sackler Gallery Archives, unless otherwise indicated.
Japanese and Chinese personal names appear in traditional style, with family names preceding given names. The pinyin style is used for Chinese romanization; where Wade-Giles is quoted from original sources, pinyin follows in brackets. In Japanese transliterations, macrons appear over the long vowel sounds, except in well-known place-names.

CHAPTER ONE

LINDA MERRILL

Acquired Taste

CHARLES LANG FREER, who traveled to regions of the world that few of his contemporaries could even have imagined, liked no place so well as his own home in Detroit (fig. 2). The house was built of limestone from the quarries of Ulster County, New York, near the town of Freer's birth; dignified but unpretentious, it embodied its resident's disposition. Over the years luxuriant ampelopsis vines enveloped the purplish stone and most of the cypress shingles facing the upper story, but balconies and bay windows opened the house to gardens riotous with roses and fragrant with honeysuckle. A gracious retreat from the clamor of the Gilded Age, Freer's residence in Detroit was an appropriate setting for the appreciation of art, a "dream of Beauty," as one friend would recall, "inside and out."[1]

Freer never dwelt on the details of his past, yet he made no effort to conceal the humbleness of his origins. He was born in 1854, the third of six children, in Kingston, New York, a small town situated between the Hudson River and the Catskill Mountains. Although he took little notice of its depiction in paintings by a school of contemporary American artists, the Hudson River landscape would be an enduring source of solace for Freer. His mother died when he was fourteen years old, and because his father proved a poor provider for the family, the boy left school and went to work in a local cement factory. Later, as a clerk in the Kingston general store, his diligence attracted the attention of Frank J. Hecker, a Civil War veteran in charge of a local railroad that ran from the river across the Catskills. Freer joined Hecker's company and soon became its accountant and paymaster. In 1876, when Hecker moved to Indiana to supervise a new amalgamation of midwestern lines called the Detroit and Eel River and Illinois Railroad, Freer followed. The move was to mark the beginning of a profitable business partnership and an enduring friendship (fig. 3). Hecker and Freer, motivated by the prospect of building freight cars in the age of railway expansion, went together to Detroit in 1880 and settled there for the rest of their lives.

Unfortunately as yet the many consider art a luxury, that is, they are blind to the fact that in its highest form it is really a necessity.

Freer to Bradley Redfield, 2 October 1893

Fig. 1. Abbott Handerson Thayer (1849–1921). *A Virgin,* 1892–93. Oil on canvas (229.7 x 182.5), 93.11.

Fig. 2. Charles Lang Freer's house at 33 Ferry Avenue, later 71 East Ferry Avenue, Detroit, ca. 1910. Built 1890–91. Wilson Eyre (1858–1944), architect.

Fig. 3. Frank J. Hecker and Freer, ca. 1900. Photograph by Sarony, New York.

As Hecker's protégé, Freer participated in the organization of the Peninsular Car Works, which manufactured rolling stock at a factory near the Detroit River. He was appointed treasurer of the company but rose quickly to the position of vice president. In 1884 the enterprise that had become the Peninsular Car Company constructed an efficient new plant on Ferry Avenue and purchased two regional railroads; in 1892, by merging with the competition, it monopolized the industry in Detroit and became the Michigan-Peninsular Car Company. Financial panic the following year ushered in what was the nation's worst depression to date; nearly two hundred railroads went down in failure, and the production of cars in Detroit came to a halt. The company managed to survive, however, and by the close of the decade the city was flourishing again, with a population that had nearly doubled. In the salubrious climate of economic revival, Freer orchestrated the consolidation of thirteen car-building companies, including his own, to create the American Car and Foundry Company.[2] After that awesome managerial feat in the spring of 1899, he retired from active business at the age of forty-five.

Envisioning a life remote from railroads and cold weather, Freer bought a vacation villa on the island of Capri to share with his friend Thomas S. Jerome (fig. 4) and left his fortune to accumulate through investment. According to the author and social activist Agnes E. Meyer, who was the recipient of many confidences, Freer's decision to retire had been an adjustment to the physical limitations that were making life in Detroit increasingly difficult.[3] Throughout the remaining twenty years of his life, Freer would endure spells of debilitating illness and eventually succumb to the devastating effects of an inherited disease, yet he would also enjoy long stretches of robust health and show astonishing physical strength and stamina on his travels around the world. In fact, Freer felt far too energetic to remain on holiday for more than a few weeks at a time. Having recovered in Capri from his initial exhaustion, he turned his retirement into a career in connoisseurship. Freer realized in retrospect that his experience in business had taught him self-discipline and "the value of time and how to use it," lessons he employed to great advantage in the study of art.[4] To his friend Charles J. Morse, Freer wrote of the advantages of "active idleness," maintaining that the "intellectual life" was the only one worth living.[5]

An American enthusiasm for art had been gathering momentum ever since the Centennial Exposition had issued in the Aesthetic movement, and it was further encouraged by the prosperity of the 1880s. Detroit was one of the cities on the itinerary of Oscar Wilde, the avatar of English aestheticism, who traveled throughout the United States in 1882 lecturing on tenets of taste. Between engagements in Fort Wayne and Cleveland, Wilde addressed an audience of prospective aesthetes in the Detroit Music Hall; he spoke on the decorative arts, describing in some detail the recent advance of English craftsmanship and prescribing practical applications for aesthetic theory.[6] James McNeill Whistler would later assert that the author had never possessed an original idea; and, indeed, many of the topics Wilde popularized in America had been taken directly from Whistler, whose own ded-

Fig. 4. Thomas S. Jerome, left, and Freer, right, in the garden of the Villa Castello, Capri, 1901.

Fig. 5. Charles L. Freer, 1880s. Photograph by C. M. Hayes, Detroit.

ication to art for art's sake would profoundly affect the collecting philosophy of Charles Freer.

In 1888 the city of Detroit manifested its interest in aestheticism with the establishment of an art museum. Its inaugural exhibition featured a selection of etchings from Freer's collection.[7] In the early years of the decade, when he still lived in rented rooms in a small house on Alfred Street, Freer had used his earnings to build a library; one of the books that he bought, *The Print Collector: An Introduction to the Knowledge Necessary for Forming a Collection of Ancient Prints* by Joseph Maberly, seems to have made a lasting impression. The opening chapter, "Of Collecting in General, and of Print-collecting in Particular," asserts that prints, relative to other categories of art, are inexpensive, portable, and easy to preserve. The argument, apparently, was persuasive. "All persons are pleased with prints," Maberly maintained,

They are not altogether caviare to the multitude; less initiation is necessary for the appreciation of their excellences. To duly admire and enjoy a fine picture, especially of any of the Italian schools, a regular professional education is almost essential. To enjoy a gallery of painting, or statuary, we must walk about it, and we must have daylight; but a portfolio of prints may be laid on the table, and give variety to the amusement of a winter's night, when variety of occupation is most in requisition, and all the circle, as they sit, may participate in the enjoyment.[8]

To a man with a modest income and a seventh-grade education venturing for the first time into the world of art, prints must have appeared the ideal objects to collect.

The birth of Freer's interest in etchings coincided with a European resurgence in printmaking. One of the most eloquent exponents of the etching revival was Francis Seymour Haden, an English physician and printmaker who was also the estranged brother-in-law of Whistler. Like Wilde, Haden lectured in Detroit in 1882, on a tour organized by the New York print dealer Frederick Keppel, who accurately predicted that Haden's presentation would stimulate the sale of his stock. Keppel himself went to Detroit the following year, taking a selection of etchings from which Freer made his first purchases. The prints were primarily by artists who had been extolled in *The Print Collector*—recognized Old Masters such as Rembrandt and Dürer, and lesser-known, modern printmakers such as Henri Fantin-Latour, Charles Jacque, and Joseph Pennell.

For several years Freer put his trust in dealers such as Keppel, who were happy to oblige with prints and information. While in New York on business, Freer would often go shopping for art; within just a few years, he had amassed an impressive collection that was especially distinguished in prints by modern etchers. From the start Freer was inclined to limit his holdings to the work of a few artists. He took an early, special interest in the Dutch etcher Carel Nicolaas Storm van 's Gravesande, whose works Keppel actively marketed in Detroit (fig. 6). Freer and Storm van 's Gravesande began a correspondence in which Freer requested the verification of signatures and asked questions about dates, states, and impressions. In this way he checked his own powers of discernment against the opinions of the artist himself, furthering his education in art and increasing his confidence as a collector. As a result, Freer assembled a focused group of works by an artist in whom he had made both a personal and a financial investment, setting a precedent for his future practice of acquisition.

One day in October 1887, when Freer was at Keppel's shop in Union Square buying etchings by Haden, Jacque, Auguste Delâtre, Johan Barthold Jongkind, and Félix

Fig. 6. Carel Nicolaas Storm van 's Gravesande (1841–1924). *On the Vecht,* ca. 1889. Charcoal and chalk on paper (33.2 x 47.4). Inscribed to Freer, lower left. The Detroit Institute of Arts, Michigan; Gift of Charles L. Freer (1905.396).

Bracquemond, he was introduced to Howard Mansfield, an attorney who owned an extensive collection of prints by Whistler. Only the previous year, Freer had purchased Frederick Wedmore's catalogue of Whistler etchings, yet he remained unimpressed with the artist's work and asked if he might see Mansfield's collection. According to Mansfield, Freer had said that he wanted to know "why anyone in the world should make any fuss over Whistler as an artist." On a momentous evening that winter in New York, Freer made his way through several of Mansfield's portfolios, which contained a total of some three hundred Whistler etchings. After studying only a few, he began pacing the floor and "uttering large adjectives." After viewing the entire collection Freer declared, "I have no words to express my admiration for the genius of this man."[9]

Even Storm van 's Gravesande recognized Whistler's extraordinary talent as an etcher and seems to have predicted the importance his work would assume in Freer's collection: having heard from Keppel about the Mansfield episode, he wrote Freer that his own etchings "could hardly stand comparison" with Whistler's.[10] Indeed, Whistler had already begun to supersede other contemporary artists in the collector's estimation. Freer would later write Mansfield that his "first sight of thoroughly fine impressions" of etchings by Whistler had marked a critical juncture in his own history. "My purchasing, I recall, began the day thereafter," he said, recollecting his acquisition of Whistler's Second Venice Set on 11 November, "and has continued ever since whenever opportunity has offered."[11]

Freer's quickly forged reputation as a print collector may have assisted his election to the Detroit Club, which had been founded in 1882 primarily by the prominent Detroit citizens who had helped establish the art museum. In 1888, Freer became chairman of the art committee, responsible for organizing the first three of the club's annual exhibitions of American paintings. With that duty, he was compelled to consider the best methods of displaying works of art, which would become a lifelong concern. His position also led to acquaintances with several leading American painters of the day, including Gari Melchers, Dwight William Tryon, Charles A. Platt, and Frederick Stuart Church.

Though better known for his magazine illustrations, Frederick Church was also a painter of anecdotal pictures in which the animals in the Central Park zoo frequently played leading parts. Church, a native of Michigan, met Freer in New York in 1889 as a result of correspondence relating to a Detroit Club exhibition, and the two became fast friends. Freer also became the artist's patron, though he bought Church's works, he confessed, primarily out of "strong personal affection."[12] The first oil painting Freer ever purchased was Church's Knowledge Is Power (fig. 7), which pictures a beautiful young woman calmly taming tigers with a rose. Her self-possession is apparently the result of

Fig. 7. Frederick Stuart Church
(1826–1900). *Knowledge Is
Power,* 1889. Oil on canvas
(51.1 x 91.4). Grand Rapids
Public Library, Michigan;
Bequest of Charles L. Freer.

higher education, suggested by her academic robe and mortarboard: Church dedicated the painting to the "College Girls of America."[13] In the 1890s, when American industrialists were becoming increasingly aggressive in their pursuit of wealth, the theme became more compelling. Sensitivity to beauty, which might be achieved through an educated appreciation of art, was considered by certain collectors, including Freer, the antidote to the materialism of the Gilded Age.

In addition to art, nature provided Freer with a means of regaining balance in a world overrun by industry and competition. Church was his chosen companion on hiking excursions in the Catskill Mountains, where Freer's spirits were invariably revitalized (fig. 8). "We spend nearly all of our hours outdoors," he wrote Frank Hecker in 1892, "and like the springs of these mountains we have a feverish desire to keep in constant motion. The springs minister to our refreshment, the air invigorates us, the scenery stimulates us, and in many other ways Nature sustains and leads us on, but finally she quietly guides us to other fields—those of sleep."[14] Freer's receptiveness to the restorative power he found in the natural world produced an abiding appreciation of landscape paintings,

Fig. 8. Freer in the Catskills, 1889. Photograph attributed to Frederick Stuart Church (1826–1900).

particularly the works of Dwight Tryon, who characteristically depicted quiet corners of New England in the early hours of the day or evening.

Tryon's landscapes were just beginning to be recognized by New York art circles in 1889, when Freer called at the artist's studio and bought *The Rising Moon: Autumn* (fig. 9) straight off the easel. Tryon warned Freer not to expect the painting to receive widespread appreciation. "It will be a picture which the average person will see nothing in, and at first sight will not reveal itself even to more cultured ones," Tryon wrote, subtly suggesting that Freer's powers of perception were exceptional.[15] If Freer would later exhibit perfect confidence in his own good taste, he may at that earlier time have felt uncertain that he could adequately judge artistic merit, especially in oil paintings, and he probably cherished Tryon's faith in the excellence of his eye. Encouraged, he purchased a second work, *The Sea: Sunset,* which the artist considered as inaccessible as the first. Freer's motives were primarily practical: he meant to hang the paintings as pendants in the "bachelor's house" he was starting to construct after years of living more modestly than his income had required.[16]

A maudlin Victorian story, frequently recounted but impossible to prove, tells of a youthful, ill-fated affair of the heart. Freer fell in love but thought himself too poor to marry, so the story goes, and his beloved died of a broken heart. Another, more plausible version of the tale ends with the lady marrying someone else. Agnes Meyer believed that a family history of syphilis accounted for Freer's determination to remain a bachelor, but he seems also to have suffered from an attitude that kept many of his contemporaries unmarried: an incompatibility with the educated, independent women who were coming into their own at the turn of the century.[17] To Tryon, Freer confided that the "modern American woman . . . with her fancies of independence, rights, wrongs, extravagance, dress and other diabolical tendencies is startling all sensible people—both male and female the world round." In Japan, in contrast, Freer found women who remained "madonna and saintlike." If he could believe for a moment that even a few such souls survived in America, he said, he would "give up the quest for art, for a while, and try to find a wife."[18] Freer apparently abandoned thoughts of marriage and devoted his energy, instead, to making a home for himself and his growing collection of art.

When their fortunes had risen precipitously in 1887, Freer and Hecker had purchased adjacent lots in a fashionable new neighborhood at the edge of the city, not far from the car-building plant. Hecker's lot was larger and faced Woodward Avenue, one of the principal thoroughfares of the city. Without delay, Hecker initiated the construction of a lavish mansion made of Indiana limestone (fig. 10), modeled on the Château de Chenonceaux near Tours as an allusion to Detroit's French heritage and an indication of his own rising status in the community. He was a sociable, ambitious, hospitable man with a large family and a love of parties, and his flamboyant house of forty-nine rooms, richly appointed in marble and onyx, matched the exuberance of his personality.

Freer, on the other hand, planned on living quietly and alone, never entertaining more than one or two guests at a time. The lot he selected was off Woodward on the first block of Ferry Avenue, a peaceful residential street where houses were set back forty feet from sidewalks lined with shade trees. Before settling on a style for his home, Freer cautiously considered several architectural examples. He toured the neighborhoods of cities he visited on business, and in the Germantown section of Philadelphia found a house he would take as a model for his own: a simple stone and shingle residence he mistook for the gatehouse of a larger estate. In 1890, Freer commissioned its architect,

Fig. 9. Dwight William Tryon (1849–1925). *The Rising Moon: Autumn,* 1889. Oil on panel (51.0 x 80.3), 89.31.

Wilson Eyre, to design a similarly modest, shingle-style house for his land on Ferry Avenue.[19]

"Should you at any time have occasion to require the services of an architect in domestic architecture," Freer later advised a friend, "you will find in Mr. Eyre . . . a man in whom you can place the utmost reliance." Not only was he honest, Freer said, but Eyre was also blessed with a refined artistic taste tempered with "thoroughly practical ideas."[20] Perhaps more to the point, as Freer wrote his business associate William K. Bixby, Eyre was "ever ready for suggestions, and at the same time always willing to fight for a principle of architecture."[21] The Freer house, almost from its conception, was the collaborative effort of client and architect. Freer worked with Eyre as he later would with Charles Platt, the architect of the Freer Gallery, to ensure that each detail contributed to the overall aesthetic effect. Although his house did not resemble the museum that Freer would later build in Washington, it set an important precedent, as one contemporary pointed out, "inasmuch as the thought of harmony has found in it adequate expression, and each and every work has been provided with a congenial environment."[22]

The interior spaces of the Freer house (fig. 11) flowed from a spacious stair hall that

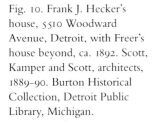

Fig. 10. Frank J. Hecker's house, 5510 Woodward Avenue, Detroit, with Freer's house beyond, ca. 1892. Scott, Kamper and Scott, architects, 1889–90. Burton Historical Collection, Detroit Public Library, Michigan.

mantel on the side of the fireplace facing the front door.

Orchestrated as an architectural ensemble, Tryon's decorations became an integral part of the Freer house. Their style and scale were determined by the architecture of the hall and their compositions adjusted to reflect the room's horizontal lines. The frames were designed by the architect Stanford White, on Tyron's recommendation, in a style consistent with other elements of the architecture. As part of his commission, Tryon selected the background for the paintings, remarking to Freer that nothing was so delightful, "and at the same time so wearing as deciding arrangements of color."[26] Working with the New York framemaker and decorator W. C. LeBrocq, Tryon eventually devised an elaborate color scheme for the walls, covering them with squares of Dutch metal, or imitation gold leaf, stippled with patches of brown and blue. At the suggestion of Maria Oakey Dewing, an authority on interior design, the border above the picture molding was painted peacock blue.

Thomas Wilmer Dewing, another rising New York artist and a friend of Tyron's, was invited to decorate the parlor, where Dewing's portrait of his daughter would hang above the mantel in a narrow frame designed by White (fig. 13). While the painting was in progress, Dewing wrote to Freer with suggestions for the room's decoration. The fireplace, he said, should be tiled in yellow, or better still, pale but distinguished Mexican onyx; the mantelpiece "rather rich with gilding"; and the walls covered with light salmon silk above a white or dark red dado with a polished white trim to avoid a "poor uninviting effect." Dewing promised Freer that the result would be cheerful—the "object of all household decorations and furnishing"—and added, "do not be afraid that this plan of mine will be tawdry or undignified. . . . It will be old fashioned 'American.'"[27] Freer, never the slave of fashion, apparently did not approve of Dewing's proposal for a colonial-revival room, preferring something more in keeping with the architectural style of the house and the color harmonies of the hall. The scheme that Dewing developed in response was similar to Tryon's, though perhaps more delicate; it would be described as an "opalescent, shimmering dream of color and pattern, comparable to a peacock's breast or the wings of a butterfly."[28]

The third American artist to take part in the Freer house project was Abbott Handerson Thayer. His participation was limited to the production of a single work, *A Virgin* (see fig. 1), but it was the largest and most expensive of the paintings Freer commissioned for his home. Seven-and-one-half-feet tall and six-feet wide, Thayer's *Virgin* would occupy a prominent position in the hall at the foot of the stairs. With its installation, as Thayer himself acknowledged, every available space would be taken: "No appreciation of its beautiful symmetry," the artist wrote Freer about the house, "could allow you to begin the usual cluttering and cramming process by putting in one more picture

Fig. 13. Thomas Wilmer Dewing (1851–1938). *Early Portrait of the Artist's Daughter,* 1894. Oil on canvas (103.6 x 172.2), 06.69. Frame designed by Stanford White (1853–1906).

anywhere."[29] Thayer and Howard Mansfield had been Freer's first official houseguests, having returned with their host from a visit to Chicago in February 1893. After Mansfield departed Detroit one morning in a rainstorm, Thayer and Freer whiled away the hours indoors by arranging for Freer to purchase Thayer's "latest masterpiece," which was, however, still unfinished. Freer subsequently confided to Mansfield that it cost so much he feared he would have to fight to keep the sheriff from his door.[30]

Thayer fretted for months over finishing the painting. In April, while it was hanging on the walls of an exhibition, he "trimmed" the drapery on the figure of the boy (modeled by his son, Gerald), then wrote to Freer that *A Virgin* belonged "to the highest class" of paintings: few works of art, he declared, represented "liver (more live) beings or a more unified all pervading (pervading every part of the group) single pure emotion."[31] Yet even after *A Virgin* arrived in Detroit at the end of May and Freer expressed complete satisfaction with the work, Thayer wanted to make alterations—to turn the clouds into wings, to "sweeten" the background, to cut off part of the border, to replace the central female figure with a "gentle white draped body with less action" that would glide, rather than stride, toward the viewer.[32] Much of the artist's discontent seems to have been founded on his fading memory of the painting, and when he realized in 1896 that only a distorted reproduction in *Harper's* had made the drapery appear so masculine, he became at last "all at rest again."[33]

Freer also invited his friend Frederick Church to contribute to the interior scheme of the house. In 1893, Freer received a curiously cute painting that Church called "The Bears," formally titled *Flapjacks, or Bears Baking Griddle Cakes* (fig. 14), to hang in the dining room. *Flapjacks* is so different in sentiment and style from the other commissioned works that it must have held a hidden personal significance; perhaps the subject was meant to recall expeditions to the Catskills, where Freer and Church would have cooked their pancakes on an open fire and may occasionally have been visited by bears. In a sketch (fig. 15) illustrating a letter written just after one of their excursions, Church depicted wild animals posing for Freer, who according to the caption had forgotten to put plates in his Hawkeye camera. The bear, in fact, was Church's emblem; and in what must have been another private joke, he designed a bronze doorbell for Freer's house that features a little bear resting on a bed of laurel leaves, his ears alert to company.[34]

Flapjacks may also allude to Freer's recent fascination with Whistler, who was known for Sunday noontime "breakfasts" at which buckwheat cakes were typically the main course. Of all the artists represented in Freer's house, Church was the farthest from Whistler in aesthetic sensibility, and *Flapjacks* can be interpreted as a play on their dissim-

Fig. 14. Frederick Stuart Church (1842–1924). *Flapjacks,* 1893. Oil on canvas (81.91 x 173.99). The Detroit Club, Michigan.

forgotten it yet.
Yours F.S.Church
58.£.13

Fig. 15. Frederick Stuart
Church (1842–1924).
Pen-and-ink sketch in a letter
to Freer, 26 July 1889.

ilarity: its scheme of white on white recalls Whistler's *Symphony in White, No. 1: The White Girl* (National Gallery of Art, Washington, D.C.), a painting of a melancholy woman in a white dress, standing on a polar-bearskin rug. Freer's dining room, significantly, was painted primrose yellow in imitation of the simple color scheme that Freer had admired on a recent visit to Whistler's London home. Although Whistler himself did not contribute to the decoration of Freer's house, his influence was everywhere apparent.

In 1902, after living in the house for a decade, Freer found that he could no longer comfortably accommodate his art collection, which was growing to unanticipated dimensions. Disliking domestic picture galleries and loath to alter a single element of the architecture, he reluctantly asked Wilson Eyre to draw up plans for an "informal large living room," or art gallery, above the stable.[35] The room (fig. 16) was sixty-feet long to provide ample space for an uncrowded arrangement of pictures, with a leaded-glass skylight so that Freer's collections could be seen by natural light; the woodwork was decorated in imitation gold leaf, a scheme inspired by a section of one of Freer's Japanese screens.[36] A few years later Freer felt compelled to add a second exhibition

gallery (fig. 17), which had walls paneled in oak and a fireplace lined with iridescent tiles from the Pewabic Pottery of Detroit, a firm founded by Freer's friend Mary Chase Perry Stratton.

Although he delighted in sharing his collection with friends and fellow connoisseurs, Freer never wanted his house to become a private museum. Even after the construction of the galleries, he continued to store most of his collection in the fireproof vault beneath the staircase. Visitors would be invited to sit in the alcove at the front of the hall to view portfolios of prints by the light that streamed through the south bay window. Annie Nathan Meyer recalled being thus "comfortably enthroned" while paintings were brought for her inspection one by one, in Japanese fashion, and propped against the back of a Davenport chair. Freer confided to her that the "bringing of the objects to the student, instead of the other way round" was to be the distinguishing characteristic of the public art gallery he had begun to envision.[37]

The Freer house remains intact on East Ferry Avenue in Detroit. Although no longer a private residence, it carries the imprint of its original owner, whose taste for simplicity was exceptional in an age remembered for ostentatious display. Freer never grew tired of what he called the "quiet, modest air" of his home, so much in contrast to the "pomp and show" of the grand houses he visited in Europe.[38] Even after spending some months in his own tastefully appointed villa in Capri, he could say with conviction that the house in Detroit was the only place he would ever feel entirely content. "The closer one can live to himself," Freer wrote in 1911, "the better he is off, and the best part that is left of me is probably represented at 33 Ferry."[39] ∎

Far left:
Fig. 16. Picture gallery in Freer's house, ca. 1906, with paintings by James McNeill Whistler. Built 1904. Wilson Eyre (1858–1944), architect.

Left:
Fig. 17. Art gallery in Freer's house, ca. 1912, with Pewabic-tiled fireplace and Davenport furniture. Built 1909–11. Wilson Eyre (1858–1944), architect.

CHAPTER TWO

LINDA MERRILL

The Whistler Collection

I N MARCH 1890, on his first trip to London, Freer devoted four days to business and the fifth to gaining an audience with James McNeill Whistler. Uncertain of the neighborhood, he took the Underground to Sloane Square and wandered down the King's Road, asking directions of everyone he met. A cabbie finally recognized Whistler's name and told Freer where to find Tower House on Tite Street, where the artist lived with his wife, Beatrix. Arriving without invitation or introduction, Freer was informed that Whistler would see him in a quarter of an hour. Freer checked his watch. Whistler made his appearance on the minute, looking just as expected, his legendary lock of white hair curling conspicuously above his forehead (fig. 19).[1]

Freer would have been aware of Whistler's reputation for contentiousness, soon to be substantiated with the publication of the artist's collected writings: his *Gentle Art of Making Enemies* is dedicated "to the rare few, who, early in life, have rid themselves of the friendship of the many." Yet, perhaps encouraged by his many recent, affable introductions to prominent New York painters, Freer seems to have approached Whistler without apprehension. Moreover, he had a mission. Having already amassed nearly one hundred Whistler prints, Freer was determined to build a comprehensive collection. In the process, he was growing impatient with art dealers, who could not always provide him with "satisfactory proofs." Making Whistler's acquaintance would assure Freer's acquisition of first-rate impressions of etchings, enabling him to build a collection similar to the one he had assembled with the help of Storm van 's Gravesande.[2]

According to a contemporary account, Freer was emboldened to call on the irascible artist because of their common nationality.[3] Through what Whistler considered an accident of birth, his life had begun in the industrial town of Lowell, Massachusetts, during the age of Jacksonian democracy. His characteristic elitism may be rooted in the years he spent in Russia as a child, when the family lived in considerable luxury in Saint Petersburg while Whistler's father directed the construction of the railroad to Moscow.

Mr. Whistler's true self, his real ideals, his natural instincts, his charity and his personal achievements are known to a few intimates only. And this is as he wished.

Freer to Howard Mansfield, 20 August 1903

Fig. 18. James McNeill Whistler (1834–1903), *Variations in Flesh Colour and Green: The Balcony,* 1864–70. Oil on panel (61.4 x 48.8), 92.23.

Fig. 19. James McNeill Whistler, 1885. Inscribed, "To Charles L. Freer—a un de ces jours" (till we meet again). Photogravure attributed to Mortimer Mempes.

After their return to America, Whistler briefly attended the United States Military Academy at West Point; but it was in Paris, in 1855, that his life as an artist can be said to have begun.

As an art student abroad, Whistler displayed scarcely more self-discipline than he had as a cadet at West Point; yet he learned to prepare his palette and to copy paintings in the collections of the Louvre. He also found an artist to emulate: Gustave Courbet, the most radical painter in Paris. In the summer of 1859, espousing the realist cause, Whistler moved to London. Taking up temporary residence in an inn at Wapping, an unsavory neighborhood bordering the river, he executed a series of etchings that would become part of the Thames Set. Prints such as *Black Lion Wharf* (fig. 20), realistic depictions of workingmen on barges or boats seen against a background of riverside wharves and warehouses, follow Courbet's injunction to record the facts of modern life.

The demand for realism did not, however, preclude the portrayal of settings with intrinsic aesthetic appeal. *Harmony in Green and Rose: The Music Room* (fig. 21), one of Whistler's first London paintings, represents the household of his affluent brother-in-law, Francis Seymour Haden. The image of the artist's half-sister Deborah is reflected in the mirror, and her daughter Annie sits at the window quietly reading a book. A visitor—a tall, striking figure in black—appears either to have just arrived or to be preparing to depart; either way, her incongruous presence disrupts the tranquility of Whistler's domestic tableau. The picture's ambiguous spatial construction contributes to the uneasy atmosphere of the room, in which two women from different spheres of modern life confront each other obliquely; but the unsettling complexities of composition and mood are resolved in the pleasing patterns of color that form the painting's main theme, the harmony in green and rose. Already Whistler's realism is tempered with aestheticism, a devotion to beauty for its own sake.

Although Pre-Raphaelitism was already past its prime, Whistler came briefly under the influence of its leading spirit, Dante Gabriel Rossetti, his neighbor in Chelsea. Like Rossetti, Whistler adopted the practice of depicting beautiful women in luxuriant settings; during the 1860s, Japanese prints, Chinese porcelains, and other oriental objets d'art began crowding Whistler's canvases as a means of dislodging painting from narrative, the prevailing Victorian style. *Caprice in Purple and Gold: The Golden Screen* (fig. 22) is a portrait of a woman in a kimono contemplating a series of woodblock prints. Evidently absorbed in their beauty, she provides a model for the apprehension of the painting itself, which Whistler meant to be enjoyed for its formal qualities alone.

Searching for a distinctive artistic style, Whistler experimented with complex figural groups in a series of paintings called the Six Projects. In one titled *The White Symphony: Three Girls* (fig. 23), women draped like Grecian goddesses are arranged to resemble figures in Japanese prints. The primary musical title emphasizes the aesthetic quality of the painting and underlines Whistler's rejection of storytelling. By the begin-

Fig. 20. James McNeill Whistler (1834–1903), *Black Lion Wharf,* 1859. Etching, second state (15.2 x 22.6), 98.271.

Fig. 21. James McNeill
Whistler (1834–1903), *Harmony
in Green and Rose: The Music
Room*, 1860–61. Oil on canvas
(96.5 x 71.5), 17.234.

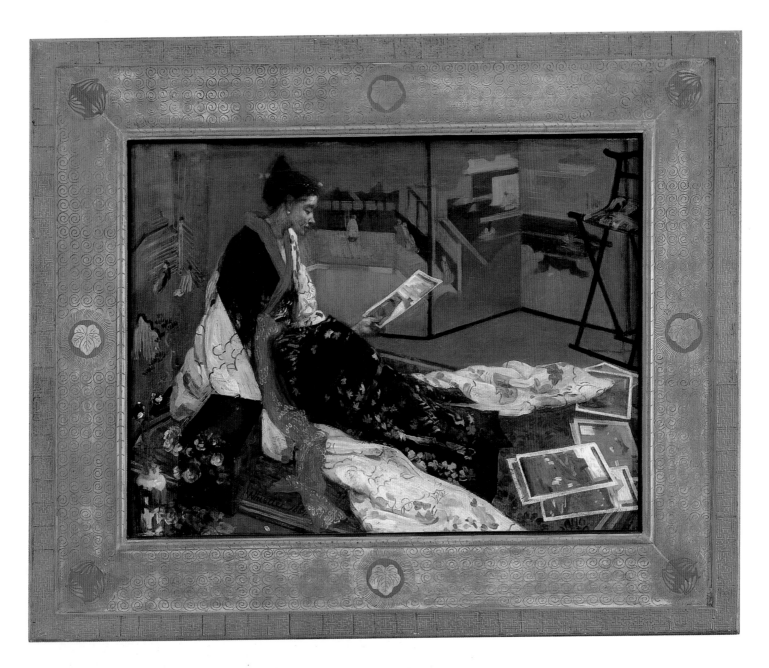

ning of the 1870s, Whistler had returned to depicting scenes he could actually see, though he was recasting those visions in the light of memory, imagination, and the influence of Japanese art. *Variations in Pink and Grey: Chelsea* (fig. 24), for example, a view of the riverside from an upstairs window of the artist's Chelsea home, is drawn from a palette reduced to a few color tones and composed from a limited vocabulary of abbreviated forms. Even the signature has become an element of design: Whistler's monogram

Fig. 22. James McNeill Whistler (1834–1903), *Caprice in Purple and Gold: The Golden Screen*, 1864. Oil on panel (49.8 x 68.9), 04.75. Frame designed by the artist.

Fig. 23. James McNeill
Whistler (1834–1903), *The White Symphony: Three Girls,* ca. 1868.
Oil on millboard mounted on panel (46.4 x 61.6), 02.138.

in the shape of a butterfly, his emblem, appears in a Japanese-style cartouche as a symbolic eviction of the written word from the realm of the visual arts.

The Thames may have drawn Whistler to London and probably kept him there even in times of dejection and disappointment; he would always live in sight of the river, finding in its aspect an ever-changing source of inspiration. During the early 1870s he began producing his most original works, paintings of the Thames at twilight when, as he later explained, "the evening mist clothes the riverside with poetry, as with a veil, and the poor buildings lose themselves in the dim sky, and the tall chimneys become campanili, and the warehouses are palaces in the night, and the whole city hangs in the heavens."[4]

Both *Variations in Pink and Grey: Chelsea* and *Nocturne: Blue and Silver—Battersea Reach* (fig. 25) present scenes reduced to their essential elements of color and form; yet the composition of the Nocturne appears less contrived, perhaps because the artist's selection had been assisted by the naturally limited light of evening. Freer once recounted the story of a young woman giving an elaborate account of an early morning walk

Fig. 24. James McNeill
Whistler (1834–1903), *Variations
in Pink and Grey: Chelsea*,
1871–72. Oil on canvas (62.7 x
40.5), 02.249. Frame designed
by the artist and signed with the
butterfly.

that had caused her to perceive, she said, how close nature came to some of Whistler's paintings. "Ah," said the artist, "so Nature is catching up, is she?"[5] Whistler's Nocturnes, visions of a transfigured modern world, are an uncompromising reply to the mundane realism of Courbet.

The principle of reduction that characterizes the Nocturnes also distinguishes Whistler's portraits, including the one that would secure his lasting fame, *Arrangement in Grey and Black, No. 1* (Musée d'Orsay, Paris), better known as "Whistler's Mother." Whistler rarely admitted to influences, yet he did consider himself the heir to Velázquez; nevertheless, when someone observed that he and the Spanish artist were the two great masters of painting, Whistler reportedly replied, "Why drag in Velázquez?" A telling example of the influence is Whistler's *Arrangement in Black: Portrait of F. R. Leyland* (fig. 26), which recalls the royal portraits of Philip IV of Spain. The allusion was not lost on Leyland, a Liverpool merchant and patron of the arts, who hung *Arrangement in Black* among the paintings by Velázquez that he had assembled with Whistler's assistance.

Although Whistler's portraits were not universally admired, they generally received a more favorable reception than did the Nocturnes, which appeared to the Victorian public uninformed and unfinished, as if the artist had not taken his work seriously. Partly to allay such allegations, Whistler mounted a one-man show in 1874 that displayed the range of his achievement; until then, despite numerous submissions to the Royal Academy and the Paris Salon, he had been known primarily as an etcher. The exhibition was also notable for its installation, which Whistler himself designed to show his works to best advantage. Two years later he embarked on another decorative project, a campaign to bring harmony to the dining room of Leyland's London home, the setting for a painting Whistler had produced twelve years earlier. That notorious redecoration resulted in *Harmony in Blue and Gold: The Peacock Room* (see fig. 120), which marked the end of Leyland's patronage and initiated a particularly spiteful period of the artist's career.

The Peacock Room brought Whistler fame but not fortune, and in the summer of 1877, hoping to recoup his losses and attract publicity to his work, he brought a suit for libel against the eminent critic John Ruskin. Ruskin had seen one of Whistler's most abstract paintings, *Nocturne in Black and Gold: The Falling Rocket* (The Detroit Institute of Arts, Michigan), at the inaugural exhibition of the Grosvenor Gallery in London and had expressed his opinion of it in an obscure publication called *Fors Clavigera*: "I have seen, and heard, much of Cockney impudence before now, but never expected to hear a coxcomb ask two hundred guineas for flinging a pot of paint in the public's face." Had Whistler not taken issue, the words might well have been forgotten; as it happened, Ruskin's piquant image of the artist pelting the public with

Fig. 27. James McNeill
Whistler (1834–1903), *Little
Venice,* 1879–80. Etching
(18.3 x 26.5), 92.16.

paint became the most famous of the many critiques and caricatures leveled at Whistler. Ruskin himself was unable to attend court when the case went to trial in November 1878, but Whistler performed admirably, professing from the witness stand the aesthetic principles that underlay his art. He was subjected to ridicule nonetheless, and although he won the verdict, he was granted only a farthing in damages.

After the trial, Whistler assailed his critics in a caustic pamphlet titled *Whistler v. Ruskin: Art and Art Critics,* then fled to Venice in hopes of executing a set of etchings that would restore his solvency and reputation. Though he planned to stay four months, he remained fourteen, having been inspired to produce a large number of watercolor paintings and nearly one hundred pastel drawings of some lesser-known sights of the city. He also completed plates for fifty etchings, including the set of twenty-six that Freer acquired in 1887. Freer would always hold Whistler's Venetian plates in special regard; he commented that *Little Venice* (fig. 27), for example, was "more beautiful than Venice herself seen from the same point of view. Not that I would detract one single item from the superb magnificence of this glorious city, but give honor to whom it is due."[6]

In London, however, the Venetian etchings were not the commercial success that

Whistler had expected, and the failure of appreciation by the English deepened the artist's disenchantment with his adopted country. He traveled continually during the 1880s, documenting his trips with small paintings. He mastered watercolor and produced dozens of paintings in a range of subjects and a variety of styles. His experience with watercolor seems to have lightened his touch in oil and suggested possibilities for the epigrammatic paintings he called Notes, which were described as "superficially, the size of your hand, but, artistically, as large as a continent."[7]

In the summer of 1888, Whistler married Beatrix Godwin, the widow of the architect who had designed the house Whistler lost to bankruptcy in the wake of the Ruskin trial. The couple moved into Tower House, just across the street from Whistler's White House, and settled into a period of contentment unprecedented in the artist's career. A studio on the top floor had a printing press to support Whistler's resurgent interest in etching. In August 1889 he went to Amsterdam and etched ten copper plates (fig. 28). As Whistler himself explained, the Amsterdam prints represented the third stage in his development as an etcher, synthesizing the early, realist style of the Thames Set and the later, impressionist manner of the Venetian etchings.[8] Indeed, the drawing was so elaborate that when Whistler finished, very little ground remained on the plates, and only a few impressions could be printed before the finely etched copper became irreparably worn beneath the pressure of the press.[9]

Whistler was printing the proofs of those rare and extraordinary etchings at the beginning of March 1890, when Freer fortuitously made his first call. Only a day or two earlier, an art critic for the *Pall Mall Gazette* had visited Tower House and found impressions of Whistler's Amsterdam plates — "the most exquisite series of etchings that he has ever produced" — framed and propped against the wall of the studio.[10] Arriving at an opportune moment, Freer was among the first to see the completed prints and to acquire a set of the last great etchings of the artist's career, which Whistler autographed for him with the butterfly.

Besides acquiring a most valuable addition to his print collection, Freer managed to frame a "mutually advantageous" agree-

Fig. 28. James McNeill Whistler (1834–1903), *Bridge, Amsterdam*, 1889. Etching, second state (16.4 x 23.9), 06.119.

ment with Whistler whereby the collector would purchase impressions of all future etchings and lithographs directly from the artist.[11] In June 1891, as he was leaving London for Paris, Whistler dispatched to Detroit an impression of his "first new etching," titled *Cameo No. 1* (fig. 29), which he had inscribed, "Selected for Charles L. Freer."[12] The print is part of a series that Whistler called "Tanagras," inspired by the Hellenistic terracotta figurines; the works picture a young model, nude or partially draped, sometimes playing with a child. That summer at his studio on the rue Notre Dame des Champs

(fig. 30), Whistler continued his work on the Tanagra etchings and on a group of closely related lithographs. The following February, at Freer's request, he sent a package containing proofs of every existing lithograph (except the color ones, which were still in progress) printed on fine Dutch and Japanese papers; although Freer owned a few of them already, the proofs in his collection could not compare, he said, with the impressions Whistler had provided, "in paper, printing and completed beauty."[13]

With the artist's cooperation, therefore, Freer nearly achieved his ambition of owning a "specimen" of every print that Whistler would ever produce.[14] His holdings increased substantially in 1898 when he purchased Seymour Haden's collection, which included some three hundred of Whistler's early prints and drawings. By 1909, Freer had given up collecting "miscellaneous etchings" to concentrate his attention and resources on Whistler; and by 1913 his print collection was virtually complete, lacking only a few unique or extremely rare impressions that were confined in impenetrable collections. Freer's remains the most comprehensive group of Whistler prints ever assembled.[15]

As that collection began to grow, Freer also cultivated an interest in the artist's work in other media. In 1889, at an important exhibition at H. Wunderlich and Company in New York, he had purchased a Whistler watercolor; the following year, on the visit to the artist's Tite Street studio, he bought a "charming pastel," *Harmony in Blue and Violet* (fig. 31), later extolled as "what we Americans call 'great.'"[16] Finally, in September 1892, in possession of new wealth from the merger that created the Michigan-Peninsular Car Company, Freer determined to buy an oil painting by Whistler. "I can afford one only," he confided to his friend and fellow collector Howard Mansfield, "but I wish it to be a good one."[17]

At Mansfield's suggestion, Freer went to Wunderlich's gallery to see *Variations in Flesh Colour and Green: The Balcony* (see fig. 18) — a painting, Whistler had assured the

Fig. 30. Whistler in his studio, 86 rue Notre Dame des Champs, Paris, 1899. Photograph by M. Dornac.

dealer, he would come to wish he could sell more than once.[18] The subject, as Whistler's mother described it, was "a group in Oriental costume on a balcony" looking "out upon a river, with a town in the distance" — in other words, models in Japanese dress posing on the artist's balcony with a view of the Thames and Battersea beyond.[19] An imaginative conflation of realism and aestheticism, the painting represents an early experiment in the application of conventions derived from Japanese prints to depictions of the contemporary London scene. Had Freer never been able to afford another oil painting, *The Balcony* would have served him well as the "fine example" he sought for the centerpiece of his collection.

In the years immediately following that signal acquisition, while the United States endured a severe economic depression, Freer bought only a handful of Whistler watercolors and pastels, though he managed to sustain his relationship with the artist through active correspondence. His letters were invariably answered by Beatrix, who became a devoted admirer of Freer's (see fig. 32). But in the summer of 1894, Whistler himself sent an important letter to Detroit, referring to a request Freer had made two years earlier for either a springtime landscape in watercolor or a single

Fig. 31. James McNeill Whistler (1834–1903), *Harmony in Blue and Violet*, late 1880s. Fabricated chalks on brown paper (27.5 x 17.9), 90.8.

figure in pastel to convey the spirit of new life, a "resurrection thought."[20] Whistler remembered only that Freer wanted a "figure—to, in a way, hint at 'Spring,'" and proposed a cabinet-size painting in oil.[21] While he worried that so important a work might exceed his financial reach, Freer was of course delighted that Whistler had agreed to accept the commission; and in November, on a visit to Paris, he was able to see *Harmony in Blue and Gold: The Little Blue Girl* (fig. 33) in progress.

A year later, "in perfect health and charmed with the experiences" of twelve months of travel, Freer wrote to Whistler to inquire whether the commissioned painting would soon be shipped to Detroit.[22] It would not. Beatrix had cancer, and Whistler was too distraught to work. She had already been ill when Freer saw her in Paris months before, when she had wished for a songbird to brighten her bedridden days. That winter, on his travels through India, Freer had searched for a shama merle, known for the full-throated song that fills the jungle at daybreak and dusk; finally in the suburbs of Calcutta, he had found a pair of shamas that a courteous sea captain agreed to deliver to Paris. One of the birds arrived safely in London, where the Whistlers had gone to seek medical treatment for Beatrix. In May 1896 she died in a cottage on Hampstead Heath.

Disconsolate, Whistler could not bring himself to write to Freer about the death of his wife until ten months later, when he recorded on mourning stationery the heartrending story of the Indian songbird:

And when she went—alone, because I was unfit to go too—the strange wild dainty creature stood uplifted on the topmost perch, and sang and sang—as it had never sung before!—A song of the Sun—and of joy—and of my despair!—Loud and ringing clear from the skies!—and louder! Peal after peal—until it became a marvel the tiny beast, torn by such glorious voice, should live!

And suddenly it was made known to me that, in this mysterious magpie waif from beyond the temples of India, the spirit of my beautiful Lady had lingered on its way—and the song was her song of love—and courage—and command that the work, in which she had taken her part, should be complete—and so was her farewell!

The painting that the singing shama, inspirited by Beatrix, had seemed to implore the artist to complete was *The Little Blue Girl*. Whistler apologized to his friend for his "apparently ungracious silence" with the explanation that he had written his letters directly on the canvas, "and one of these days, you will, by degrees, read them all, as you sit before your picture." He hoped, he said, that with his "refined sympathy and perception," Freer would be able to discern in the painting signs of his late wife's pleasure, the "interest taken in the perfection of it, by the other one who, with me, liked you."[23]

Fig. 32. Sketch of Charles Lang Freer, early 1890s, attributed to Beatrix Godwin Whistler (1857–1896). Pen and ink on paper (9.5 x 11.2). Hunterian Art Gallery, University of Glasgow, Scotland.

With such a history, it is little wonder that Whistler could not bear to part with the painting during his lifetime or that even today *The Little Blue Girl* is almost painful to behold: the features of the girl's face are obscured by mantles of paint that form a tortured surface pattern betraying the artist's "forlorn destruction" over the death of his wife. But even apart from that technical difficulty, the painting conveys the uncomfortable impression of an artist whose reach has exceeded his grasp; Whistler may have been making a final attempt to produce a monumental female nude in the academic tradition that had always eluded him. For Freer, Whistler's *Little Blue Girl* epitomized "the most mysterious and beautiful qualities" of the artist's oeuvre. Although he would not declare it Whistler's masterpiece, he considered the painting "one of the great productions of modern times" and treasured it as well for the personal associations connected with its origin and execution.[24]

From the beginning of their acquaintance, the reputedly antagonistic Whistler had always been entirely amiable with Freer, who would long remember the artist's unexpected hospitality on that first occasion in 1890. Freer later resolved to say little about his relationship with Whistler, deploring "the many who are trying to gain a little personal notoriety out of their acquaintance with the master." In private correspondence, however, he took pains to correct prevailing misconceptions.[25] In 1900, for example, he wrote to a friend that the widespread impression that Whistler was difficult and unsociable was altogether unfounded. "Naturally enough, from strangers he expects the formality and courtesy due a gentleman and an artist, and when so approached he returns all he expects, and more. To those who know him well, he is the very soul of politeness and good fellowship."[26] On their first afternoon together (when Freer must have shown the necessary deference), Whistler had entertained his visitor with a collection of press cuttings documenting the criticism he had sustained over the years. This caused Freer to surmise that the "warlike propensity" Whistler occasionally displayed was only the outcome of "thirty years of constant warfare with the dull-minded art critics of England." Freer himself had never encountered a "gentler, sweeter, more refined nature."[27]

■

IN JULY 1899, just after Whistler turned sixty-five, he made an immodest proposal. "I think I may tell you without the least chance of being misunderstood," Whistler wrote to Freer, "that I wish you to have a fine collection of Whistlers!!—perhaps *the* collection."[28] At the time, apart from an extensive group of prints and drawings, Freer's collection of works by Whistler consisted of a few watercolors and pastels and two oil paintings: *The Balcony* (see fig. 18), acquired in 1892, and *Nocturne in Black and Gold: Entrance to Southampton Water,* purchased from Whistler in 1897. But as Whistler may well have been aware, Freer was poised to become a professional collector: his company had

recently monopolized the car-building industry in the United States, and as a result he possessed sufficient wealth to allow a life of art and leisure. Freer's reply to Whistler's proposition has not survived, but in his next communication the artist referred to Freer's "very delightful letter, of which I hope next week to talk to you," which suggests that his idea had been favorably received.[29]

Freer was then on his way to Liverpool to see a painting in the collection of Alfred Chapman, *Nocturne: Blue and Silver — Bognor.* It was precisely because such paintings were for sale in England that Whistler determined to have an American possess the premier collection of his works. In the early 1870s, Whistler had considered the Bognor one of his finest Nocturnes, "perhaps the most brilliant," and expected it to sell for three hundred guineas; eventually the painting went for a trifling fifty pounds to Chapman, who sold it to Freer in 1899 for one thousand pounds more than he himself had paid.[30] While Whistler took some "mischievous pleasure" in the enormous sums his works were beginning to fetch, he also felt acutely the "lack of all communion," as he phrased his cause for discontent, "between the artist and those who held his work," and looked forward, he said, to other relations.[31]

Freer had already indicated an interest in expanding his Whistler holdings by offering to buy two paintings he had seen on display at the second Exhibition of International Art in London. Whistler and Freer may have discussed the scheme for "*the* collection" later that summer, when the artist presented Freer with a watercolor design for a fan and a copy of his most recent literary production, *Eden versus Whistler: The Baronet and the Butterfly,* signed with the butterfly and inscribed "with affection" to "a determined friend." Although the collector bought only a few works on paper that year and the next, he became better acquainted with Whistler and his art on trips to London in 1900 and to Paris in 1901. Those brief visits left Whistler with the fervent wish for a span of several weeks to go over with Freer the works he thought most interesting. "I have my plan!" Whistler wrote Freer, "and hurry is an abomination."[32]

The plan was apparently in place by October 1901, when Whistler informed Freer that John J. Cowan, a collector in Edinburgh, was selling some of his paintings. He advised Freer to buy at least two of them "in a poke," if necessary, or sight unseen. "They will cost money," he said, "but I should be sorry to know they went anywhere else. Besides I think you will never forgive yourself if you miss them."[33] Freer instantly sent a cable to Cowan, who replied with a price that was immediately accepted, and by December the paintings were hanging in Detroit. *The Thames in Ice* (fig. 34), one of Whistler's early oils, turned out to be "the very type of the period of Mr. Whistler's work," Freer wrote Cowan, "which I have long been wanting to add to my little group"; and the watercolor portrait of Mrs. Charles Whibley exhibited "certain rare

qualities of composition and color which, it seems to me, no one but Mr. Whistler can paint."[34] Cowan, who was selling the paintings from financial necessity, was happy to know they were going to a friend of Whistler's in the United States, since he believed the artist's work had never been properly appreciated in Britain. Freer replied, "I have never been able to understand why so intelligent and advanced a country should be so short-sighted concerning the work of the greatest figure of the Nineteenth Century in the broad field of the Fine Arts."[35]

On May Day 1902, Freer arrived in Liverpool, where he was "feasted and filled with art and champagne."[36] It was an auspicious beginning to a banner year. Although he originally intended to stay in England for only a couple of weeks, in the end Freer spent all of May and most of June casting his net for acquisitions. He did not waste an hour in attempting to see every important work by Whistler remaining in England and Scotland, an awesome undertaking that kept him "extremely busy," he wrote Frank Hecker, "and most instructively entertained." He purchased paintings from almost everyone he met, and he visited virtually every relevant private collection in Britain. The experience of seeing so many of Whistler's works at once was, he said, both delightful and valuable, and confirmed the opinions he had been forming throughout the past fifteen years "on certain matters of beauty."[37] Periodically he would write to Hecker to wire more funds and sell more stock, if necessary, to finance his purchases. "What I am picking up here is

Fig. 35. James McNeill
Whistler (1834–1903), *Purple
and Gold: Phryne the Superb!
—Builder of Temples*, ca. 1898.
Oil on panel (23.6 x 13.7),
02.115.

worth much more to me than Pressed Steel," he explained. "A good name for my new findings would be pressed or compressed joy."[38]

Freer spent much of his time in the company of Whistler himself, who undoubtedly orchestrated his patron's travel itinerary and social schedule and seems to have offered continuing counsel. He advised Freer, for example, to buy at any cost *The White Symphony: Three Girls* (see fig. 23), the only one of the Six Projects not in his own possession; and when at length Freer succeeded in wresting the painting from the hands of its owner, Thomas Way, Jr., he declared the purchase to be "the most important one artistically" of the many he had made that year.[39] Freer also bought several works directly from Whistler; among them were some pastels related to the Tanagra prints and a small oil painting called *Purple and Gold: Phryne the Superb!—Builder of Temples* (fig. 35), examples of the artist's recent production that he needed to round out his collection. Whistler's late work, Freer observed, possessed "a certain dignity, amounting almost to solemnity, that keeps one while in its presence constantly reminded of the efforts of the early Greeks and Egyptians."[40]

Whistler had moved to a new house in London beside Chelsea Old Church and was "in great feather," Freer wrote Hecker, "and insists upon painting my head before I leave." Freer hoped he would be able to talk Whistler out of wasting "valuable time upon a valueless theme," but the artist persisted and Freer eventually acquiesced.[41] Having decided on the color scheme for the portrait, Whistler sent a telegram to Freer's hotel on 13 May directing him to bring a brown jacket when he came to the studio that afternoon. The work (fig. 36) was well under way by the middle of June, when Freer reported to Hecker that Whistler was making him look like a pope—"but then that is all right for there will of course be little of Freer in it. It will surely be all Whistler!"[42]

While many of Freer's days were spent with Whistler, many of his evenings were spent with Miss Goddard, otherwise known as Romaine Brooks, the artist whose visit to London had been "foreordained," Freer said, and to whom he had partially lost his heart. The greater part of his affection was committed to the thirty-one works by Whistler in oil, watercolor, and pastel belonging to H. S. Theobald of Hyde Park. Many of them had been acquired in 1884 at the close of Whistler's one-man show at Messrs. Dowdeswells' gallery on New Bond Street, when Theobald had purchased all of the paintings that remained unsold. He apparently had a penchant for miniatures: the major work of the collection (which Freer bought separately), *Nocturne: Silver and Opal—Chelsea* (fig. 37), is only eight by ten inches, the smallest of Whistler's Nocturnes in oil. Freer described Theobald's lot of pictures as "most varied and beautiful and the finest single group known" and took particular pleasure in the acquisition, which nearly doubled the size of his own Whistler holdings.[43]

On the last day of May 1902, when the Boer War was brought to an end, Whistler invited himself to dinner with Freer at the Carlton Hotel, where he drank gin slings and told anti-English jokes all evening long.[44] Three weeks later there was another cause for celebration, the coronation of Edward VII. Freer lamented that in preparation for that event the dignity of London was being all but lost to a "wilderness of senseless decorations and illuminations." Ugly, rough-timber barriers were being constructed along the parade route—presumably, he observed, to prevent the English from crowding each other to death. "It's horrible," he wrote on 20 June, "and tomorrow Whistler and myself, the only two sane men left, run away from it all, escaping to Holland, where we hope for quiet and reflection."[45]

Freer's time in England had seemed so enchanted that he was given cause to wonder "why all of this charm and joy should come into my little life."[46] But hardly had he left London when his pleasures came abruptly to an end. En route to Amsterdam, Whistler suffered a heart attack, and the party, which included Whistler's sister-in-law, Rosalind Birnie Philip, got no farther than The Hague. Whistler remained critically ill, and in marked contrast to previous weeks, Freer's days in the Netherlands dragged by. Abandoning his plan to continue on to Spain, Freer made the wry reflection, " 'Why drag in Velasquez' seems prophetic."[47] He sat faithfully at Whistler's bedside, observing that even the artist's unconscious gestures were reflected in the brushwork of his paintings. Finally, on the morning of the artist's sixty-eighth birthday, after twenty-one days of "gloom and misery," Whistler appeared much improved and the doctor predicted a rapid recovery.[48] By the end of July he was well enough to move to a private house, and Freer departed The Hague, leaving a gift of butterflies that was worthy, Whistler said, of a daimyo or a doge.[49]

The next summer, Freer returned to Europe, stopping briefly at the villa in Capri on his way, at last, to Spain. In Madrid he saw a bullfight and visited the Prado, noting the latter in his daybook with an exclamation. He reluctantly left the city for London, where Whistler, again gravely ill, had been expecting him for most of June. "He could say next to nothing this afternoon," Freer reported to Hecker, "until just as I was leaving, when he whispered 'come tomorrow sure.'"[50] Practically every afternoon, Freer took his failing friend for a drive in the park, but when he called at the studio on 17 July, he found that Whistler had died only minutes earlier. Freer wrote the news to Hecker, telling him for his "personal information (which the world knows nothing about) that up to the last moment there was seen and felt that same old-time knightly but gentle acceptance of all things fine and true." He added as a postscript, "Need I say that in all things of perfect refinement of beauty the greatest masters are now all gone."[51]

Fig. 36. James McNeill Whistler (1834–1903), *Portrait of Charles Lang Freer,* 1902. Oil on panel (51.8 x 31.7), 03.301.

Fig. 37. James McNeill Whistler (1834–1903), *Nocturne: Silver and Opal—Chelsea,* early 1880s. Oil on panel (20.3 x 25.7), 02.146.

Freer remained in London for Whistler's funeral and burial beside Beatrix's grave in the churchyard at Chiswick. In the following weeks he rendered practical assistance to Rosalind Philip (fig. 38) and her sister Ethel Whibley, to whom he became so indispensable that they called him "General Utility." Freer also bought works of art. "The bonds you may sell to provide funds for my purchases, I care nothing about," he wrote Hecker. "I can live happily, fortunately, without them. But the things I am getting are surely beyond price. Some day: many days after bonds or anything else can serve me, others will be served, well served, intelligently served by my slight efforts of this year."[52]

Freer acquired paintings from Thomas Way, Jr., and from William Burrell of Glasgow, but most of the acquisitions of 1903 came directly from Whistler's studio, sold from the estate by the executor, Rosalind Philip. Freer secured the remaining Six Projects, referring to them as "schemes in oil," and several other works to which he had laid a prior claim. He recovered the portrait of himself (see fig. 36), probably untouched since the ill-fated trip to Holland the previous year, yet "even in its incomplete state," Freer observed, "a wonderful example."[53] He also at last obtained *The Little Blue Girl* (see fig. 33), which, with Whistler's death, had become additionally charged with emotional intensity.

Freer continued purchasing paintings he had been advised by the artist to acquire, as well as others that simply took "strong hold" of his affections.[54] Many of the negotiations were founded in friendships that had started during Whistler's lifetime. When, for example, John Cowan decided to dispose of additional paintings in the autumn of 1902, he thought first of Freer, who had recently sent Cowan's daughters a gift of Japanese "picture books."[55] As a result, Freer was able to buy *Variations in Pink and Grey: Chelsea* (see fig. 24), a painting that provided "exactly the note needed," he said, for the still incomplete collection of works by Whistler.[56]

Other works, such as *Nocturne: Blue and Gold—Valparaiso* (fig. 39), had been long admired. Freer had first seen the Valparaiso Nocturne in 1893 at the World's Columbian Exposition in Chicago, where it hung among a group of Whistler's works that "completely overshadowed everything in the Fine Arts Department," Freer reported to the artist, "and gave pleasure and inspiration to many more people than you imagine."[57] Whistler had begun painting *Valparaiso* in 1866 on his mystifying trip to South America, where from a safe distance he had witnessed a Spanish attack on the Chilean harbor. Temporarily removed from European influence, he had cast off the conventions of Western painting in favor of an asymmetrical composition derived from Japanese prints. In London several years later, Whistler apparently returned to the Valparaiso picture, which he may originally have painted as a daytime scene, and transformed it into a Nocturne. Perhaps Freer recognized the painting's importance in the evolution of

Whistler's style, for it seems to have made an indelible impression: fourteen years after seeing it in Chicago, having heard that its owner had died, Freer wrote to a London art dealer that even though the recent "financial disturbance" in America (the Panic of 1907) had caused him to curtail his spending, he would in the case of the Valparaiso Nocturne "willingly make considerable sacrifices to obtain it."[58]

When the prized Nocturne arrived in Detroit in the summer of 1909, Freer was not there to receive it; he was on an expedition to China. His interest in Asian art was beginning to absorb most of his time and financial resources, but the new enthusiasm did not conflict with his ambition to possess "*the* collection" of Whistler's work. He suggested the duality of his taste in a letter of 1901 to Frederick Keppel, the art dealer who had fostered his early interest in European etchings: "I find my interest in Art centering more strongly, year by year, in the early productions of the Japanese and Chinese painters and potters. Of course, Mr. Whistler's work interests me very much, and the more I study it the greater its fascination."[59] Indeed, until the end his life, Freer continued to develop and refine the Whistler collection, considering it a complement to his collection of Asian art; for it was Whistler himself who had incited Freer's effort to acquire prime examples of the "early productions" of China and Japan.

Fig. 38. Rosalind Birnie Philip (1873–1958), ca. 1903. Photograph by W. and D. Downey, London.

In 1892, coincidentally the year that he bought *The Balcony,* Freer had purchased a selection of Japanese prints after seeing an exhibition of Hokusai prints at the Grolier Club in New York and detecting "points of contact" with the Whistler etchings in his own collection.[60] When he related his "discovery" to Whistler some years later, the artist informed Freer that he had known about Japanese woodcuts as early as 1864, citing *The Golden Screen* (see fig. 22) as evidence. When, in 1902, Freer saw the painting at the country home of Lord Battersea, he found it to be "one of the most perfect things in composition and colouring in the whole range of Mr. Whistler's art," noting in his diary that the Chinese screen was "wonderfully painted" and the porcelain vase a "marvelous bit of blue and white." The prints in the picture, presumably part of Whistler's personal collection, were recognizably by Hiroshige (1797–1858).[61]

Freer himself collected Japanese prints until about 1905, when he disposed of them all, "not because they impressed me unfavorably," he explained, "but solely for the rea-

Fig. 39. James McNeill
Whistler (1834–1903), *Nocturne:
Blue and Gold—Valparaiso*,
1866/ca. 1874. Oil on canvas
(75.6 x 50.1), 09.127.

son that I deemed it wiser to replace them with specimens of ancient paintings."[62] The turning point in the evolution of his taste for Japanese art seems to have come in 1894, when Freer spent a fortnight with Whistler in Paris discussing their common interest in Japanese art. Regrettably, there is no contemporary account of their conversations, but many years later Freer recounted to Agnes Meyer the tantalizing theory that Whistler had expounded: namely, that import objects such as the prints and porcelains widely available in London and New York were only the "last gasp of a great tradition," faint indications of a "far earlier and higher culture." Whistler reportedly extracted Freer's promise to search the Orient for those little-known treasures. Shortly thereafter, Freer would make his first trip to Japan, launching his quest for masterpieces of Asian art.[63] ■

CHAPTER THREE

THOMAS LAWTON

The Asian Tours

CHARLES LANG FREER was forty years old when, on 29 September 1894, he boarded the night train in Detroit for New York to begin an eleven-month tour that marked his initial exposure to Asia. While Freer the successful businessman was already a noted collector of American prints and paintings, he remained circumscribed in his awareness of Asian cultures and spoke no foreign languages.[1] With the intrepid determination that distinguished every aspect of his life, he embarked on what would be the first of five trips to Asia, each signaling a further development of his knowledge and understanding of Asian culture.

Freer had begun to collect Asian art, but those first purchases were made through dealers in New York. As early as 1887, Freer had bought a small Japanese fan (fig. 41) from Takayanagi Tōzō, an importer of "high class Japanese art objects and a choice collection of bric-a-brac" who had a shop at 160 Fifth Avenue. From the same dealer, Freer also acquired, in 1892, his first Japanese ceramic: an eighteenth-century Satsuma ware jar with an underglaze blue decoration (fig. 42) that reminded Freer of Whistler's landscapes. The following year Freer bought from Takayanagi his first Chinese painting, a small, modest Ming dynasty scroll of herons (fig. 43). Each of these works was quite unlike the more elaborately decorated examples of East Asian art collected by other Westerners in the late nineteenth century. Already Freer was following his own inclinations.

On his first Asian trip Freer was essentially a tourist who was also anxious to rest. The economic depression of 1893 had meant that Freer, habitually hardworking, spent even longer hours than usual attempting to minimize the financial impact on his railroad-car business. Having driven himself for so long without a vacation, he was physically and mentally exhausted, and determined, he said, "to free myself from work for a year and seek rest and pleasure in the old world."[2]

The journey that began in September 1894 would lead Freer far beyond any paths

Fig. 40. In 1907, Freer posed with Hara Tomitarō and Hara's wife (front right) and daughter (front left). In the second row, from right to left, are one of Freer's ricksha men from his 1895 trip; a Yokohama art dealer, believed to be Nomura Yōzō, from whom Freer and Hara purchased objects; and a woman believed to be Miss Margaret Watson, a Detroit friend of Freer's. The group is standing in front of an ancient temple on Hara's estate, Sannotani.

he could have imagined. The terse entries in his diaries pertain mostly to practical matters, but longer comments in letters to friends record Freer's reactions to people, places, and events and reveal his desire to understand the cultures with which he was coming into direct contact. With each of his tours, Freer probed ever more deeply into the complexities of Asian civilizations. By 1909, when he planned an extended stay in China, he was confident that his own perceptions were as valid as those of many experts on Asia. By 1911, at the end of his final tour, Freer was an internationally recognized collector and connoisseur of Asian art.

First Impressions

Freer's transatlantic crossing, which began promptly at noon on 22 September 1894, was uneventful. Elated at experiencing no seasickness, he arrived in Genoa after an enjoyable twelve-day journey. He carried with him a letter of credit for four thousand pounds and many letters of introduction, including one from the governor of Michigan. For more than a month he toured the major cities of Italy before going to Paris for two weeks. The tightly packed itinerary in Italy and the French capital was but a small segment of the entire tour around the world, however. Freer was soon in Marseilles, whence he would embark on his voyage across the Mediterranean to Alexandria and through the Suez Canal across the Indian Ocean to Ceylon (modern Sri Lanka).

When, on 13 December, Freer reached Colombo, the capital of Ceylon, he took his first steps onto Asian soil.[3] For Freer and other Westerners of his generation, Ceylon was regarded as the repository of the original teachings of the Buddha. The relative ease of internal travel and prevalence of English-speaking people made Colombo an excellent starting point, from which Freer caught his initial glimpse of Asia. Even Ceylon's small size was an asset, since it proved considerably less intimidating than the

Fig. 41. Folding fan with spurious signature and seal of Ogata Kōrin (1658–1716), Japan, Edo period, 19th century. Ink and color on paper (17.9 x 49.0), 87.1.

populous Indian subcontinent or the sprawling provinces of China that Freer would eventually experience. He was able to climb to the summit of Adam's Peak (7,360 ft.) and admire the object sacred to pilgrims: an impression in the natural rock traditionally said to be that of the foot of the Buddha. To his friend Frank J. Hecker, Freer wrote of Adam's Peak as the "holy of holies" and admitted that while en route to Ceylon he had exercised daily on shipboard to prepare for the strenuous climb up the mountain.[4] Freer's preparations may have been prompted by Murray's *Handbook for Travellers in India and Pakistan,* the trusted guide for Westerners, which cautioned that the ascent to Adam's Peak was "steep, and to those easily made giddy not altogether safe, but English ladies have been to the summit and it is annually ascended by thousands of pilgrims of both sexes and all ages."[5]

On Christmas Day 1894, Freer stood alone enjoying the sunset from Abhayagiriya (Mount of Safety), the largest of four main reliquary mounds at Anuradhapura in the northern half of the island. During the eleven months of his tour, he frequently spent long periods alone, excepting the company of native servants, most of whom spoke little or no English. Yet Freer gives no indication that he was lonely; in his view it was necessary to see cultural monuments by oneself. Apparently he was intent on learning as much as possible and regarded any diversion as a waste of time and energy. His successful business career was based largely on a comparable ability to set aside distractions and concentrate on the realization of specific goals.

On 3 January 1895, on an overnight steamer, Freer took the approximately two-hundred-mile trip from Colombo across the Gulf of Mannar, arriving on the southeastern coast of the Indian subcontinent. Undoubtedly echoing the comments in his guidebook, Freer noted that the Buddhist *chaitya* hall at Karle, which dates to the first century A.D., was the largest and best preserved in India. But the teeming port city of Bombay, as indeed all of the major Indian cities where European influence was predominant, received negative reactions from the discriminating Freer: he emphatically advised Hecker, "When you are in India waste no time at Calcutta, Madras, Bombay or Delhi." Traveling to Ellora, he explored the rock-cut temples, dedicated to Hindu and Buddhist deities, that extend three-quarters of a mile along the western face of a hill. If he did not care for all of India, overnight in

Fig. 42. Bottle, Satsuma ware, attributed to Kanō Tangen (1679–1767), Japan, Edo period, 18th century. White body with underglaze cobalt decoration (21.7 x 17.5), 92.26.

Fig. 43. Artist unknown,
Herons (detail), China, Ming
dynasty, 17th century. Hanging
scroll; ink and color on silk
(44.3 x 29), 93.32.

Ellora he slept in the state guesthouse of the nizam of Hyderabad, which he pronounced "splendid."[6]

In search of cooler weather, Freer journeyed north, where he had an audience with H. H. Sir Jaswant Singh Bahadur, the maharaja of Jodhpur in Rajputna, whose "princely courtesies" to Freer included the unlimited use of his private stables and servants and whose "jewels would fill a hogshead" (fig. 44). The maharaja sent one of his friends, who spoke English perfectly, to show Freer the sights, "many of which are seldom seen by any one."[7]

With remarkable physical stamina for a person concerned about his health, Freer included Delhi, Lahore, and Peshawar on his route to the northwestern frontier between India (modern Pakistan) and Afghanistan. There, protected by an armed escort, Freer chose to visit the Khyber Pass, which was "open only two days each week" and "where no European is allowed to enter without a pass and escort and under no circumstances to travel beyond Ali Mashid Fort."[8] The Taj Mahal at Agra and the city of Fatehpur Sikri were principal monuments on Freer's itinerary. But his extraordinary endurance began to flag, and by the time he reached Benares (modern Varanasi), his right leg, aching from so much walking, prevented him from doing as much as he would have liked in that holy city on the Ganges. A tour of Bodh Gaya also was curtailed by his ailing leg. Finally, in Calcutta, Freer was in such pain that he was forced to seek medical advice. The doctor prescribed a rest at Darjeeling, located high in the mountains and justly famous for its moderate temperatures and spectacular view of the Himalayas. The setting provided Freer with a much-needed rest as well as an opportunity to reflect on all he had seen before he returned to Calcutta—a "fearful hole"—to continue his journey to Japan.[9]

On March 20, Freer left Calcutta, bound for Colombo, then to Singapore, with the heat becoming more intense as the ship neared its destination.[10] He complained about the tropical weather and his troublesome leg but was relieved when, after an overnight stop in Singapore, he was able to sail north to Hong Kong and its more bearable weather. Hong Kong and Shanghai were Freer's only Chinese ports of call during his first Asian tour, and the intrigue of their distinctly European atmosphere juxtaposed against crowded native quarters compelled him to consider a future visit. His six days in Shanghai were, Freer wrote, "enough to show me a finer, higher side of Chinese life than I had supposed existed. Also a coarser, lower level than I had dreamed of."[11] The "finer, higher" aspects of Chinese life may well have been a reference to several pieces of Chinese pottery that he had purchased before leaving Shanghai for Japan.

After arriving in Nagasaki's foreign settlement, grateful to be able to enjoy the cherry blossoms, Freer recorded, "India is entirely unlike Japan; and Indian life and adventures will, I think, leave more lasting and precious impressions upon my mind."[12] Given those reactions, it is ironic that Freer never again visited the Indian subcontinent yet made several extended trips to Japan. Moreover, he did not begin to acquire Indian art—which formed a surprisingly small portion of his total holdings—until 1907, although he assembled an extensive collection of Japanese pottery, painting, and sculpture. Freer enjoyed the smooth water and picturesque scenery of Japan's scenic Inland Sea, which took him to Kobe, a Japanese port city favored by late nineteenth-century foreigners for its dry, clear air and its proximity to many scenic areas.

Fig. 44. H. H. Sir Jaswant Singh Bahadur, the maharaja of Jodhpur, 1880s. Photograph by P. A. Johnson for Johnson and Hoffman. From Clark Worswick and Ainslie Embree, *The Last Empire: Photography in British India, 1855–1911* (New York: Aperture, 1976), pl. 117.

In Kyoto, one of Freer's goals—closely related to his business interests—was to attend the Naikoku Kangyō Hakuranki (Japanese Industrial Exposition). Similar large-scale domestic expositions had been held in Tokyo in 1877, 1881, and 1890 as a result of foreign interest in Japanese art and culture following the international expositions of 1873 in Vienna and 1876 in Philadelphia. Freer had attended the latter, organized as part of the American Centennial celebration, where the first Japanese artifacts were presented to the American public. After studying the displays at the Kyoto exposition, Freer turned to more traditional Japanese culture. He had planned his itinerary on the basis of the routes recommended in Murray's reliable *Handbook for Travellers in Japan;* his copy of the guide-book is well thumbed, with copious notes and underlining that demonstrate the meticulous way in which Freer went about his tour.[13] When he interrupted his investigations of Buddhist temples to enjoy the excitement of the Hōzu Rapids, he first had to pass over a "hilly and rough" road from Kyoto to Hōzu that required riding in a ricksha, a mode of transportation very different from the American railroad cars with which he was so

Fig. 45. Freer and two ricksha men, Kyoto, 1895. Freer wears a rumpled suit and loose tie; perhaps as a concession to the dusty Kyoto streets, he rolled up the cuffs of his trousers. On several occasions Freer took extended trips into the mountains—sometimes for as long as ten days—accompanied only by his reliable Japanese ricksha men, some of whom, he wrote in his diary, could "cover forty or more miles a day."

familiar. Yet Freer adjusted quickly. Shortly after arriving in Japan, he had found two ricksha men whom he engaged for the rest of his stay, and in Kyoto posed with them for a studio photograph (fig. 45).

Freer's itinerary in Japan included many highlights. The scenery at Lake Biwa, where Freer spent a day, enjoys a unique status in Japanese poetry, painting, and calligraphy. By mid-May, obviously relishing Japan's varied landscape and historic monuments, Freer was in the ancient capital of Nara, where he visited the Buddhist temple Hōryūji; in his guidebook he penciled a single word, "delightful," beside the detailed account of Nara, and another, "superb," next to the description of Hōryūji. At Uji, a short distance from Kyoto, with its picturesque town and enterprising cormorant fishermen, Freer admired the serenely elegant Byōdōin (Phoenix Hall), one of the most beautiful of all Japanese Buddhist temples. For many Americans the Phoenix Hall had become a symbol of Japan when a replica of the eleventh-century structure was constructed in Jackson Park, Chicago, for the 1893 Columbian Exposition. Freer would return to the Phoenix Hall on subsequent trips to Japan, always receptive to the quiet harmony of Buddhist architecture.

In Nagoya, Freer hoped to see the screen paintings by Tanyū, Eishin, Motonobu, and other Kanō school artists housed in the castle, towering over the city, of the Owari branch of the Tokugawa family. To expedite his access to the paintings, he had obtained a formal document from the American minister in Tokyo. But bureaucrats in Nagoya detected inconsistencies in the paperwork, and Freer had to be content with seeing only the outside of the building. He was not happy about his experience with Japanese officialdom or with the hospitality of Nagoya, and was further irritated at being followed throughout the city by a Japanese detective. It was with considerable relief that Freer left Nagoya for Nikko, where he spent almost a week admiring the elaborately crafted mausolea of the Togukawa shoguns, located high in the mountains some one hundred miles north of Tokyo. With characteristic thoroughness, Freer allocated a separate day for each of the two mausolea and set about comparing the temple of Ieyasu (1542–1616) with that of his grandson, Iemitsu (1603–1651).

From Nikko, Freer took an excursion to the Kirifuji-no-taki (Mist-Falling Cascade). A teahouse on the hill above the waterfall provided a fine view of the cascade and a panoramic vista of the surrounding countryside. Freer also went to Chūzenji, which, with its beautiful lake, was regarded as one of the principal points of interest in those environs. While it was possible, according to Murray's guidebook, for "sturdy pedestrians" to walk to and from Chūzenji in a day, Freer apparently made the trip in a ricksha, stopping at teahouses along the way.

To the south, in Kyoto, Freer visited the Kurodani Buddhist monastery. The architecture and art treasures obviously impressed him, for he made profuse notes in the margins of his guidebook and carefully underlined certain sections. The Ginkakuji (Silver Pavilion) was equally exciting. Freer's comment, "Yes, very interesting," only partially conveys his preoccupation with the small, two-story structure situated in a quiet garden, for his guidebook also contains a pencil sketch he drew of the floor plan of the four-and-one-half-mat tearoom.

On three consecutive days in Kyoto, Freer visited the imperial palace, where he observed the contrast of its imposing scale and opulent decoration with the austere refinement of the Katsura and Shigakuin imperial retreats in the suburbs of the city. With his first stay in Japan rapidly drawing to a close, Freer went twice to the Kinkakuji (Golden Pavilion), located in a Zen garden. By 1895 the modest wooden structure retained little of its original gold leaf, but the phoenix-shaped finial was eloquent proof of its former elegance.[14] He also visited the Nishihonganji, a large, imposing Buddhist complex known for its architecture and paintings, and noted with satisfaction that August was the "best time" to appreciate the monumental site.

On 21 August, Freer left Kobe for his return voyage to the United States and by 12

September was in Detroit. Ceylon, India, and Japan had been the highlights of his trip, with China little more than a footnote. Freer had seen a great deal as a private individual. He would never again enjoy such anonymity in Asia.

Splendid Opportunities

When Charles Freer traveled to Asia again in 1906–07, twelve years after his first tour, he was fifty-three years old and a well-known art collector. A carefully planned trip, it lasted eight months and enabled Freer to see even more Asian countries than before. In letters and in his diary, Freer expressed an assurance that contrasts sharply with his more tentative reactions of 1895.

In mid-November 1906, during a raging snowstorm, Freer sailed from New York for Naples. He made excursions to Ischia, Bosco, and Pompeii but was impatient to renew his acquaintance with Asia. Within two weeks, he sailed for Egypt, stopping first in Alexandria, where he visited Pompey's Pillar, the Catacombs, and the Greco-Roman Museum before proceeding to Cairo, then a popular winter resort for international travelers. Continuing his relentless investigation of cultural monuments, he used as a general guide the newly published *Caire, Le Nil et Memphis* by Gaston Migeon, curator at the Musée du Louvre, and meticulously recorded the date of his visit beside the illustrations of buildings, including the Citadel, the Mosque of Sultan Hassan, the Great Mosque of Sultan Bhikuk, the Mosque of Anvin, the Blue Mosque, the Red Mosque, the Coptic Church, the Obelisk, the Virgin Tree, the Cairo Museum, the Arab Museum, and the bazaars.[15] As a change of pace, he made the obligatory trip to Gizeh and contemplated the battered ruins of the Pyramids and the Sphinx silhouetted against restless desert sand.

In business correspondence to Frank Hecker, Freer described some ancient Greek biblical manuscripts of "exceeding interest" that he had purchased in Cairo for sixteen hundred pounds. Normally measured in his comments, he related in this instance that the manuscripts "carried me completely off my feet." He wrote, further, "As I wish the purchase kept quite private, I trust you will not mention it outside."[16] Freer had good reason to urge Hecker to remain silent about his latest acquisition, for he had ventured into an area that was new to him, and the claims made by Ali Arabi, the dealer, about the age and importance of the manuscripts were too extravagant to accept without reservation. The parchment pages were bound within wooden covers bearing encaustic portraits of the Four Evangelists, depicted in the order in which their Gospels appear in the manuscript: Matthew and John on the left cover, Luke and Mark on the right (fig. 46). The Greek text was written in dark brown ink on thick parchment, and the leaves were brittle, especially at the edges; many of the pages were firmly stuck together and held desert sand in the wrinkles. Even the positive comments of two Greek scholars had not completely relieved Freer's doubts about the wisdom of his uncharacteristically impulsive purchase. By the time Freer traveled to Egypt again, in 1908, the importance of his acquisition was internationally recognized and biblical scholars were busily analyzing the

manuscripts, which would be referred to, when published several years later, as the Washington Manuscript of the Gospels.[17]

Throughout Freer's travels in Egypt—to Luxor, Abu Simbel, Aswan, and as far south as Nubia and the Sudan—he was formulating wide-ranging plans for the future of his collection. He wrote to Hecker about the need for specimens of Egyptian art:

Another branch of the question is whether my collection can express the power of line and forms to their full value and as I have so long desired without including stone and wood sculptured figures, unglazed, of certain Egyptian dynasties. I now feel these things are the greatest art in the world—greater than Greek, Chinese or Japanese. My mind, so far as the Chinese and Japanese are considered may slightly change and further light concerning these branches is really my great hurry to reach Japan.

Fig. 46. Covers to the Washington Manuscripts, with portraits of the Four Evangelists, Egypt, 7th century A.D. Encaustic painting on wood; each panel (21.3 x 14.3), 06.297-98.

During my study on the wonderful old mosques in Cairo and the Arabic library and muse-
ums in the same city—and in meeting intelligent Arabs and Syrians and private Egyptian collec-
tors, I learned enough additional facts to confirm my early impressions that my pieces of Rakka
[Syrian pottery] are all genuine and fully as rare and beautiful as I had supposed.[18]

Although Freer would change many of those opinions, they are important to the evolution of his thinking about the nature and scope of his collection and the museum in
which it would be installed. In correspondence with Hecker, Freer noted that his collection would lose much of its interest to future scholars if not classified properly and accurately.[19] His custom of saving all documents relating to his acquisitions may well reflect
his meticulous business practices; whatever the impetus, the registrarial and archival
records preserved in the Freer Gallery are remarkably complete.

In spite of Freer's intentions to acquire representative examples of Egyptian sculpture, he made relatively few purchases in 1907, perhaps partially in response to the local
dealers. "Business practices here are shocking," he wrote to Hecker. "I have bought a
few things and have struck some pretty tough men. Honor in business affairs is unknown
and many others of the traits in mankind which we in America are taught to admire,
here are entirely unseen."[20]

In January 1907, Freer set sail for Colombo. He described his second visit to
Ceylon as an opportunity to see the "buried cities" and "Buddhistic ruins" of the island.
The general itinerary of his 1895 stay in Ceylon was replaced by a set of specific goals
that were intimately related to the Asian acquisitions he had made during the intervening twelve years. This trip, Freer stated, would be the "last effort I shall ever make" to
view those monuments.[21]

The guidebook Freer used this time, *The Buried Cities of Ceylon: A Guide Book to
Anuradhapura and Polonaruwa with Chapters on Dambulla, Kalavewa, Minintale and Sigiri,*
was a gift from his guide, L. Peter Rodrigo, the assistant archaeological chief of Ceylon.[22]
From the extensive notes Freer wrote in the margins of the slender volume, it becomes
obvious that he studied the contents with his usual care. Above the description of the
"deathlike stillness" of a circle of Buddha images at the Maha Vihare, Freer recorded his
own experience: "But the noisy priests ruin the effect with their quarrelling of the tips. I
could only get silence by having my guide tell them they would get no further money
unless they closed their mouths and kept them tight." In other comments, he relates his
annoyance when the Buddhist priests, a "fearful gang," began "greedily demanding gra-
tuities from strangers." "A great pow wow followed my contributions," he wrote,
"each one claiming for himself the silver pieces I gave in each temple for the temple
reparation and care."[23]

Having completed his tour of Ceylon, Freer sailed for Singapore and Batavia, capital of the Dutch East Indies. He arrived in Java excited by the prospect of seeing the Buddhist and Hindu temples about which he had heard and read so much. Members of a Dutch organization concerned with the preservation of the ruins helped Freer to plan his itinerary, which included "about a half dozen temples . . . which they tell me not a half dozen foreigners have seen since the Dutch took possession."[24] The redoubtable Sir Stamford Raffles, lieutenant governor of Java from 1811 to 1816, had been the first Westerner to discover and describe the temples at Prambanan in central Java.

In "fine weather and perfect view," Freer spent a day touring the "eight groups of Hindu ruins" on the plain near Prambanan. His unofficial guide was *A Padre in Partibus: Being Notes and Impressions of a Brief Holiday Tour through Java, the Eastern Archipelago and Siam* by the Reverend George M. Reith, a book he had purchased in Singapore several days earlier.[25] But he was not dependent on Reverend Reith's rambling descriptions; he had prepared himself for his examination of the tenth-century temples by reading the scholarly analyses of Dr. Isaäc Groneman, honorary president of the Archaeological Society at Jakarta.[26] Without expressing approval or disapproval, Freer marked a passage in Reith's book about the reliefs on the temple of Shiva:

They depict scenes from the Ramayana, some of which are lewd and obscene. In this point they present a great contrast to the Buddhist sculptures of Boro Boedoer [Borobudur] and elsewhere, which are pure and chaste, and the most careless observer comparing the two cannot fail to note how great was the moral advance of Buddhism beyond the parent religion. One could spend many a pleasant hour, however, in these galleries of pictured stone, for the indecency is only occasional—one has to take it with the rest—and the crowded bas-reliefs are both beautiful and interesting.[27]

From Prambanan, Freer traveled by carriage to the great Borobudur complex, arriving on 8 March. Once again he referred to a study of the site by Dr. Groneman[28] and the reminiscences of Reverend Reith. Freer purchased an album of photographs that record the condition of Borobudur at the beginning of the twentieth century, before extensive conservation would remove the moss, lichen, and intrusive vegetation and restore many of the stones to their original positions. He spent the entire day studying the ninth-century Buddhist narrative bas-reliefs and freestanding esoteric Buddha images that envelop and surmount the imposing monument. At dusk he watched from the top of the great stupa as the sunset slowly transformed the surrounding countryside. It was, Freer wrote in his diary, the "most beautiful view of my life."[29] Like the Reverend Reith and many other travelers before him, Freer spent the night at the guesthouse located near the stupa. Freer may well have signed the visitor's book to which Reith refers and read some of the remarks about Borobudur, ranging from the deadly earnest to the irreverent, that had been left behind by earlier travelers.[30]

From Batavia, Freer passed through Singapore and Saigon before reaching Hong Kong on Easter Sunday. When he went ashore the following day, he enjoyed the panoramic view of the harbor from Victoria Peak, saw the "native town," and purchased pottery from local dealers. On a short trip to Canton, he walked around a portion of the walled city and bought more ceramics. Then, in Shanghai, he noted that among other great changes since his earlier visit, "Huge buildings have sprung up and immense business operations are started."[31] One of the few objects that Freer obtained from Chinese dealers in the "old native city" was an earthenware model of a tower made for an Eastern Han dynasty burial (fig. 47). After centuries in the earth the green lead glaze on the tower had developed a shimmering iridescence that further enriched its visual appeal.

Freer was soon journeying to Japan. Although he still regarded Japan as the major cultural center in East Asia, he left China with lingering regret that his visit had been so brief:

Already I am dreaming of some old inland cities lying between Saigon and Peking—which someday I would like to search as I did Canton and Shanghai, only more slowly and thoroughly. From Egypt to the temples of Ceylon and Java and thence to the treasure houses of China and Japan is to me an experience of indescribable delight.[32]

Every aspect of Freer's second visit to Japan was different from his previous tour in 1895. An unknown foreigner with an affinity for the subtle beauty of Japan's ancient traditions, Freer had spent most of his first visit trekking through the mountains to various scenic spots and avoiding large cities. But by 1907, Freer's reputation as a collector of Asian art preceded him, and the galaxy of Japanese art collectors who opened their homes and collections to him provides ample evidence of his new and favorable situation. Although Freer had bought a great deal of Asian art from 1895 to 1907, he had traveled during that time only as far as Europe. For his second Asian trip, no less a figure than Ernest Fenollosa, the American specialist in Asian art, had provided letters of introduction, organized an elaborate travel plan, and entreated Freer to use his name "for all it may be worth." Fenollosa assured Freer nonetheless, "You may safely trust to your own judgment of paintings, better than anybody's."[33] In 1907, Fenollosa's was certainly a fair evaluation of Freer's connoisseurship, but Freer had become increasingly more confident about his own expertise and needed little urging to rely on his own opinions.

One of the most extraordinary events in Freer's 1907 visit to Japan was his meeting with Hara Tomitarō, a prominent Japanese banker, silk merchant, and art collector (see

Fig. 47. Model of tower, China, Eastern Han dynasty, 2d century A.D. Glazed clay (84.4 x 44.0), 07.68. Pottery models of this type, a two-story tower set within a bowl-shaped moat, with sentries and archers standing guard, were made for burial during the Han dynasty.

fig. 40).[34] Hara invited Freer to stay at Sannotani, his large villa overlooking Yokohama Bay, and turned over his estate and his art collection to Freer for as long as Freer remained in Japan.[35] Freer recalled:

[Hara] traced me from Shanghai, sent men to Nagasaki, where my ship did not stop, then to Kobe to meet me and escort me to this wonderful fairy land. He secured one of my old time servants to attend to my personal requirements, has a flock of other servants at my call, horses, etc.[36]

According to Freer's description, Sannotani consisted of more than two hundred acres, upon which were temples, shrines, and teahouses in addition to the traditional Japanese house in which Freer stayed. Hara's storage building, or *kura,* was attached to the guest quarters, which gave Freer full access to Hara's magnificent treasures (fig. 48). "It completely overwhelms me and I really don't know what to do," he wrote to Hecker. "It is one of those extraordinary manifestations of Oriental hospitality of which I am extreme-

Fig. 48. Room in Hara Tomitarō's villa, Sannotani, ca. 1915. Hara's son, Hara Zenichirō, is on the right.

ly unworthy and which I can never repay."[37] In two weeks at Sannotani, Freer studied Hara's art collection, walked in the gardens, entertained in the elegant surroundings, and exchanged opinions with Hara about their East Asian collections. The two collectors also became friends, and for the remainder of Freer's life their friendship was punctuated by exchanges of gifts of art. Each of Freer's two subsequent visits to Japan included a visit to Sannotani.

On his 1907 trip, Freer reveled in his distinctive status among the most outstanding and influential art collectors in Japan. His requests to view individual objects or entire collections were granted promptly, with quiet Japanese courtesy. Almost gleefully, Freer wrote to Hecker of having spent the afternoon with Masuda Takashi, head of the Mitsui business enterprises.[38] Freer described Masuda as the "richest collector of Japan," then related how Masuda had invited a few other Japanese collectors to meet him:

It was an extraordinary little event. You should have heard their congratulatory remarks concerning the manner in which I bought the Ririomin [Chin.: Li Longmian; see fig. 70] rakans from under "our feet" as they put it. The loss of these sixteen paintings to Japan created great excitement and now they stand ready to make great sacrifice to get them back again. Fortunately for America, I could not return them even if I wanted—they are in the Smithsonian lot.[39]

The stay in Japan was not without some distasteful incidents, however. The "shocking" behavior of some dealers and their associates, some of whom were Buddhist priests, provoked strong outbursts from Freer. Although he was reluctant to record in writing the denouement of his struggle with Japanese dealers, he was fond of telling the story to friends: Evidently some of the dealers, from whom Freer had determined never to purchase another object, managed to arrange a visit to a dilapidated temple where, Freer was told, everything was for sale. For two days Freer studied the collection. Just when he was about to purchase most of the objects, he learned that the priests actually were dealers in disguise, and all the monks were equally bogus—they were, in fact, relatives of the dealers who were playing their crucial parts in the drama. In an effort to circumvent further unpleasant experiences that might compromise his relationships with private collectors, Freer avoided shops he had previously frequented:

This course I found necessary in order to see the many private collections to which they are not admitted and also to protect myself against contemplated conspiracies, which I quickly discovered after my landing at Kobe, were aimed in a big way, and most devilish, at my purse. . . . The story is an amazing one, particularly the part played by dealers, long enough for a sensational novel, unholy enough to satisfy a missionaries's [sic] dream and beset with the greatest aesthetic pitfalls I have thus far met. The closing act, I dare not put on paper.[40]

The "closing act" was Freer's taking one of the fraudulent Buddhist priests by the scruff of his neck and physically removing him from his hotel room. As a postscript, Freer wryly told friends that most of the antiques he had seen in the temple soon reappeared on their accustomed shelves in dealers' shops.[41]

Encounters with nefarious Japanese art dealers were only part of a transformation that Freer noted in his letters. He also lamented the loss of the quiet, gracious country he had observed twelve years earlier: "Japan is undergoing tremendous changes and in the fierce race for wealth and power, its traditions and authentic ideals are being trampled in a mire hideous beyond description." A few days later he would write, "The changes going on in Japan are terrible—everything is being Europeanized! Were it not for my study here I would leave Tokyo tonight and get off to the country where a trace, at least, of Japan's tradition may still cling."[42] It is doubtful that Freer repeated those remarks to his scrupulously courteous hosts, men of noble or business families who were guiding Japan toward a future in which Western technology was crucial.

After bidding farewell to the friends who had come to see him off, Freer sailed from Yokohama, arriving in San Francisco on 14 July. Five days later he was home in Detroit.

To Understand Beauty in a Wider Way

When in the following year Freer traveled to West Asia, his goal was to broaden his knowledge of his Egyptian and West Asian holdings in general and his Rakka pottery in particular. He stated his purpose in a letter to Hecker: "My quest to the 'Holy Land'—Racca pottery. You know I have invested pretty heavily in this line of 'fayence' and I consider it necessary to learn what I can."[43] Arriving in Port Said, Egypt, Freer was greeted by Ibrahim Aly, his former interpreter, or dragoman, who awaited Freer eagerly, impatient for a promised gold watch.[44] In Cairo, Freer quickly found "Old Arabi," the dealer from whom he had acquired the biblical manuscripts eighteen months earlier (fig. 49). Almost at once Freer became immersed in the game of bargaining for art treasures, a pastime that he had grown to enjoy and in which he clearly could hold his own: "Poker and all other games are as nothing," he wrote to Hecker. "It's real living, real experience and beats winning a big contract for cars quite out of sight. In dealing with these Eastern devils one's imagination is really stirred."[45]

After Freer left Alexandria for Jerusalem, where he spent several days visiting all the major sites of the old religious center, he spent the next several weeks in Beirut and the ancient cities of Damascus, Baalbek, and Aleppo. The multilayered history of the West Asian cultural centers impressed him. As always, he was looking at objects—particularly ceramics, whether in museums, private collections, or dealers' shops—with an eye to learning more about their quality, history, and provenance. In West Asian ceramics, as in Japanese paintings, he was gaining confidence in his own connoisseurship. He wrote to Hecker, "I have already learned how inaccurate [is] much of that which has been hitherto said about the potteries of Damascus and the vast field north and east of here. This information alone is worth more to my personal collection than I had dared dream."[46]

Given Freer's interest in Rakka ware, it is understandable that he wanted to reach the place where the pottery was said to have been made: the city of Rakka (ancient Nicephorium) on the Euphrates River in north central Syria. The nearest Freer came to that destination, however, was Aleppo, where he purchased several pieces of pottery from street vendors. Freer had obtained his first example of so-called Rakka pottery, a singled-handled pot (fig. 50), from Dikran Kelekian in 1902;[47] so impressed was Freer with its rich greenish blue glaze that he continued to acquire the ware. Freer's enthusiastic response was apparently influenced by his earlier acquisitions of Chinese, Japanese, and Korean ceramics, in which he admired foremost the subtle nuances in the glazes. When commenting on his initial purchases of Rakka ware, Freer invariably stressed his appreciation of their rich iridescent surfaces rather than their shapes.

Along the Mediterranean coast Freer made stops at Rhodes and Smyrna, then continued through the Dardanelles to Constantinople (modern Istanbul). He responded to the historic city, the capital of Byzantium, in the qualified way that many foreign visitors have, noting a few "drawbacks" in "one of the handsomest of cities."[48] Among the mon-

Fig. 49. Freer and colleagues in Cairo, 1909. From left to right are Dr. Thomas Mann, Freer, Ibrahim Aly, and Ali Arabi. At the time he purchased the Washington Manuscripts (see fig. 46), Freer promised Ali Arabi's son a gold pocket watch if the manuscripts proved to be genuine. When they did, Freer presented him with a watch and sent one to Ali several months later. Freer continued to give watches to dealers and guides throughout Asia.

uments Freer saw was the "Chinese Pavilion" in the "Old Seraglio." His interest in that remarkable collection of Chinese celadon and blue-and-white porcelain—which had been assembled by the Ottoman sultans mainly during the sixteenth through eighteenth centuries and is now housed in the Topkapi Palace Museum—is prophetic. Almost a half-century later John A. Pope, the third director of the Freer Gallery (fig. 51), would write a scholarly volume about a portion of that collection[49] and acquire a small group of outstanding examples of the ware from the important Jingdezhen kilns in southeastern China (fig. 52).

Athens, Corinth, Patras, Olympia, Corfu, Trieste, Vienna, and Budapest were on Freer's itinerary before he boarded the Orient Express for Paris, where he enjoyed a few days with friends, such as Gaston Migeon, curator at the Louvre; Marcel Bing, the art dealer; and Raymond Koechlin, the writer and art critic. Most of Freer's time in Paris, however, was devoted to arranging shipment to the United States of the pieces he had purchased in Syria; his other acquisitions had been sent directly to Detroit.[50] On 26 August, Freer sailed for New York, arriving home on 6 September.

Scientifically and Determinedly

Freer's fourth trip to Asia, in 1909, began with stops in Europe and England. Freer had designed an itinerary based on correspondence with Asian art scholars. Dr. Ernst Arthur Voretzsch, the German consul-general to China, had urged Freer to spend more time in China searching for important examples of early Chinese art. Freer had also communicated with Isaac Taylor Headland, professor of science and psychology at Beijing University from 1890 to 1907,[51] who had assembled a collection of Chinese art, a portion of which was exhibited under the auspices of the Art Society of Pittsburgh; Freer had subsequently purchased two of the scrolls that were purported to date from the Song dynasty (figs. 53 and 54). Headland's advice on the need for a longer stay in "interior China" to attract dealers, which was reinforced by Voretzsch, prompted Freer to make definite plans for his trips to Asia in 1909 and 1911.

Again, Freer was ailing when he left the United States. Although an ulcer on his left foot had to be lanced before he boarded ship, Freer nevertheless maintained a busy schedule at his first stop, Paris. Throughout his stay his companion and interpreter was Marie Nordlinger, to whom he had been introduced in 1904 by Siegfried Bing, the French art dealer and father of Marcel. Born in Manchester, England, Miss Nordlinger had first worked for Bing in his Art Nouveau workshop as an enamelist and, subsequently, when he was disposing of his Japanese print collection, as his representative in New

York. While in the United States, she had assisted Freer with cataloguing portions of his collection in preparation for the formal acceptance of his gift by the United States government; she recorded her observations in letters to the French writer Marcel Proust.[52] In Paris, Freer and Miss Nordlinger met with various art dealers, including Dikran Kelekian, Marcel Bing, and Edgar Worch, and they called on Migeon at the Louvre and Koechlin at his home. Departing from the formality usually extended to Freer even by his closest friends, Miss Nordlinger invariably began letters to him with "Dear Charlie." She would maintain a close friendship with Freer until his death in 1919.

On a brief trip to London, Freer dined with Laurence Binyon, who was for many years keeper of the Department of Prints and Drawings at the British Museum. Binyon frequently discussed objects from Freer's collection in his publications, and in 1916, at Freer's request, would take time from relief work to write an essay on a sixty-foot-long handscroll that Freer had acquired in Beijing five years earlier (fig. 55).[53] Freer also conversed with the redoubtable archaeologist and collector Sir Aurel Stein about his "splen-

Fig. 50. Pot, Rakka ware, Syria, 11th–12th century. Glazed clay (12.9 x 19.8), 02.244.

Fig. 51. John A. Pope (1906–1982), seated second from right, in Xi'an with the Committee of the China International Famine Relief Commission, 1929. John Alexander Pope Papers, Freer Gallery of Art and Arthur M. Sackler Gallery Archives.

Fig. 52. Dish, Jingdezhen ware, China, Ming dynasty, early 15th century. White porcelain with underglaze cobalt blue decoration (08.9 x 44.7), 53.77.

did work in Turkestan, Bhutan, and Western China" and saw "hundreds of his discoveries—seventh-century Chinese paintings, etc., etc."[54] Although Freer was in London only briefly, he made a number of important purchases. The four pieces he acquired from T. J. Larkin of New Bond Street, London, were, in his view, the "greatest collection ever exported from Persia."[55] Although scholars have modified Freer's original estimation, the thirteenth-century fragment of a Seljuk tile depicting an assembly of youths is still considered to have been an important acquisition (fig. 56).

In Berlin, Freer maintained his enthusiasm over his latest purchases. After five visits to see the collection of Persian pottery given to the Kaiser Friedrich Museum by the German archaeologist Friedrich Sarre, he wrote to Hecker: "It is the best collection in Germany and probably second best in Europe, but the whole collection does not include a single specimen equal to any one of at least eight of those recently bought by me in Paris and London and in numbers my collection is easily three times larger than his including my late additions."[56]

At the Museum für Völkerkunde (Ethnological Museum), Freer met Albert von Le Coq, keeper of the Indian collection, who showed him the Central Asian wall paintings and manuscripts that he and Albert Grünwedel, director of the museum's Indian

Department, had brought back from the first of several expeditions sponsored by the German government.[57] Keenly interested in transcultural relationships, Freer had followed closely the activities of the various groups from Russia, Sweden, England, and Germany that were investigating ancient sites in Central Asia. Having read published reports of the expeditions as soon as they became available, he concluded that the "Chinese-Turkestan objects in Berlin . . . must be of priceless value to all who are interested in Oriental art; they are undoubtedly the great connecting link between the early Buddhistick art of India and all that grew out of it in later periods in the further east."[58]

Freer also visited Brussels, Ghent, Bruges, Antwerp, Cologne, and Dresden, as well as the Italian cities of Milan, Rome, and Naples, before sailing for Alexandria. Proceeding to Cairo without delay, he engaged his favorite dragoman, Ibrahim Aly, and visited the art dealer Ali Arabi; he also acquired an important collection of some fourteen hundred pieces of ancient Egyptian glass (fig. 57). While many of the objects—including 750 beads—are small, the collection is remarkable for its quality and range.[59]

Accustomed as Freer was to the intrigue that attended all aspects of the Cairo antiquities market, he was not surprised to receive a visit from

Maurice Nahman, a local banker active as an art dealer, whom Freer had met on his previous visit to Cairo. The two men had recently been engaged in correspondence negotiating for a treasure cache called the Gold Treasure, believed to have consisted originally of thirty-six pieces. Early in 1909, Nahman had shown all thirty-six of the objects to the scholars who attended an archaeological congress in Cairo, including Dr. Walter Dennison, professor of Latin at the University of Michigan, Ann Arbor. Dennison was so impressed with what he saw that he immediately cabled to Freer a description of the most outstanding pieces of the "marvelous Byzantine Gold Treasure," listing among its contents a "Medallion Theodosius in frame, Crystal Statuette of Theodosium. Two Earrings, Two Bracelets with pearls, Three small Medallions."[60] The original Gold Treasure is said to have come either from Antinoë on the east bank of the Nile or from Tomei near Assiût in Upper Egypt;[61] recent scholarship has confirmed that the objects included in the Gold Treasure date from the sixth and seventh centuries and probably were made in Constantinople. While Freer realized the importance of the find, he was reluctant to purchase any of the objects without having actually seen them. The necessity of making a quick decision and his confidence in Dennison's judgment prompted him, however, to set aside his hesitation, and he instructed Dennison to purchase those nine pieces (fig. 58). In Cairo, Nahman was already offering to buy them back,[62] but Freer declined. Not until late December 1909, upon his return to Detroit, was he able to see the objects for himself and assess their significance.

From Cairo, Freer set out for Hong Kong, stopping at Colombo, Penang, and

Fig. 53. Artist unknown, *Pavilion of Rising Clouds*, China, Song dynasty, 12th century. Hanging scroll; ink on silk (150.0 x 78.8), 08.171. Although this landscape is no longer attributed to the Northern Song master Mi Fu (A.D. 1052–1107), it is still regarded as the most important surviving painting based on Mi Fu's large-scale compositions.

Fig. 54. Artist unknown, *Dwellings of the Immortals* (detail), China, Ming dynasty, 17th century. Handscroll; color on silk (56.6 x 638.1), 08.170. Freer and his contemporaries valued this scroll more highly than the Song dynasty landscape once attributed to Mi Fu (fig. 53). Formerly attributed to the Song master Fang Chunnian (1st half 12th century), it is little studied today.

Fig. 55. Artist unknown, *Landscape* (detail), China, Ming dynasty, 15th–16th century. Handscroll; ink and color on silk (66.4 x 1842.7), 11.169. Freer believed this landscape to be a genuine work by the late twelfth- to early thirteenth-century artist Ma Yuan, but today the scroll is considered a Ming dynasty copy of *A Pure and Remote View of Streams and Hills* (Palace Museum, Beijing) by Ma Yuan's contemporary, Xia Gui. The opening passage of the scroll is based on a now-missing section of the original Xia Gui painting.

Singapore on the way. At his destination, he stayed with Voretzsch, whose residence was filled with Chinese antiquities he had collected in East Asia. Perhaps without realizing how far-reaching his influence would be, Voretzsch introduced Freer to several prominent Chinese collectors. For the first time, Freer had the opportunity to discuss traditional Chinese connoisseurship with native collectors and to study individual antiquities with the same intimacy he had experienced in Japan.

By September, Freer had traveled from Hong Kong to Tianjin, where he engaged Nan Mingyuan, a Chinese guide and interpreter who would serve faithfully throughout Freer's sojourns in Beijing. Freer was soon aware of his good fortune in having hired the chubby and good-natured Nan, who enjoyed a remarkable success escorting Westerners through the delicate web of Chinese social, economic, and political life. In a letter to Hecker, Freer extolled Nan's virtues:

I am most fortunate in having secured the services of a native expert . . . in Chinese ancient art, who, during the last twenty years has served many foreign and native collectors and merchants. . . . I have never known his equal in ancient things Chinese—in fact, in Chinese art he is fully [Ernest] Fenollosa's equal in Japanese art. He lives in Tientsin [Tianjin] where I first met him, but he knows everyone in Peking [Beijing].[63]

In turn, Freer's kindness and generosity impressed Nan, who regarded Freer as a paragon among the Westerner visitors. It may have been an even greater surprise for Nan to learn of Freer's status as a famous collector and connoisseur; but in later years, when Nan was seeking a new post with foreign visitors to China, he took full advantage of his former relationship with Freer.[64]

During his monthlong stay in Beijing, Freer found time for mandatory sightseeing: he visited the Temple of Heaven, the Temple of Agriculture, the Drum Tower, and the great gates at the southern center of the wall that then surrounded the city. He also traveled outside Beijing to view the Summer Palace, the Ming Tombs, and the Great Wall. For the most part, however, Freer devoted himself to the acquisition of Chinese objects for his collection. In a letter to Hecker, Freer outlined his strategy with exuberance:

I have hired a couple of rooms in the Tartar City where the natives think I am a buyer for some American auction house. I allow no one with things to sell to see me in my hotel, thus preventing the guests in this large and excellent hotel [Grand Hotel des Wagons-Lits], excepting two or three reliable Americans to learn my plans or the location of our claims. It beats California in 49!

I spend all of my daylight hours in the Tartar City, the scenes surpass those of the bazaars of Cairo and Constantinople and in their dealings the natives are apparently very reliable.[65]

Freer did not have long to wait. Chinese dealers flocked to his rooms in the Tartar City in response to his inquiries about early Chinese paintings. As he purchased large numbers of scrolls, Freer cabled Hecker for additional funds and, perhaps to reassure him, justified his unusual expenditures: "It will please you to know that these funds have helped me to buy early paintings by the greatest of Sung [Song] and Yuan painters such as no European or American museum—and I can safely add Japan has—including Ririomin [Chin.: Li Longmian] in superb style and condition—two specimens—and others of almost equal rank."[66] Eight days later he again wrote to Hecker:

Thanks to Fenollosa's superior teachings and the splendid opportunities given me in Japan during the summer of 1907, when I saw practically all of the early Chinese paintings owned publicly and privately in Japan, I knew what to search for when

Fig. 56. Square tile, Iran, Seljuk period, early 13th century. Clay with luster glaze over opaque white glaze (20.7 x 21.8), 09.118. This rare, luster-painted tile is apparently the only surviving portion of a large multi-tile panel portraying courtly activities.

Fig. 57. Egyptian glass, Egypt, New Kingdom period, ca. 1450–1250 B.C. Glass (largest piece, 13.2 x 9.2), 09.430, 09.413, 09.428, 09.423. The collection assembled by Giovanni Dattari, a wealthy resident of Cairo, also included bronzes, terra-cottas, outstanding glass vessels, mosaic inlays, amulets, earplugs, and game counters.

Fig. 58. Pieces from the Gold Treasure, Turkey, 6th–7th century B.C. Gold (diameter of large medallion, 10.7), 09.62–65, 09.67–70. Freer purchased from the Gold Treasure a pair of armlets, linked medallions, a large single medallion, earrings, and a crystal statuette (09.61, not shown).

I began my quest here—I mean Peking [Beijing]—scientifically and determinedly for paintings of the Tang, Sung [Song] and Yuan dynasties. The result carries me off my feet and almost out of my head. Had I during all my stay in China secured a full half dozen specimens of the great men of the three dynasties named, I would have considered myself extremely lucky. But the fact is, I have already in my possession here, over ten times that number. I am already thinking and planning for a return visit here another year.[67]

Freer still had a great deal to learn about the connoisseurship of Chinese painting. Most of the scrolls he purchased in Beijing in 1909 were not as old as he had been led to believe, and during the next few years he gradually removed them from his holdings, occasionally presenting them as gifts to friends and colleagues. A few of the scrolls, however, were of excellent quality, one of the finest being the long handscroll *Wang Wei's Villa at Wangquan* (fig. 59).

Among the most memorable experiences of Freer's 1909 stay in China was his trip to Tianjin to meet the powerful Manchu official Duanfang (see fig. 61) and see his enormous collection of antiquities. Once again, Freer expressed his pleasure in having access

Fig. 59. Song Xu (1523–1605), *Wang Wei's Villa at Wangquan* (detail), China, Ming dynasty. Handscroll; ink and color on silk (30.0 x 1076.2), 09.207. When Freer purchased this painting in Beijing, the proprietor of the Riu Cheng Chai assured him that it was a genuine work by the Yuan dynasty master Wang Meng (ca. 1301–1385) and had been in the collection of a "mandarin." More recent study has shown it to be by Song Xu of the Ming dynasty.

to the private holdings of an important Chinese personality. He wrote to Hecker that "interesting collections of ancient bronze and painting and pottery, including the one most famous in China, that of Viceroy Tuan Fang [Duanfang], have been opened for my study as freely as in Europe or America, notwithstanding all that has been reported from this country heretofore."[68]

On 12 October 1909, Freer embarked on an eight-hundred-mile train ride to Hankou, Hubei Province, where he transferred to a steamer for the remaining six hundred miles down the Yangzi River to Shanghai. Fleeting impressions from the deck of the steamer of Wuhu, Nanjing, Zhenjiang, and other cities made a profound impact. Never before had he been so aware of the sprawling distances of China's geography, reflected in its vast history. After his arrival in Shanghai he wrote to Hecker, "The glimpses I am getting of old China during this hurried trip confirm the impression I have received from various sources during recent years. In comparison, Japan seems only an imitative doll!"[69] That brief comment was in marked contrast to Freer's earlier, more cautious reactions to China and signaled his decision to focus his time, energy, and money on learning more about Chinese culture. For the remainder of his life, Freer would concentrate increasingly on acquisitions of Chinese art. By the time of his death, his Chinese holdings would outnumber all others.

Freer left Shanghai for Kobe and then Kyoto, where he spent several days revisiting familiar sites such as the Ginkakuji, the Nanzenji, the Kiyomizudera, the Kitano Tenjin temple, and the Kinkakuji garden. In Kyoto he also visited the tomb of Honami Kōetsu, the seventeenth-century Rimpa artist whose work he particularly admired. His visit there coincided with a memorial service for Ernest Fenollosa, who had died in London in September 1908 (see fig. 101). With his friend Hara Tomitarō, Freer attended the solemn ceremony in which Fenollosa's ashes were interred at Miidera, the Buddhist temple at Otsu overlooking Lake Biwa where Fenollosa had studied Buddhism.[70] On that mid-November day, Freer was impressed by the quiet serenity of the temple grounds, which continues to affect visitors today.

Before leaving Japan, Freer visited several art dealers. From his friend Nomura Yōzō in Yokohama he purchased a thirteeth-century wooden Bodhisattva (fig. 60), formerly in the collection of Count Tanaka Mitsuaki, a prominent Japanese government official. Leaving Yokohama for San Francisco, Freer arrived in Detroit in time for the Christmas holiday.

Respect and Esteem

Freer's preoccupation with China during his fifth and last trip to Asia was evident from the outset. In August 1910 he took the more direct overland route for the first time, sailing from San Francisco for East Asia aboard a Japanese steamer. Although Freer's immediate goal was China, he interrupted his journey for a few days in Japan to visit friends, including Hara Tomitarō, whose villa, Sannotani, once again provided a pleasant refuge. From Sannotani he traveled to Tokyo and called on several Japanese acquaintances, but he was soon back in Yokohama, bound for Kobe, Nagasaki, and Shanghai.

In Shanghai, Freer devoted his time to meeting dealers and collectors, including A. W. Bahr and Dr. John C. Ferguson, in whose company he visited several private collections. But Freer's sights were set on travel to inland China, and he was anxious to begin that journey. When he arrived at Taku on 18 September he was met by Nan Mingyuan, who would again serve as his translator and guide. Nan was wearing the engraved gold watch that Freer, in keeping with his habit, had sent him a few months earlier.[71] At the Grand Hotel des Wagon-Lits in Beijing, Freer was pleased to be given the same room and assigned the same servants as in 1909. He also was pleasantly surprised at being able to rent the same quarters in the Tartar City—complete with the staff, ricksha, and ricksha driver—that he had enjoyed the previous year. Comfortably settled, Freer contacted Beijing's art dealers.

Even though Freer attended foremost to improving his collection of Chinese antiquities, he could not ignore the demands of the city's international community. Almost immediately Freer was plunged into a social whirl, beginning with a reception in his honor given by the American Ambassador William James Calhoun and his wife, Lucy. Mrs. Calhoun made thoughtful comments to Freer about his collection and, to his even greater pleasure, mentioned specific pieces she had seen on exhibition in the United States. In the face of such hospitality, Freer had little choice but to play the part of a visiting celebrity, though he protested to Frank Hecker, "Of course I don't deserve such attentions and as you know, I really don't care for them, but the things I unearthed in China last year and some of those recently secured have got known in Legation circles and they think me either a saint or a fool and I fancy they are trying to learn which."[72] Ambassador Calhoun and his wife obtained special permission for Freer to see portions of the Forbidden City. Freer also accompanied Mrs. Calhoun and a group of Westerners on a visit to Duanfang, who was then in Beijing, for what would be Freer's last meeting with the viceroy (fig. 61). When Duanfang was assassinated in 1911, during the turbulent period that preceded the founding of the Republic, his family was forced to sell pieces from the collection. Freer was among those to acquire some of his greatest treasures, including *Nymph of the Luo River,* the most famous painting in Duanfang's collection, which was offered to Freer in 1914 (fig. 62).

Although Freer appreciated the efforts Mrs. Calhoun and others made on his behalf, he remained steadfast in his plans to tour the interior of China, where he hoped to travel to the ancient capitals of Kaifeng, Luoyang, and Xi'an.[73] To Freer's surprise, Nan Mingyuan, who on Freer's previous visit had refused to journey from Beijing for fear of the dangers of the road, agreed not only to accompany Freer but to manage the venture as well.[74] The notes Freer made during his 1910–11 trip in China are remarkably detailed. Clearly he regarded his tour of ancient Chinese cities as the culmination of his long study of Asian history and culture. The description of the rigors of the journey conveys the difficulties that he and other intrepid turn-of-the-century travelers had to face:

I start on my little expedition to the ancient interior capitals, now called Kai Feng-fu [Kaifeng]—Honan-fu [Luoyang] and Sian-fu [Xi'an]. The road to the latter city from Honan-fu is considered

Fig. 60. Bodhisattva, Japan, Kamakura period, 13th century. Lacquer and wood with traces of gilt copper, and glass. (62.8 x 43.2), 09.345. The plasticity of the figure's high chignon and drapery folds as well as the use of inset glass eyes to achieve greater realism are typical features of Kamakura sculpture.

by all authorities the hardest in China and it is now badly flooded. My friend Marcel Bing, the Parisian expert, came over it recently and required twenty-four days for a journey which usually takes twelve. In addition his expedition was held up by bandits and every cent of his money was taken. A Mandarin . . . lent him enough cash to get back to Honan-fu, where he sold two of his horses to reach Peking [Beijing]. . . . His collection of art objects was not taken by the bandits. His experience clears the route for me as the government has arrested the bandits and is now guarding the road. My visits to Kai Feng-fu and Honan-fu will give time for the floods to recede and the road to dry. The Chinese Government has given me a passport and will provide a military guard.[75]

As planned, Freer traveled from Beijing to Kaifeng, the location of which on northern China's central plain had been a strategic factor during the several dynasties when the city served as a capital. For Freer, Kaifeng's ancient status, especially during the Northern Song dynasty of the tenth through the twelfth centuries, imbued the site with an almost mystical significance. He visited the remains of secular and religious structures such as the so-called Iron Pagoda, whose origins date from the eleventh century, and the Dragon Pavilion, constructed on the site of the Song imperial palaces. It was a momentous experience for Freer to stand on Chinese soil that had seen the passage of generations of Chinese rulers. He described Kaifeng as being to him what Hōryūji had been to Fenollosa on his first visit to Nara.[76]

A particularly significant and fruitful excursion, for which Freer prepared in advance, was the trip by sedan chair from Luoyang to Gong Xian to study the sixth-century sculpture carved into the face of the Mang Hills. Freer had studied photographs of the caves published by the distinguished French sinologist Edouard Chavannes to familiarize himself with the cultural monuments in the area.[77] Although Freer had also intended to visit Xi'an, two Danish missionaries in Luoyang had advised against it, since flooding and bandits apparently made the roads extremely dangerous. Because their advice echoed what Chinese authorities and others had told Freer about his proposed expedition, he abandoned his plans in favor of a shorter trip to Longmen. The Buddhist caves there were famous for the sculptured images, begun in the fifth century, and their inscriptions (fig. 63).

Freer was not the first Westerner to visit Longmen, but he intended to produce the most complete record ever made of the caves and their surroundings. With Nan as his interpreter, he made arrangements with local Chinese officials. His party—which included Nan, a photographer, a cook, a servant, two men to make rubbings, six Chinese soldiers, and several sedan-chair bearers and cart drivers—arrived at the caves at the end of October, nearly a month after leaving Beijing. Freer seems to have been unconcerned about his personal safety despite his awareness of potential danger. The Chinese members of his entourage were less sanguine:

Enroute here my photographer was stoned and received an ugly blow over his right eye, but Pond's Extract put him back in harness again, although the dropping of a pin now startles him. My cook sleeps with the new bread knife I bought in Peking [Beijing], my interpreter wraps countless blankets around him when he lies down, the photographer never sleeps, my servant wept last night when the temple cat mewed outside; so if the brigands overpower the guard, I shall dive under my folding cot.[78]

Fig. 61. Duanfang (1861–1911), 1906. During an eight-month tour of the United States and Europe to observe Western forms of government, Duanfang was received at the White House by President Theodore Roosevelt in January 1906. While in Washington, he sat for this portrait by the noted woman photographer Frances Benjamin Johnson (1864–1952).

Although the Chinese rarely ventured to Longmen, preferring to study the Buddhist sculpture and inscriptions from rubbings in the safety of their homes, and more timid travelers might have lost sleep or become agitated, Freer remained remarkably unperturbed. Concerned for his safety, the lieutenant governor of the province and his chief of staff paid an official visit two days after Freer arrived in Longmen. Insisting that Freer accept a larger guard for night protection, they left six additional soldiers behind, two of them assigned at all times to the temple where Freer lived. Although he never passed through the temple gate without at least four soldiers, Freer was able to work happily and without interruption, recording his impressions of the caves in a sixty-five-page manuscript in which he described all aspects of his experience there.[79]

The Chinese photographer, whom Freer refers to only as Utai, quickly went to work,[80] as did the men whom Freer had engaged in Kaifeng to make rubbings of the sculptures that were impossible to photograph. Freer also sketched the ground plan of the colossal Tang dynasty Buddhist images in the Fengxian Temple, which he called the "Great Open Roofless Temple," a complex that dominates the Longmen caves. Unable to read the inscriptions, Freer would not have known that the notorious seventh-century Empress Wu had contributed funds from her cosmetics budget to support the creation of the main image of the temple, which is probably Vairocana, the Cosmic Buddha. So exhilarating was the experience of seeing important Buddhist images firsthand that Freer made plans for future pilgrimages to other Buddhist sites. In his Longmen notebook, he recorded his determination to visit Yungang in Shanxi Province on his next trip to China. If he could see the caves at Yungang, Freer wrote, and someday travel to Angkor Wat in Cambodia, he would feel that he had seen the best sculpture in the great centers of Buddhist art.[81] Just before leaving Longmen, Utai took a photograph of the entourage (fig. 64). The condition of the road in the foreground suggests how rough the journey must have been. Freer, of course, traveled in a sedan chair.

By mid-November, back in Beijing, Freer turned his attention once more to the acquisition of objects for his collection, although he did make an excursion beyond the Great Wall. By late December he was in Mukden (present-day Shenyang), where he visited the Qing imperial palace on Christmas Day. Despite the rare opportunity of seeing

the impressive palace complex, Freer concluded that Mukden was a "pretty desolate place to spend Christmas."[82] In Darien on 27 December, Freer was pleased by the prospect of leaving the cold and snow of Manchuria. He left Port Arthur on the first day of January 1911, bound for Shanghai.

In Shanghai, Freer attended a meeting of the North China Branch of the Royal Asiatic Society in the company of John C. Ferguson, its president. Except for a few Chinese and Japanese businessmen, all of the members were Westerners, a condition that reflected Shanghai's social restrictions. Freer was pleased when he was elected to membership in the prestigious organization. Ferguson introduced Freer to Pang Yuanji, whose collection of Chinese paintings was one of the largest and most famous in Shanghai. According to Freer, Pang was willing to sell some of his finest scrolls because

Fig. 63. General view of Buddhist caves at Longmen, Henan Province, China, 1910. Photograph by Utai. As a result of the dangers involved in journeying to Longmen, the caves were desolate in 1910. Today, in contrast, thousands of visitors descend on the site every month.

he needed money to pay gambling debts, as tradition decreed, before the end of the lunar-calendar year. Whatever the reason, Freer purchased several important paintings from Pang's collection. Among the finest is a long narrative handscroll, *Admonishing in Chains* (fig. 65). In Freer's judgment those final purchases in China constituted his crowning acquisition, contributing a "matchless note to the group."[83]

After celebrating Chinese New Year in Shanghai, Freer decided to explore another historically famous place in southeastern China. In early February he left with several American acquaintances for Hangzhou, the capital of the Southern Song dynasty. Traveling by houseboat, the party reached its destination the following evening and immediately arranged an itinerary that included the West Lake and the Buddhist rock sculptures in the Lingyin Temple. As Freer looked out over the mist-filled vistas of the West Lake, he was reminded of the many Chinese paintings inspired by that famous scenery; he also thought of the six-fold Japanese screen he had purchased in the Waggaman sale (see fig. 95). The artist Sesshū Tōyō is said to have traveled to Hangzhou, and Freer speculated that his screen might indeed depict the West Lake.

Freer left China without returning to Beijing, sailing for Japan from Shanghai on

20 February. News of Freer's trip to the interior of China excited considerable interest in Japan, and a number of his Japanese friends in Tokyo, including Marquis Inouye, Baron Takahashi, and Viscount Kaneko, gave a reception and dinner in his honor. Obviously touched by their thoughtfulness, Freer described the events to Hecker:

The kind-hearted men who assembled yesterday at the informal reception, made the trip an excuse for complimenting me. However, the affair was very enjoyable to me and all present seemed to be happy. Many speeches were made, and I talked an hour on comparison between early Chinese and Japanese art, based on recent investigation made by myself in China and Japan. A most audacious performance on my part—think of an American with cheek enough to draw comparisons on Chinese and Japanese art before an audience made up almost entirely of Japanese experts. I told them that they having drawn us together would have to suffer for their kind persistence.[84]

Several days later, in Yokohama on 30 March, Freer talked about Longmen with Hara Tomitarō and other friends at Sannotani; that discussion was one of the earliest detailed analyses by a Westerner of the historic Buddhist site. Evidently Freer used the extensive

Fig. 64. Members of Freer's entourage preparing to leave Longmen, 12 November 1910. Nan Mingyuan is on the far right. Photograph by Utai.

notes he had made at the site as talking points, passing around photographs of the monuments as he spoke. Nothing could be more indicative of Freer's status as a collector-connoisseur than his presentations in Tokyo and Yokohama. With confidence, Freer was able to speak on equal terms with Japanese connoisseurs about crucial aspects of their own culture. For Freer, those occasions were among the high points of his last Asian tour.

On 14 April 1911, after eight months in Asia, Freer sailed for home, arriving on 27 April. His hope of visiting Xi'an and Yungang was not to be realized, for he died in 1919 without having traveled to China, or indeed to Asia, again. ∎

Fig. 65. *Admonishing in Chains* (detail), China, Song dynasty, 12th–13th century. Handscroll; ink and color on silk (36.9 x 207.9), 11.235. A historical event is illustrated in this handscroll: Chen Yuanda, a fourth-century Chinese official, chained himself to a tree and admonished Liu Cong (r. A.D. 310–18), a Turkic ruler of Chinese territory, for his extravagant plans to erect additional buildings in the palace. The story is presented as a series of three tableaux (the opening tableau is shown here), each evoking a different mood. The painting conveys a concept basic to Chinese thought, that Chinese culture, with its emphasis on restraint and moderation, has a humanizing power.

CHAPTER FOUR

THOMAS LAWTON

Colleagues and Dealers

CHARLES FREER WAS precise and exacting in his business affairs, and when he turned to art collecting, he brought a similar firmness and shrewdness to his negotiations with dealers. Throughout the years he collected Asian art, Freer was training himself—tirelessly and relentlessly—just as he had persevered, as a young clerk, to master the rules of corporate enterprise. At the outset, during the 1890s, Freer had only a general awareness of the complexities of Asian art; few antiquities of outstanding quality were available for comparison, and even fewer experts in the West were discerning in matters of connoisseurship. Freer realized that he had to depend upon the integrity and knowledge of the people from whom he purchased Asian objects for his collection.

A transaction between Freer and an art dealer involved more than a simple exchange of money. Unlike many other contemporary Western collectors of Asian art, Freer insisted on learning as much as possible about every Asian object that passed through his hands. He asked for, and usually received, details relating to the provenance of a particular artifact; he obtained translations of inscriptions and sought to understand the achievements of individual artists and particular schools. Wherever possible, Asian art dealers responded to Freer's requests and provided the information he wanted. When substantive details were lacking, less scrupulous dealers may have invented impressive pedigrees. But Freer's natural intelligence alerted him to such instances of benevolent guile and enabled him to move through the hazards of Asian connoisseurship with surprising success.

Invariably as courteous as he was demanding, Freer maintained friendly relationships with many Asian colleagues. Just as he was a steadfast client and friend, however, Freer could also be a formidable adversary if he believed a dealer had behaved improperly. Among the many Asian art dealers whom Freer met, several exerted an especially sig-

Detail, figure 79.

nificant influence on his personal development and the growth of his Asian collections.

Matsuki Bunkyō (1867–1940)

Of the many art dealers from whom Freer acquired Asian art, none had a more remarkable background than Matsuki Bunkyō (fig. 66). Born in Nagano Prefecture on the Japanese island of Honshū, Matsuki learned the rudiments of connoisseurship from his father, who was knowledgeable about calligraphy and painting and familiar with Japanese antiquities.[1] At a young age, Matsuki became interested in Buddhism and, at fifteen, entered a Buddhist temple in Tokyo as a novice monk of the Nichiren sect. A good student, Matsuki studied Chinese and Japanese Buddhist texts and eventually received permission to attend English language classes. At eighteen, Matsuki was allowed to return to secular life, his Buddhist superiors apparently having reached the curious decision that the young man was "too talented" to be a monk. He subsequently went to China, where he spent two years studying and traveling to such major cities as Shanghai, Tianjin, and Beijing.

In mid-May 1888 the twenty-one-year-old Matsuki returned to Japan, only to sail for San Francisco the next day. He had eighty dollars in his pocket and twelve letters of introduction from his friends in China and from one of his teachers in Japan. Impressed by the self-reliance of Benjamin Franklin, whose autobiography he had read, Matsuki headed for Boston, where he expected to find American culture. Shortly after reaching the East Coast, he called upon Dr. Edward Sylvester Morse at his home in Salem, sixteen miles northeast of Boston (fig. 67).

Morse, a man of choleric disposition, had been trained as a zoologist at Harvard University and had taught Darwinian evolutionary theory at Tokyo University from 1877 to 1879 and 1882 to 1883.[2] He lost no time in showing Matsuki the more than five thousand pieces of pottery from all over Japan that he had collected and eventually would sell to the Museum of Fine Arts in Boston, where he would be keeper of Japanese pottery from 1892 until his death. Morse soon was talking enthusiastically to Matsuki about questions of provenance and the significance of pottery marks. He tested Matsuki's general knowledge of Japanese ceramics and was especially impressed when the young man was able to decipher some difficult characters, a skill partially owed to his Buddhist training, for which familiarity with Chinese was essential. The meeting with Morse made a deep impression on Matsuki and helped to determine his future. That summer Dr. and Mrs. Morse became his guardians, and the following September, with assistance from Morse, Matsuki entered Salem High School.

In 1892, after his graduation, Matsuki went into business in Boston selling Asian artifacts at 380 Boylston Street. At first, he handled modestly priced Japanese woodblock prints but gradually expanded his activities and eventually could offer his clients Chinese and Japanese works of extraordinary quality. Indeed, some of Freer's finest Chinese and Japanese objects were purchased from Matsuki.

Freer and Matsuki first met in the summer of 1896, when Freer visited the shop on Boylston Street. The two men seem to have gotten along well, and in September of that year Matsuki called on Freer at his home in Detroit. From the beginning, Freer offered the dealer many courtesies: he ordered two ginkgo trees, "as perfect specimens as you possibly can," to be sent to Matsuki and his wife after Matsuki had admired the ones in Freer's garden.[3] In the summer of 1897, when Matsuki traveled to Europe, Freer gave him a card of introduction to James McNeill Whistler and suggested cultural sites he should see in London and Paris.[4]

Time and again, usually when Matsuki was preparing for his annual buying trip to Japan, Freer loaned him large amounts of money to enable him to buy stocks of objects. Although the dealer was energetic in locating outstanding pieces, he had difficulty making a profit. Many of the letters between dealer and client mention the current status of their accounts. Although Freer was a stickler for accuracy, especially in financial matters, he was remarkably accommodating with Matsuki:

The reference you make to financial matters between us is noted, and whatever there may be still due me can be adjusted any time in the future convenient to you. . . . Whatever little assistance I may have rendered you financially you have much more than offset by the many errands you have attended to for me in Japan and elsewhere. Besides this, you must remember that I am indebted to you for the possession of many beautiful art objects which I would not have had but for your intelligent attention to my wants.[5]

In return for his financial support, Matsuki always gave Freer the first choice of his finest objects. On his way to Japan, Matsuki usually stopped at Freer's home in Detroit en

Fig. 67. Edward Sylvester Morse (1838–1925), ca. 1873. Peabody Museum of Salem, Massachusetts.

Fig. 68. Maruyama Ōkyo (1733–1795), *Geese Flying over a Beach,* Japan, Edo period. Four-fold screen; ink on paper (154.8 x 349.6), 98.143. The theme of descending geese originated in China during the late Northern Song dynasty (A.D. 960–1126) as one of the "Eight Views of Xiao and Xiang." In China the "Eight Views" usually were painted on handscrolls and occasionally on hanging scrolls; in Japan the theme was more popular on screens or, as in this example, on sliding doors or partitions.

route to the West Coast and invariably cabled Freer just before sailing from San Francisco, Seattle, or Vancouver. Freer, in turn, would write or cable Matsuki on the eve of Matsuki's overseas departure to extend best wishes for a good trip. Each fall, on his return to the United States, Matsuki would travel to Detroit to show Freer his most important acquisitions.

One of Freer's purchases from Matsuki, a four-panel screen painted by Maruyama Ōkyo in the eighteenth century, remains a major Japanese painting in the Freer Gallery (fig. 68). The screen, which depicts two geese flying low over a shore where breaking waves emerge from the mist-filled distance, originally served as four sliding partitions (*fusuma*) in a Japanese interior. No doubt the four panels make up a portion of a complete depiction of "Eight Views of Xiao and Xiang," a theme borrowed from Chinese art that celebrates the scenery along the Xiao and Xiang rivers in southern China; eight specific views, each bearing a poetic title, were believed to epitomize the natural beauty of the region.[6] Matsuki, perennially enthusiastic about the antiquities that passed through his hands, was so certain of the authenticity of the screen that he wrote Freer:

Okio geese are still growing in my heart. I hope it will prove [to be genuine] some day and hope you [will] say "Matsuki did not make mistake after all." For myself as Japanese [I] still hold that you can beat any Okio under the sun in the land of rising sun. I am perfectly happy it stays with you as I meant [the screen] to stay in your house.[7]

Another painting that Freer purchased from Matsuki was of the Bodhisattva Fugen by Takuma Eiga (fig. 69). The Buddhist deity of teaching and meditation is depicted with remarkable informality. Seated atop a reclining elephant, the figure departs from the traditional hieratic treatment of the image, which is usually executed in polychrome. Only the simply outlined halo suggests the divine status of the long-haired Fugen.

Freer bought the four-panel screen in October 1898 and *Fugen* in 1904. During those early years of their relationship, Freer frequently turned to Matsuki for advice as well as objects. In 1902, when he was considering the purchase of several contemporary Japanese paintings from Ernest Fenollosa, Freer wrote to Matsuki:

I have an opportunity to buy a kakemono by Kano Hogai and another by Hashimoto Gaho. As I have never purchased any of the work of either of these two painters, I write to enquire of you, confidentially, what such things are valued at in Japan. By this I mean, how much ought I pay for important examples of these men's work.[8]

But even as Freer was asking for Matsuki's comments about those paintings, he had begun to regard Fenollosa's knowledge of East Asian art as superior to that of anyone else, relying more and more on Fenollosa's judgment when making decisions about purchases. In Japan in 1904, for example, Matsuki obtained a set of sixteen paintings of Buddhist *luohan*, or disciples, attributed at the time to the Chinese master Li Longmian of the Northern Song dynasty (fig. 70). Freer was impressed by the paintings: he admired the quality of the brushwork and noted the gnarled faces of the sixteen disciples. But it was only after Fenollosa had verified that they were genuine examples of Li Longmian's work that Freer agreed to purchase them:

The sixteen [hanging scrolls] by Ririomin [Chin.: Li Longmian] Professor Fenollosa says are absolutely the originals, and I am much pleased to add the lot to my collection. Please feel that in securing this lot of pictures for me you have done yourself great credit, and have placed me under many obligations to you.[9]

The Buddhist paintings soon were regarded as among the most important objects in Freer's collection. In the summer of 1906, when the celebrated scrolls were in New York City for special photography, Freer agreed to have them taken to the home of his friends Mr. and Mrs. Henry O. Havemeyer, who also collected Asian art. The Havemeyers opened their Fifth Avenue home just for the day to study the Buddhist images. As late as 1907, when discussing his collection with Fenollosa, Freer considered setting aside a special gallery in his museum expressly for the paintings. Recent scholarship attributes them to the fourteenth-century Japanese artist Ryōzen on the basis of their style and the inscriptions. Freer, too, ultimately changed his mind about the authenticity of the scrolls; by the time of his death, he still believed they were Chinese paintings by a Song dynasty artist but no longer insisted on the Li Longmian attribution.

The Chinese painting Matsuki offered Freer that gave rise to the most animated discussion between Freer and Fenollosa is a long handscroll, then attributed to the Southern Song artist Xia Gui, who was active in the twelfth or thirteenth century (fig. 71). Matsuki initially asked fifty thousand dollars for the scroll—a tremendously high price at the time—informing Freer that that amount was demanded by the Japanese owner. He urged Freer to consider the scroll, adding that he would be willing to mortgage his own home in Salem, if necessary, to guarantee the purchase: "If you cable half the value I negotiate Konoike bank for mortgaging all my property and instead will raise the rest and guarantee that I will bring said genuine Kakei [Chin.: Xia Gui] roll at my risk."[10] Always the astute businessman, Freer made a counteroffer of twenty-five thousand dollars. He confided to Fenollosa that he suspected Matsuki would have to pay precisely that amount for the scroll:

Confidentially, I must tell you that in my opinion the Kakei [Xia Gui] roll was his own property at the time he sent me word by cable that the price was $50,000. By this I mean he had the option

Far left:
Fig. 69. Takuma Eiga (active late 14th century), *Fugen,* Japan, Namboku-chō period (1334–92). Hanging scroll; ink and color on silk (67.7 x 41.1), 04.202. The use of mono-chrome ink and the casual treatment of Fugen reflect the influence of Chinese innova-tions that would be associated in Japan with Zen devotional imagery. Judging from the composition, which is directed toward the right, the scroll may originally have formed part of a triptych.

Fig. 70. Ryōzen (active ca. 1328–ca. 1360), *Buddhist Luohan,* Japan, Namboku-chō period. Hanging scroll; ink, color, and gold on silk (113.1 x 58.8), 04.297. This is one of sixteen scrolls originally attributed to the twelfth-century Chinese artist Li Longmian (Jpn.: Ririomin). According to documentation Matsuki provided Freer, they formerly belonged to the Sanshōji, a subtemple of the Tōfukuji monastery in Kyoto. When the Sanshōji burned in 1856, the paintings were sold to the famous lacquer artist Shibata Zeshin (1807–1891). At his death Zeshin left the scrolls to his son, who used the paintings as collateral for a loan from the Yokohama Specie Bank, where they remained until Matsuki negotiated their sale in 1904. Inscriptions on the scrolls identify each *luohan* and give the name of the Sanshōji.

to buy the Roll at $25,000—the sum which he asked me by wire to cable him—and whatever amount he could obtain from me in excess of $25,000 would be his property.[11]

At Freer's request, Fenollosa wrote to the Japanese connoisseur Kanō Tomonobu, asking him to look at the handscroll and give an opinion about its quality. Fenollosa further asked Tomonobu to prepare a *shimpitsu* (true brush) authentification certificate if he believed the painting to be genuine and of exceptionally fine quality. The consultation was carried out with discretion: Fenollosa's letter was taken to Tomonobu by Matsuki's brother, Kihachirō, who also accompanied Tomonobu to the home of the owner of the painting. Tomonobu's reaction was finally forwarded to Fenollosa in the United States. His advice to Freer, based on Tomonobu's opinion, was enthusiastic:

I telegraphed you yesterday, that I thought it a good plan to make the offer of $25,000 to Matsuki, for the Kakei [Xia Gui] roll, and await his response. It is my opinion that, since I believe Kakei to be the greatest landscape painter the world has seen and since this roll is probably the best specimen of his now existing, it is intrinsically worth $50,000 or whatever else a man who could afford it would have to pay to get it. But your conjecture is also probably true that no one at present, either

Fig. 71. Artist unknown, *River Landscape* (detail), China, Ming dynasty, 15th–16th century. Handscroll; ink and color on silk (34.1 x 934.0), 06.228. *River Landscape* was formerly attributed to the Chinese artist Xia Gui (Jpn.: Kakei) of the Southern Song dynasty (1127–1279).

foreigner or Japanese, is likely to offer more for it than $25,000. Your cable to Matsuki will go far to test this fact, and put him on his mettle to obtain the treasure on some more favorable terms. It will encourage him to learn that you are still in the field.[12]

Acting on Fenollosa's opinions, Freer agreed to purchase the handscroll. Then, perhaps feeling some guilt, he added a fee of twenty-five-hundred dollars—for a total price of $27,500—to enable Matsuki to realize some profit from the transaction. Matsuki accepted the offer. Fenollosa wrote to congratulate Freer on his latest acquisition, at the same time voicing undeservedly harsh criticism of Matsuki:

It is a good thing that there are men of the energy, interest, and even wildness of Matsuki; for they "do" things, though they are untrustworthy and hard to manage. I congratulate you most heartedly on the acquisition of the Kakei [Xia Gui] treasure, which is of secondary importance to the Ririomins [Li Longmians] alone. Those two [artists] head the two greatest schools of Chinese art.[13]

Although Freer and his experts believed the so-called Xia Gui handscroll was dated to the twelfth or thirteenth century, today it is assigned to the Ming dynasty and the fifteenth or sixteenth century. It is important to realize that Matsuki, Fenollosa, Tomonobu, and Freer made their judgment about the painting when the few genuine examples of Xia Gui's work, either in private hands or in the Qing imperial collection, were virtually inaccessible. Several decades were to pass before Chinese, Japanese, and Western specialists could gain entrance to those collections and establish a firmer basis for the connoisseurship of Chinese painting. Even today, despite continuing research, questions of connoisseurship of early works remain among the most vexing to scholars. While some writers have stated that Freer turned more and more to China after 1902 or 1903 as Japanese art commanded higher prices on the international market, his purchase of the Xia Gui handscroll demonstrates that he paid large sums of money for Chinese art if and when he believed he was acquiring works of importance.

Freer consulted Edward Sylvester Morse about the authenticity of his collection of Japanese pottery, a considerable portion of which he had purchased from Matsuki. Morse was characteristically candid in expressing his opinions, and his evaluations of some of the pieces Freer had bought from his protégé were distinctly unfavorable. Of a small jar decorated with birds and fishing nets that Freer had purchased from Matsuki in 1898 as a genuine example by Ogata Kenzan (fig. 72, *right*), Morse said, "Don't believe Kenzan ever made that in the world. Rotten signature—fresh out of the furnace." Equally devastating was his evaluation of a small bowl with a coarse clay body, white slip, and bluish glaze that Freer had purchased in 1898 from Yamanaka and Company in New York (fig. 72, *left*). He had asked, in passing, Matsuki's opinion of it, and Matsuki had identified it as an example of a ware made in Settsu Province, two hundred or 250 years old. Morse had quite a different reaction: "Settsu? Don't believe it. Brand new—one of Matsuki's lies!"[14] In that instance, Matsuki's opinion has been partially vindicated: modern specialists identify the bowl as an example of Kosobe ware, made in Settsu Province in the nineteenth century.

In October 1908, Matsuki advised Freer of his plans to retire from his antique business and devote himself to managing the affairs of several Japanese companies. Surprised by Matsuki's sudden decision, Freer wrote him an extremely formal letter in which he turned, inevitably, to their long-standing financial entanglement. In addition to the loans that Freer had made, there was also the sensitive matter of an exchange of artifacts in 1906: After Freer had made extensive alterations to his Ferry Avenue house to obtain more and better exhibition space, he had reviewed his holdings and found a number of pieces unsuitable for the collection. Matsuki asked to be given an opportunity to purchase those objects for resale at his shop in Boston. Freer agreed, and the objects were shipped to Boylston Street. But Matsuki never reimbursed Freer, even though he had sold the objects when closing his shop. In his October 1908 letter, Freer referred only to the outstanding loans: "I deem this an appropriate time to call your attention to your account with me, a statement of which I beg to enclose herewith, showing a total indebtedness to date of $11,990.91."[15] Evidently Freer was not satisfied with Matsuki's response, for in March of the following year he wrote again:

I must . . . say to you that I am surprised to learn that you are counting upon paying the sum of money due me from your future business. I certainly feel, that when you were selling out the stock of goods carried in your Boston store (many of which you had purchased from me) you should have paid me out of the proceeds of your Boston sales. . . . I must further say, that the manner in which you have chosen to practically ignore my account against you, is scarcely the kind of treatment I had expected to receive from you. I shall hope to receive promptly from you, something more tangible than the indefinite statements contained in your letter of February 21st, or I shall consider it my duty to start legal proceedings for the collection of the money due me.[16]

It must have been extremely unpleasant for Freer to have to write such a letter to a friend of many years.

By 1909, Matsuki obviously was in serious financial difficulty. In an effort to resolve his monetary problems with Freer, he assembled a collection of Chinese Buddhist and Daoist sculpture that he described as having come from Hayasaki Kōkichi, a Japanese dealer who had spent long periods in China. The sculptures varied in quality and condition. Although several pieces were important for their inscriptions, Westerners, including Freer, were not attuned to the subtleties of Chinese calligraphy at the time. Freer, therefore, regarded most of them as suitable only for study, not for exhibition, and declined when Matsuki offered the collection for twenty-two thousand dollars.

To press his case as strongly as possible, Matsuki told Freer that the Tang dynasty Eleven-Headed Guanyin (fig. 73), clearly the finest piece in the group, was part of a larger ensemble from the old Tang capital of Chang'an (present-day Xi'an). He also pointed out that three pieces from the same group were in the Tokyo National Museum, one was in the Museum of Fine Arts, Boston, and another was owned by Hara Tomitarō of Yokohama. Since Freer and Hara were good friends, and Freer admired

Fig. 72. *Right,* Tea-ceremony water jar with spurious signature of Ogata Kenzan (1663–1743), Japan, Meiji period, late 19th century. Glazed clay (17.6 x 18.8), 98.52. *Left,* Bowl, Kosobe ware, Japan, Edo period, mid-19th century. Glazed clay (7.6 x 18.3), 98.463.

Hara's art collection, Matsuki's psychological strategy was sound.

It is uncertain whether Matsuki knew how the dealer Hayasaki had gained possession of the group. As a nineteen-year-old student at the Tokyo Art School in 1893, Hayasaki had accompanied the noted Japanese scholar-connoisseur Okakura Kakuzō on his trip to China, where the two men saw the Tang sculptures from the Tower of Seven Jewels in Xi'an. The group had originally been installed in that structure, which was built in A.D. 703 by the formidable Empress Wu. In 1906, Hayasaki acquired twenty-six of the original thirty-two sculptures and had them set up in the garden of his Tokyo residence. By the time Matsuki offered the Eleven-Headed Guanyin to Freer in 1909, Hayasaki had already sold several of the sculptures.

Still stung by what he regarded as Matsuki's unprofessional behavior regarding his financial irresponsibility, Freer cabled that the price for the group of Chinese sculptures was too high. As an alternative, Freer offered to purchase only the Eleven-Headed Guanyin. But as both men were aware, without that piece the collection was valueless. Matsuki therefore reduced the price of the entire collection to fifteen thousand dollars, ending his cable to Freer with the plaintive plea, "Am hard pressed. Save me."[17]

Freer, who was almost ready to leave for an extended 1909 trip to Asia, relented. In doing so, he acquired a group of pieces that included one of the finest Tang dynasty sculptures in the Freer Gallery collection.[18] But, having paid what Matsuki would finally accept, he made clear his resentment of the dealer's dereliction by pointing out that $9,051.32 remained unpaid on his account.

While Freer met Matsuki's brother, Kihachirō, on subsequent trips to Japan, it seems that he never saw Matsuki again. In 1934, Matsuki returned to the Buddhist church and died six years later in a temple at Akasaka, Tokyo. According to people who knew him, Matsuki, whose family had remained in Salem, spent his last years as a lonely monk, refusing to talk about his life in America.

Dikran Kelekian (1868–1951)

The artful, calculating talents of Dikran Kelekian hover around every aspect of his long and successful career (fig. 74). Modesty was not a quality that Kelekian recognized. Others might have hesitated to herald the collector's achievements, but he himself had no such reservations. Kelekian's business stationery proclaimed in suitably large type that he had been awarded the highest prize in every category at the World's Columbian Exposition of 1893, a distinction he earned at the age of twenty-five. Kelekian's letter-head also pointed out that he had been a member of the jury for the 1900 Exposition Internationale Universelle in Paris and had served as the Imperial Commissioner-General for Persia at the Saint Louis Exposition in 1904. As a reward for his services at the Paris exposition, the shah of Persia had awarded him the honorific title of khan.

In truth, Kelekian was a remarkable man. Born in Caesaria, Turkey, he was only seventeen years old when he followed his father and brother, George, in taking up anti-quarianism as a calling.[19] According to Kelekian, it was his father, trained as a jeweler, who sold a group of gold medals struck in honor of Alexander the Great—the so-called Tarsus treasures named for the find-site in Turkey—to the French government.[20] Success came early to Dikran Kelekian: by 1894, the year after he showed objects from his collection at the Chicago exposition, he was able to sell a valu-able chalcedony Venus to Baron Edmond de Rothschild of the celebrat-ed international banking family. Within a short time, Kelekian had opened a shop in Paris, followed by others in London, Cairo, and New York. His first in New York was called the Musée du Bosphore; the pri-mary purpose of the Cairo establishment was to acquire objects that could be sold abroad.

Despite Kelekian's unsteady command of idiomatic English, he was unequaled in zeal when advocating Persian art to potential clients. In one of his earliest letters to Freer, Kelekian managed to compliment, cajole, and criticize all at once:

Allow me to congratulate you for your noble action of the donation of your very valuable collection to the Washington University [i.e., Smithsonian Institution]. I do not think that the people who are the head will yet appreciate the real impor-tance of such valuable collection, but the future will give you all the necessary glory, I am sure.

Fig. 73. Eleven-Headed Guanyin, China, Tang dynasty, early 8th century A.D.. Stone (height 108.8), 09.98.

Fig. 74. Dikran Kelekian (1868–1951), ca. 1934. From *Art News* 32, no. 20 (17 February 1934): 11.

Freer's collecting of Rakka ware began in 1902, when he purchased a one-handled pot from Kelekian (see fig. 50); later that year, Kelekian sold him five more pieces described as Rakka ware. Freer continued to collect the pottery in increasing numbers from dealers in New York and Paris, mainly from Kelekian and Siegfried Bing. But after 1908, perhaps because he felt Kelekian's prices were too high, Freer purchased little of the West Asian ware from him. Nonetheless, as late as 1914 he was so impressed by the rich, coloristic glaze on a large, three-handled twelfth–thirteenth century jar, he bought it in spite of the price (fig. 75).

As Freer became increasingly interested in Chinese art, the wily dealer expressed his displeasure by sending Freer reminders, heavy with innuendo, of more enlightened clients and their collections:

Sir Burton [sic] Clarke the Director of South Kensington Museum [Victoria and Albert Museum] who has been director of the Metropolitan Museum has seen the collection of Mr. Havemeyer and told him that he had the most valuable collection [of] pottery in America and in the world. I am proud of it. Mr. Havemeyer was kind enough to come to my place afterwards and buy $7200 [of] the things he had already seen. And I am so glad he bought them as I know that they are priceless pieces. Time will talk.[22]

When it became apparent that Freer's interest in Chinese art could not be dislodged, Kelekian, ever the realist, was equal to the challenge. A "magnificent Chinese head and a very interesting stele by Wu Tu Zu [Wu Daozi]" were dispatched from the New York shop to Freer for consideration.[23] After Freer purchased the stele, Kelekian continued to offer him Chinese examples, some of which were of extremely high quality. The Tang dynasty Bodhisattva that Freer purchased from Kelekian in 1916 combines the lithe body and dramatic movement characteristic of Chinese Buddhist images of the early eighth century (fig. 76).

On one occasion, Kelekian, ever alert to a possible sale, also advised Freer of the availability of a Whistler painting; Freer quietly demurred. Even after Freer had purchased several Chinese pieces, Kelekian, still eager to promote his stock of Persian art, continued to lament what he regarded as Freer's abandonment of West Asian art: "Why do you not continue to add a few more pieces to your fine Persian collection? Do you not think that Persian potteries stand with the greatest art in the world?"[24]

In November 1917, Kelekian called on Freer in Detroit. He was en route to Chicago, where his Chinese ceramics and Freer's Chinese paintings were on display at the Art Institute.[25] Freer considered Kelekian's collection of Chinese ceramics "one of the three or four finest in existence";[26] he had decided it was not necessary to send any of his own ceramics to Chicago since Kelekian's holdings would be on view. Kelekian wrote to Freer after visiting the Chinese exhibitions:

I went this morning to see your paintings at Art Institute. They are magnificent. Only sorrow I have that unfortunately neither your paintings nor my potteries are appreciated. How long are we going to wait I do not know? I have been waiting quarter of century, I commence to be discouraged. I wish I could make some money in other kind of business and buy fine things for me and not sell them.

Your paintings, sculptures, and my potteries look very fine.

There were only few persons. I stayed from 9:30 to 1, and from 3 to 5. There were not 20 people, most of them stayed 5 minutes. Helas.[27]

Freer did not share Kelekian's concern about the small number of museum visitors. His reponse to Kelekian mirrors his elitest view of the importance of appealing to "people of the right sort":

The attendance is to me extremely gratifying. Many people of the right sort are really studying and attempting to imbibe information and inspiration and I think more good will follow the show. The Museum authorities are efficient in making attractive appeals to the public, and I am positive that

Fig. 75. Three-handled vase, Rakka ware, Syria, 12th–13th century. Glazed clay (66.2 x 42.7), 14.58. The deep turquoise-blue glaze, largely covered by greenish gray encrustation and further enriched by pale gold iridescence, appealed to Freer's taste for intricate surface quality.

when the exhibition closes you will take great personal satisfaction from your generous action in loaning your treasures.[28]

A description of Kelekian by Frank Crowninshield, the well-known writer and editor, captures the irrepressible spirit of the man whose informed judgments and consanguine interests had so impressed Freer:

He is a creature so curiously compounded that under his grim and sometimes awesome visage he combines, in one person, the qualities of a Persian satrap and a properly accredited archangel; of Ghenghis Khan and the Chevalier Bayard; of Thor, the God of Thunder and Saint Francis of Assisi.[29]

Siegfried Bing (1838–1905)

Siegfried Bing played a pivotal role in introducing Japanese art to the West. Born in Hamburg, Germany, Bing became a naturalized French citizen and spent most of his life in Paris.[30] He began his career in his family's firm, Bing Frères et Cie, which produced French porcelain and glass; he turned to the manufacture of decorative arts and, in the 1890s, became a major force in the Art Nouveau movement.

By the 1870s, Bing was a dealer in Japanese artifacts. His personal collection of East Asian art, which was sold at public auction in 1876, focused on Japanese bronzes, ceramics, and woodblock prints that were popular in France at the time and becoming increasingly available in the West. The Japanese pavilion at the Paris World's Fair of 1878 generated even greater interest in Japanese objects; Bing took advantage of public attention when he opened his shop on the rue Chauchat.

Turn-of-the-century Paris was the center of activity for many prominent collectors and dealers of Japanese art. A small group of those collectors, calling themselves Les

Amis de l'Art Japonais, convened at monthly dinners to discuss Japanese art and exchange opinions about their recent acquisitions. Bing and Hayashi Tadamasa, one of the principal Parisian dealers in Japanese art, served as genial hosts. Members included the printer Charles Gillot, the writer Louis Gonse, the Louvre curator Gaston Migeon, the painter Claude Monet, the critic Raymond Koechlin, the jeweler Henri Vever, and Michel Manzie, an artist and printer who occasionally dealt in art. Many among the illustrious group were instrumental as well in formulating the tenets of the Art Nouveau movement. Les Amis had been in existence for more than a decade when Bing introduced Freer to the membership in 1904.[31]

Unlike many of his French colleagues who made most of their purchases in Paris, Bing went to East Asia on several occasions. On his first trip, in 1880, he spent a year traveling in China, Japan, and India. When he returned to Paris at the end of the year, he opened a new shop at 13 rue Bleue as a showcase for the objects he had purchased in Japan. In 1883, the year that Gonse published *L'Art Japonais,* a pioneering attempt to discuss Japanese art within an art historical framework, Bing organized the first Salon of Japanese Painters. It was sponsored by the Ryūchikai, a Japanese association that included Ernest Fenollosa among its members. Bing also was involved in the Exposition Universelle of 1889.

Although Bing had arranged sales of his East Asian holdings in New York as early as 1887, he did not visit the United States until February 1894, when he arrived in New York to prepare an auction at the American Art Galleries. The title of its sales publication, *Catalogue of Antique Chinese and Japanese Porcelains, Pottery, Enamels and Bronzes, Cabinet Specimens in Jade, Agate, and Crystal, Sword-guards, Netsukes, Kakemonos, Old Fabrics, Etc., Etc.,* indicates the remarkable scope of the sale, which numbered 1,853 individual lots, some of which consisted of several objects. Bing also organized sale exhibitions of Japanese woodblock prints in New York and Boston. But Freer and Bing apparently did not meet each other in 1894; Freer did not attend the New York sale or purchase any of the objects being auctioned, nor is there any indication that he called at Bing's shop when he traveled to Paris in November of that year, at the beginning of his first tour of Asia.

In March 1897, when the East Asian collection of the French collector and art critic Edmond de Goncourt was sold at the Hôtel Drouot in Paris, Bing wrote the introduction for the catalogue, beginning elegiacally, "Edmond de Goncourt est mort."[32] Freer bid on several objects through Enrique Baer, Bing's nephew and agent in the United States, and acquired three pieces of pottery from the sale. One was a small, sturdy celadon bowl, identified at the time as Korean and "very old"; the two others (see fig. 77) are Japanese and date to the nineteenth century.[33] Freer had already acquired several

Fig. 76. Bodhisattva, China, Tang dynasty, 1st half 8th century A.D. Stone (height 101.7), 16.365.

pieces of Korean pottery in 1896 from Yamanaka and Company in New York and wanted to strengthen his holdings.

Although Freer was in Paris in 1900 for the "rush and roar" of the Exposition Universelle, which, like the 1878 exposition, featured an elaborate Japanese pavilion, and although he had purchased several pieces of Japanese pottery from dealers there, he did not have an opportunity to meet Bing. When the two finally did meet, in Paris in July 1901, Bing was a gracious host. On his first evening in Paris, Freer had dinner at Bing's home, and during his remaining four days in the city he called at the shop at 19 rue Chauchat in the company of James McNeill Whistler, who knew Bing well. At some point during his stay, Freer purchased three Japanese paintings that Bing attributed to three of Japan's greatest artists: Ogata Kenzan, Ogata Kōrin, and Tawaraya Sōtatsu. The scroll he attributed to Kōrin, *Red and White Poppies* (fig. 78), today is regarded as a nineteenth-century work.[34]

Fig. 77. Tea-ceremony water jar, Satsuma ware, Japan, Edo period, 19th century. Glazed clay (16.2 x 17.3), 97.10. This elegant buff-colored water jar decorated with elaborate overglaze enamels is one of three pieces of ceramics that Freer purchased at the Edmond de Goncourt sale in 1897.

Fig. 78. Artist unknown, *Red and White Poppies*, Japan, Edo period (1615–1868), 19th century. Hanging scroll; color and ink on paper (119.3 x 48.2), 01.26.

In February 1903, Freer was again in Paris, where he attended the sale of Japanese art assembled by Hayashi Tadamasa. Bing, who was the expert for the catalogue—another indication of his pervading influence in Paris art circles[35]—assisted Freer in purchasing what would be one of his greatest Japanese treasures, *Moonlight Revelry at the Dozō Sagami* by the ukiyo-e artist Kitagawa Utamaro (fig. 79). Bing also helped Freer acquire a pair of hanging scrolls by the Japanese master Katsushika Hokusai (fig. 80). Shortly after the Hayashi sale, Freer wrote to Bing with understated pleasure: "The two Hokusai kakemono were very satisfactory, and the Utamaro I am glad to have, notwithstanding the fact that it is a very difficult piece to handle."[36] Later in 1903, when Freer was in Paris (after Whistler's death), he had lunch with Bing and viewed his private collection at rue Vezeley. He also met Raymond Koechlin, whose home he visited on the Ile Saint Louis. Afterward he wrote to Hecker that Koechlin's was the "finest collection of Oriental art in Paris." The same letter described his extensive 1903 purchases from Bing and included a barbed generalization: "Today, Mr. Bing threw me high into the air. . . . [He] is mighty kind but very seductive. All Frenchmen love money."[37]

An unexpected treat for Freer during that trip was the comprehensive exhibition of Islamic art at the Pavilion de Marsan of the Musée des Arts Décoratifs, organized by Gaston Migeon. Its scale was impressive: more than one hundred Persian and Indian paintings and manuscripts afforded Freer and other collectors their first chance to study in detail the relationship between Islamic painting and decorative arts. Freer described it as a

special collection of Spanish-Moresque, Persian, Arabic and Babylonian art — the great fore-runners — loaned from the private collections of Paris — i.e. Baron de Rothschild, Gillot, Vever, Koechlin, et al. The whole including the first thoroughly good exhibition of these arts ever publicly made. It has offered us a great opportunity to continue our study and compare the various periods, mediums and wares. The exhibition closes July 1st. It is said that every one of the finest specimens of the early pottery owned in Paris are shown in the exhibition.[38]

Freer made notations in his pocket-size catalogue, *Exposition des arts Musulmans,* although he also purchased the large, folio catalogue, *Exposition des arts Musulmans au Musée des Arts Décoratifs,* which reproduced one hundred of the finest pieces in the exhibition. He would have been delighted to know that several decades after the Islamic exhibition, three of those objects were acquired by the Freer Gallery. One, a Syrian brass basin (fig. 81), was then in the collection of the Duc d'Arenberg. The others, two glass pieces then owned by Baron Gustave de Rothschild, reflect comparable quality: a fourteenth-century mosque lamp with enameled and gilded decoration and an elegant, long-necked Syrian glass bottle dating from the mid-fourteenth century (fig. 82).

In addition to these important 1903 purchases that Bing facilitated, two other events marked Bing's increasing involvement in Freer's exposure to Asian art. The first centered on the sale of Charles Gillot's collection of Chinese and Japanese art, for which Bing prepared the catalogue. Freer had seen the pieces

Fig. 79. Kitagawa Utamaro (1754–1806), *Moonlight Revelry at the Dozō Sagami,* Japan, Edo period. Ink and color on paper (147.0 x 318.6), 03.54. This large ukiyo-e painting—almost ten-and-one-half feet in width—presents a panoramic view of life in a traditional geisha house. The influence of Western art is apparent in the artist's use of linear perspective: the composition recedes through the crowded room to the distant horizon.

with Bing in Paris and later, in the summer of 1903, they corresponded about the objects they had observed together.[39] The Gillot sale, held in Paris in February 1904, was enormously successful and set new records for prices paid.[40] With Bing acting as his agent, Freer placed several bids, one of them for a folding screen then attributed to Ogata Kenzan, which proved to be the sensation of the sale (fig. 83). The preauction estimate was six thousand francs, but the bidding rose dramatically until the screen was purchased by Yamanaka Sadajirō for fifty thousand francs (approximately $28,000). When Bing told Freer of the price paid for the screen, Freer responded, "Who bought it? And was the buyer sober at the time?"[41] But Bing was successful in purchasing for Freer a painting of Avalokiteshvara, the Bodhisattva of Mercy, seated on a rock (fig. 84). According to the Gillot catalogue, the painting was Japanese, from the fourteenth century; today the date is considered accurate, but Freer actually had purchased not a Japanese but a Korean painting—his first. Freer would later acquire several of Gillot's Japanese lacquers from Yamanaka in New York (fig. 85). About those purchases, Freer declared, "I am not a buyer of lacquer, but these few specimens were so beautiful, I felt I had to have them."[42]

Fig. 80. Katsushika Hokusai (1760–1849), *New Year Rituals,* Japan, Edo period. Pair of hanging scrolls; ink and color on silk (each scroll 115.8 x 44.2), 03.52-53. Young girls perform traditional New Year rituals: one prepares to wash her face with lemon water, while the other ties a picture of a treasure boat onto her pillow to ensure good fortune.

Fig. 81. "D'Arenberg basin,"
Syria, 13th century. Brass with
silver inlay (22.5 x 50.0), 55.10.

Fig. 82. *Right,* Mosque lamp,
Egypt, ca. 1360. Glass with
enamel and gilt (33.6 x 24.8),
57.19. *Left,* Bottle, Syria, mid-
14th century. Glass with enamel
and gilt (49.7 x 24.8), 34.20.

The second significant event in Bing and Freer's relationship at that time was Freer's introduction to Les Amis de l'Art Japonais. Freer must have valued the friendship and scholarly aspirations of his French colleagues, and Bing took advantage of that situation to encourage Freer to send photographs of pieces from his collection to Gaston Migeon for reproduction in a new folio-size publication, *Chefs-d'oeuvre d'art Japonais,* which Migeon was preparing in an effort to broaden the Western view of Japanese art.[43] It is a testament to Bing's powers of persuasion that Freer agreed, even though he had not yet met Migeon and was generally reluctant to grant permission to reproduce objects in his collection.[44] Migeon selected as many objects as possible that had not previously been published; Freer was the only non-French collector represented. Clearly the finest object Freer submitted was *Geese Flying over a Beach* by Maruyama Ōkyo, the screen he had obtained from Matsuki in 1898 (see fig. 68).

Beginning in 1904, Bing experienced a series of financial problems, circumstances serious enough to prompt him to send his assistant, Marie Nordlinger, to the United States to negotiate the sale of his collection of Japanese woodblock prints. Surprised that Bing would consider disposing of his private holdings, Freer calculated that the decision had been financially motivated. When Miss Nordlinger visited Freer in Detroit, she

Fig. 83. Artist unknown, *Landscape of the Four Seasons*, Japan, Edo period (1615–1868), Sōtatsu school. One of a pair of six-fold screens; color on paper (121.92 x 312.42). The Metropolitan Museum of Art, New York, Rogers Fund 1915.

brought, among other objects, three cases of Egyptian antiquities. Freer bought two pieces of Rakka pottery but declined to purchase any of the Egyptian objects, writing to Bing:

The Egyptian antiquities are very interesting, and I have enjoyed studying them very much. I must say, however, that it is a kind of art with which I find myself without the appreciation which is probably its just due. The art of China, Japan, and Central Asia appeals to me more deeply. [45]

Of the nine Tibetan paintings that Miss Nordlinger encouraged Freer to purchase, Freer later recounted to a friend:

I saw the Tibetan paintings and I fear their beauty carried me completely off my feet. I brought back with me nine of the paintings, a very selfish act I fear. However, in the remaining lot there are two or three excellent ones. The most expensive one, priced at $320, I rejected because of the price. It seemed to me cheap enough in one sense, but ridiculously high in comparison with those still finer which were marked as low as $60 and $80 each. I rejected another one because it seemed to me entirely lacking in beauty. [46]

Fig. 84. Artist unknown, *Avalokiteshvara with Willow Branch,* Korea, Koryŏ period, 14th century. Hanging scroll; ink, color, and gold on silk (98.4 x 47.8), 04.13.

Although Bing at that time was confined to his home because of illness, he remained a gracious host and even arranged a party for Freer. [47] By late June, however, he was in the hospital for surgery and his son, Marcel, was playing a major role in the family business. Before Freer left Paris early in July, he went to the hospital to say goodbye to his old friend. Bing died in September 1905 at the age of sixty-seven. The obituary in *Brush and Pencil* gave an accurate account of Bing's artistic accomplishments, a description that Freer would have endorsed:

The news of the death of Siegfried Bing . . . will come as a personal loss to scores of collectors in Europe and this country who owed many of their treasures of Japanese art and no little of their love of Oriental art, to this indefatigable dealer, who did so much to make known the transcendent qualities of the best porcelains, bronzes, lacquers, and prints of the Far East. . . . He was a typical dealer of the old school, the friend and guide of his customers, but while keen enough at a bargain, his chief ambition was to make Oriental art felt as an influence for good upon designers.[48]

Colonel Henry Bathhurst Hanna (1839–1914)

When Charles Freer visited the Indian subcontinent for the first and only time early in 1895, he was still a fledgling collector of Asian art. On that trip he purchased only books and a few unassuming objects, none of which would be included in his gift to the nation. It was not until 1907 that Freer began to collect Indian art seriously, and then his acquisitions came from British and American collectors. Among Freer's Indian holdings, the paintings and manuscripts he acquired from Colonel

Fig. 85. Mask box, Japan, Edo period (1615–1868), 17th century. Lacquer on wood with lead and mother-of-pearl (23.2 x 29.2), 04.36.

Henry Bathhurst Hanna deserve special mention.[49]

Hanna had assembled the collection during his long military career as an English officer in the Indian army. In 1857, while still in his teens, he had taken part in quelling the Indian Mutiny. He also served in the Oudh Campaign in 1858–59, the Hasara Campaign in 1868, and the Afghan Wars of 1878–80. From 1860 to 1861 he was in China with his regiment for the final phase of the Opium Wars. In addition to his military service, Hanna published his views on military matters relating to the campaigns in which he took part.

Assembled over thirty years, Hanna's collection of paintings and manuscripts was remarkably varied. It comprised seventeenth- and eighteenth-century Mughal works of imperial quality as well as some later copies; Deccani and provincial illustrations; and miniatures executed under English patronage and influence. Hanna made most of his purchases outside the larger Indian cities in the course of military duties. "Many of my books and pictures I have discovered in out of the way places," he wrote, "whilst great cities, where such things might fairly be looked for, have not yielded one to the most patient search."[50]

The pride of Hanna's collection was an abbreviated version of the Persian translation of the great Hindu epic the *Ramayana* (Story of Rama). In some instances, portions of the Persian text are integrated with the 130 full-page illustrations, which glorify Rama's epic battles with Ravanna, the demon king of Lanka, or Ceylon, to rescue his wife, Sita.[51] In Hanna's opinion—not an unbiased one—his *Ramayana* manuscript was "far superior to anything of the kind in the British Museum, or South Kensington Museum [Victoria and Albert Museum], or amongst the Oriental manuscripts in India House."[52] While Hanna believed the manuscript had been commissioned by Akbar the Great in the sixteenth century and was the Mughal emperor's personal copy, recent scholarship has shown it was commissioned by Abd ar-Rahim (shown in fig. 86), a leading noble at Akbar's court who was commander in chief of the armies, and is therefore not an imperial work. An inscription in the manuscript records that it was produced from 1587 to 1598, although a few illustrations may well have been added somewhat later.

Hanna's *Ramayana* presents an interesting fusion of Mughal and Hindu traditions. While Muslim court art supported by the Mughal rulers in the sixteenth century was extremely refined, the ancient and distinctly Hindu artistic traditions remained strong. Two of the best pages in the manuscript, *Rama and Lakshman Battle the Demon Rakshasas* and *A Group of Dancing Girls Sent to Entice the Youthful Ascetic Rishyashringa* (fig. 87), provide excellent examples of the meeting between these aesthetics.

As early as 1890, Hanna began seeking a suitable repository for his collection, which eventually included some 130 items. In May 1890 his Indian paintings and manuscripts were exhibited at Dowdeswell and Dowdeswells in London; in the preface to the catalogue, Hanna

Fig. 86. Hashim (active 2d quarter 17th century), *Portrait of Abd ar-Rahim, Khan Khanan,* India, ca. 1626. Ink and gold on paper (14.9 x 8.2), 39.50.

Fig. 87. Folios from a
manuscript of the *Ramayana*
(*Story of Rama*), India, Mughal,
late 16th century. Ink and
opaque watercolor on paper
(each 27.5 x 15.2). *Left,* Mohan
(active late 16th century), *Rama
and Lakshman Battle the Demon
Rakshasas,* 07.271.35v. The
brilliant orange and green of the
demons on two sides and the
pool of red blood at the bottom
of the composition are elements
indebted to Hindu sensibilities,
while the clear and direct
presentation of the action stems
from native Indian traditions.
Right, Govardhan (active late
16th century), *Dancing Girls Sent
to Entice the Youthful Ascetic
Rishyashringa,* 07.271.19r.
Although the *Ramayana* is a
Hindu epic, the sophisticated use
of color, the modeling of figures
to suggest physical substance—
influenced by European prints
brought to India by missionaries
and traders—and the incorpora-
tion of naturalistic flora and
fauna are elements drawn from
earlier Mughal works.

specifically identified four works that he
considered the "gems" of his miniature
collection, one of which is usually identified as *Jahangir and Prince Khurram Feasted
by Nur Jahan* (fig. 88). When Hanna failed
to find a purchaser, he made the collection available on long-term loan to the
Laing Art Gallery of Newcastle-on-Tyne,
which had opened in 1904.

Freer first wrote to Hanna about his
Indian paintings in April 1907. He told
Hanna in May that the collection interested him a great deal but, always cautious, asked Hanna not to hold the collection for him if another purchaser
should appear. If, however, Hanna still
had possession of the paintings in
September, Freer would go to England to
inspect them.[53]

After studying the collection at the
Laing Art Gallery on 24 September, Freer
again wrote to Hanna, describing the
collection as "wonderful."[54] Obviously
pleased by such a favorable reaction,
Hanna replied, "I am confident there is
nothing like it in the world. When in
India people, both European and native,
used to come from far and near to see it."[55] Freer also conveyed his reactions to Hecker:
"The Hanna collection far surpasses in importance in all directions my deepest hopes. I
am amazed that it should have been on the market nearly twenty years without finding a
buyer. It is doubtless unique in the world."[56] Freer went on to compare the rarity of the
Hanna collection to the Korean ceramics that Hecker had acquired on his behalf from
Ambassador Horace N. Allen earlier that year.

All that remained was for Freer and Hanna to agree on the price. Hanna initially
suggested seventy-five-hundred pounds, explaining that he had settled on that amount
after considering the time and difficulty assembling the collection had involved as well as
the rarity of comparable examples. While he would have been able to garner higher

prices for the paintings if he disposed of them individually, Hanna was loath to break up the collection. He also told Freer that the need to provide financial support for two younger sisters had been the determining impetus in his decision to part with his paintings.[57]

When Freer, pleading ignorance of the current market value of such a collection, requested permission to seek advice from specialists in Paris, Hanna urged him to do so. Following a five-day visit to Paris, Freer meticulously assigned a price to each item in the collection and offered Hanna thirty-one-hundred pounds (approximately $15,000), considerably less than the original asking price. With a graciousness that characterized all of the correspondence between the two men, Hanna replied, "It would not be truthful to say that I was not disappointed at the offer you made me, but I see that the calculation by which you have arrived at the price to be a fair one."[58] The sale was made in October 1907.

As Freer and Hanna concluded their negotiations for the transfer of the collection of Indian paintings, Hanna expressed his appreciation for the courtesy and consideration Freer had shown throughout their brief acquaintance. Freer's dealings with Hanna were confined to one transaction, unlike his relationship with Matsuki, Bing, and other dealers, which spanned years. Yet the way in which it was handled was typical of the manner in which Freer conducted all of his business. The combination of civility and prudence that had enabled him to become professionally successful served him equally well as he assembled his art collections, regardless of any complicating circumstances, such as being thrown "high into the air" or "carried . . . completely" off his feet by an art dealer. Once Freer had ascertained the importance of a single object or a group of objects and decided the acquisition would enhance his collections, he was able to set his enthusiasm to one side and manage the purchase with detachment. When the prize had been won, Freer's emotional fervor and aesthetic appreciation were further heightened by the realization that he had also concluded a sound financial settlement. ■

Fig. 88. Artist unknown, *Jahangir and Prince Khurram Feasted by Nur Jahan,* India, Mughal, ca. 1617. Opaque watercolor and gold on paper (25.2 x 14.2), 07.258.

CHAPTER FIVE

THOMAS LAWTON

Freer and Fenollosa

As FREER BEGAN to acquire the East Asian objects that would form the basis of the extraordinary collection he eventually presented to the American people, he met most of the specialists who studied Asian art and culture. Among those scholars, Ernest Francisco Fenollosa (fig. 89) played a particularly important role in helping Freer understand the fundamentals of connoisseurship and determine questions of authenticity.[1] Being teacher and consultant to Freer were but two of Fenollosa's roles, however; the financial relationship between the two men that began from their first meeting continued for several years thereafter.

Fenollosa was born into a family of modest means in Salem, Massachusetts. He graduated from Harvard College in 1874 with honors in philosophy and, supported by a fellowship, continued to study the subject for another two years. He also enrolled in a training program for art teachers at Boston's Normal Art School, at the same time attending studio courses in drawing and painting at the Museum of Fine Arts. His training in philosophy and art laid the foundation for what would become a career as an international advocate of Japanese culture.

With the recommendation of Edward Sylvester Morse (see fig. 67), Fenollosa, then only twenty-five years old, was appointed to the founding chair of philosophy at Tokyo University, a position he held from 1878 to 1886. Those years of involvement in all facets of Japanese life were a watershed in his personal development. He taught a wide range of courses—logic, philosophy, the history of philosophy, sociology, political economy—to students destined to become the leaders of modern Japan. Fenollosa also found time to investigate traditional Japanese culture and, as he learned of the neglect of native cultural values in deference to Western models, emerged as a fervent proponent of the need to preserve Japan's heritage.

Even as Fenollosa was urging the Japanese to safeguard their cultural traditions, he took advantage of his extremely liberal government salary to assemble, with considerable

Detail, figure 96.

discretion, an excellent private art collection. He benefited from the sweeping changes that accompanied the Meiji Restoration of 1868 and forced formerly privileged families and temples to dispose of their art treasures in order to survive in an unfamiliar and unsympathetic environment. During those tumultuous years some of Japan's greatest treasures changed hands for a fraction of their cultural or market value. Fenollosa was but one of a group of concerned and informed Westerners who were collecting Japanese art; in the summer of 1882, for instance, Fenollosa joined Morse and William Sturgis Bigelow, a rich Boston physician, on a buying trip to Kyoto. Fenollosa, Morse, and Bigelow were no doubt motivated by a genuine love of Japanese art and a concern for the preservation of traditions that might otherwise be lost in Japan's race toward Westernization. But they would not have been unaware of the extraordinary financial advantages being offered to them at a time when so much of Japan's cultural patrimony was tumbling onto a curious international market. Conscious of the ethical contradictions of his actions, Fenollosa wrote to Morse in 1884:

I bought several pictures dating from 700 to 900 A.D. Already people here are saying that my collection must be kept here in Japan for the Japanese. I have bought a number of the very greatest treasures secretly. The Japanese as yet don't know that I have them. I wish I could see them all safely housed for ever in the Boston Art Museum [Museum of Fine Arts]. And yet, if the Emperor or Mombusho [Ministry of Education] should want to buy my collection, wouldn't it be my duty to humanity all things considered to let them have it? [2]

From 1886 to 1890, Fenollosa served as one of the Imperial Commissioners of Fine Arts in Japan. In that prestigious capacity he traveled to the United States and Europe, in the company of Japanese colleagues, to study Western art education systems, part of the planning for the establishment of a national art school in Tokyo. When the commissioners arrived in the United States in 1886, Fenollosa's personal belongings included approximately one thousand paintings, which he had already sold to Charles G. Weld, a wealthy Bostonian, with the understanding that the collection would remain in the Museum of Fine Arts. At the time of the sale Fenollosa also stipulated that his name be associated with the paintings; on Weld's death in 1911, they were bequeathed to the museum as the Fenollosa-Weld Collection. [3]

When the Tokyo Fine Arts Academy opened in 1889, Fenollosa put his expertise to full use, teaching courses in aesthetics, art history, and studio techniques. His international reputation as a scholar ensured his successful candidacy for yet another unprecedented appointment: the following year he was named curator of the newly formed Department of Japanese Art at the Museum of Fine Arts, the first department of Asian art to be established in an American museum. The original Museum of Fine Arts, a fussy neo-Gothic building in Copley Square—on the site now occupied by the Copley Plaza Hotel—had opened in 1876; the present, more staid structure was completed in 1909. Before leaving Japan to take up his position in Boston, Fenollosa was decorated by the Emperor Meiji for his twelve years of service to the Japanese government.

As curator, Fenollosa was a vital force in organizing the outstanding Japanese collection at the museum. Within a remarkably short time he planned a number of special exhibitions and began the long-term task of cataloguing his department's holdings. Perhaps even more influential were his lectures on all aspects of East Asian culture. Fenollosa's reputation continued to grow, and he was accepted by the discriminating leaders of Boston society, but his career met with a severe setback in 1895, when his wife, Lizzie Goodhue Fenollosa, was granted a divorce. Fenollosa soon married Mary McNeil Scott, his assistant at the Museum of Fine Arts, who was twelve years his junior. Following a discreet six-month leave of absence, Fenollosa resigned from the museum. He then embarked on the most intense period of his life as he, his wife, and her two children traveled to New York, Europe, and Japan in search of a stable livelihood for Fenollosa.

Fig. 89. Ernest Francisco Fenollosa (1853–1908), ca. 1890.

Different dates have been given for the meeting of Freer and Fenollosa.[4] Freer referred to Fenollosa in his correspondence as early as 1898, when, to Howard Mansfield, author of a descriptive catalogue of Whistler prints, he wrote of Fenollosa's collections of Japanese prints and painting:

When I was in New York I met W. H. Ketcham and he told me of the collection of Fenollosa prints and paintings and of the division being made to give his wife an interest therein. Ketcham told me that the lawyer having the matter in hand had asked him to sell what he could of the lot belonging to Fenollosa. Ketcham also told me in a general way what there was in the collection, and in discussing values he said that he believed they could be bought at very low prices, and wanted to know if he could not send them on to me for examination with the understanding that if I cared to buy any of them, I would do it through Ketcham in order that he might receive a commission on the sales.[5]

Several months later, Freer offered the lawyer, Edward S. Hull, Jr., two thousand dollars for "two lots of kakemono, panels, pottery, screen[s] and the two kakemono by Shunsui and Yeishi, being sold by Fenollosa, also the Hokusai kakemono, 'Cock and Drum.'" Hull accepted the offer.[6] Among the hanging scrolls was *Boy and Mount Fuji* by Katsushika Hokusai, a painting that would become one of the most popular paintings in the Freer Gallery (fig. 90). In September 1898, again acting for Fenollosa, Hull sold Freer five Japanese woodblock prints.[7] Freer was still acquiring Japanese woodblock prints during those years, but as their prices rose as high as those of Japanese scrolls, he withdrew from the market and by 1904 was no longer actively purchasing prints.

When Freer acquired Hokusai's dynamic *Thunder God* in 1900, Fenollosa was in Japan and Hull still handled the negotiations (fig. 91). Freer, who had already begun to assemble detailed records of his acquisitions, requested that Hull send him a copy of Fenollosa's comments on the painting:

It will be interesting to file it away with the Kakemono, and I think that the next time he comes to America I can show him a much finer painting of the same subject by [Tawaraya] Sotatsu. The Hokusai is certainly fine, but I think when I show him the one by Sotatsu, he will take off his hat to the latter.[8]

Apparently Freer had second thoughts about the Sōtatsu painting, for it would not be included in his gift to the nation. *Thunder God,* which carries an inscription dated 1847, remains a powerful, almost terrifying, image; Fenollosa prepared a comprehensive description of the painting in 1900 for the catalogue of the first exhibition of works by Hokusai and his students ever held in Japan.[9]

A letter from Freer to Hull of October 1900 suggests that a meeting with Fenollosa was imminent: "I appreciate your desire to have me meet Professor Fenollosa, and I assure you it will give me much pleasure to do so when I am next in New York."[10] Although Fenollosa was in the United States on a lecture tour in the winter of 1900, he and Freer appear not to have met until late February 1901, when Fenollosa spent a week as Freer's guest in Detroit viewing examples of East Asian and American paintings in Freer's collection. He sold several Japanese scrolls to his host, writing the receipt in longhand on Freer's stationery. A month later, from New York City, Fenollosa wrote in his first letter to Freer that he would soon send some art objects to Freer in Detroit. Those purchases mark the beginning of a series of sales that continued until 1906.

Fenollosa's thanks to Freer for his hospitality were phrased with exquisite courtesy, ensuring that his discriminating host would recognize a kindred spirit:

I can't tell you in adequate words what light of encouragement and color of joy you made that all

too short week shed over my winter in America, and forward along my life-work. I feel like a new man, warmed with your sympathetic comprehension and frank friendship. . . . Next to your friends, the joy was in your rare works of art. In your house one takes a perpetual bath in the True and Beautiful. Koyetsu [Kōetsu] and Whistler and Thayer and Rossetti are spiritual brothers, singers of supreme utterance. As the old Chinese said of his garden, "In this open pavilion I make wise men my friends."[11]

Fenollosa also spoke of having a cold. Throughout the years of their acquaintance, the two connoisseurs regularly exchanged comments about their health; they seem to have suffered from a series of respiratory problems, including influenza and grippe as well as a variety of nervous complaints. In this, also, they were kindred spirits.

Freer's warm regard for Fenollosa almost immediately took the form of what can be interpreted as an oblique criticism of Matsuki Bunkyō, on whose judgment and attributions Freer had depended heavily since 1896. He wrote to Matsuki:

Professor Fenollosa left last night for New York, having spent just one week with me. I enjoyed his visit immensely. We had an opportunity to make careful examination of all the screens and Kakemono, and I wish you could have been present at times and listened to his very instructive criticism and appreciation.[12]

Although Freer asked Matsuki on at least one occasion to comment on Fenollosa's appraisal, and Matsuki continued to offer Freer objects for sale, their relationship gradually cooled. As Freer attempted to distinguish the "fraudulent" from the "good," he turned increasingly to Fenollosa for assistance:

I have chosen seven kakemono [from Matsuki], all of which are attributed to important early Chinese and Japanese artists, but I feel entirely incompetent to judge either of the genuineness of the specimens or of their financial or artistic value. I have discussed the matter very fully with Matsuki, and have arranged with him that he is to submit the seven paintings to you for inspection and criticism. If you decide the specimens are really representative of the masters named, I am to take them at the prices mentioned. Otherwise, I do not want them.[13]

Freer also purchased Japanese paintings from Fenollosa's first wife, Lizzie Goodhue Fenollosa. He took considerable pleasure in reuniting a pair of Hokusai screens that had been separated by the Fenollosa divorce (fig. 92). Negotiating with the owners independently, Freer did not allow sentiment to interfere with business: he paid $1,750 to Fenollosa for one screen[14] and only fifteen hundred to Lizzie Fenollosa for the other.[15]

Fenollosa was compelled to sell paintings from his collection for funds needed to complete construction of Kobinata, his new home in the suburbs of Mobile, Alabama, close to the family residence of his second wife;[16] Kobinata was the name of a street in Koishikawaku, Tokyo, where the Fenollosas had lived during their last days in Japan. In one of his longest letters to Freer, he wrote in detail about the paintings, which included contempory works by Kanō Hōgai and Hashimoto Gahō.[17] Hōgai was one of the artists whom Fenollosa knew personally and had supported during his years in Japan. His painting of the Buddhist deity Kannon (fig. 93), which Fenollosa referred to as the "Creation of Man," was completed in 1883 and shown in Paris the same year.[18] At the close of the exhibition, Siegfried Bing acquired the painting, together with others by living Japanese artists. Three years later, when Fenollosa was in Europe as one of the Japanese commissioners of fine arts, he bought "Creation of Man" from Bing. The information he provided obviously impressed Freer, who had not previously purchased contemporary Japanese paintings. Freer agreed to buy the scrolls, but only after asking Matsuki and Ushikubō Daijirō, who worked at Yamanaka and Company, for estimates of an appropriate price.

Fenollosa described another of the scrolls in his collection as an "old Chinese Sung [Song] painting," explaining to Freer that it was part of a set of scrolls from the Daitokuji, the great Zen temple in Kyoto (fig. 94). He provided a brief history of the scrolls, beginning with their traditional attribution to the Northern Song master Li Longmian, or Ririomin.[19] Fenollosa's statement that *Luohan Laundering* "surely dates from the twelfth century" has been confirmed by subsequent research; an inscription in gold-colored pigment along the lower right edge of the scroll gives the date and the name, Lin Tinggui, of the little-known Chinese artist.[20]

During the first years of their relationship, it is clear that in regard to Asian paintings Fenollosa was the teacher and Freer the student. Freer acknowledged those roles to the American painter Dwight W. Tryon when he wrote, "Professor Fenollosa has been my guest for the last four days, during which he has been giving me further instructions in Japanese and Chinese painting. He is a thoroughly intelligent man, and has remarkable appreciation of beauty."[21]

While correspondence between Freer and Fenollosa was initially limited to descriptions of Fenollosa's collection and his ambitious plans for lectures, Freer asked Fenollosa for advice on objects that he was considering for purchase on several occasions

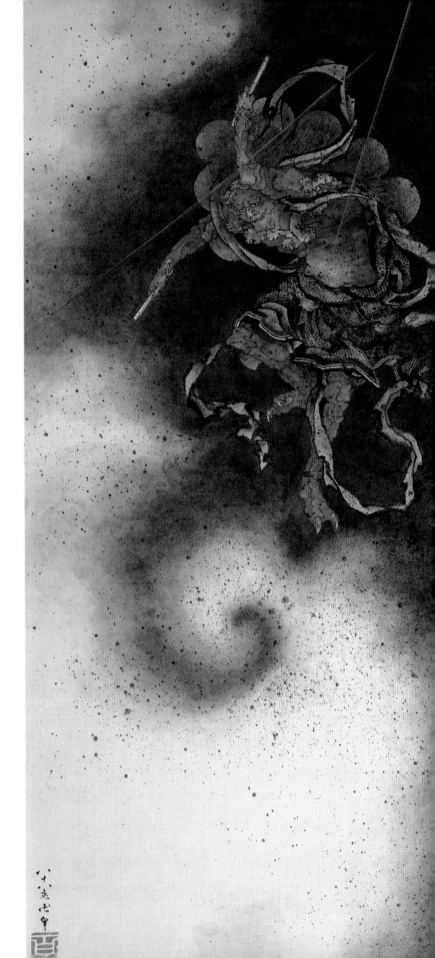

during the years following their first meeting.[22] When, for example, Freer received a catalogue of the important Hayashi Tadamasa sale of Japanese art in Paris,[23] he turned to Fenollosa for guidance:

The complete catalogue of the forthcoming Hayashi Sale reached me this afternoon, and I have already examined the complete list of paintings. I am wondering if you have not had access to the finished catalogue, and, if you have, whether or not you have noticed anything in the early schools which you think it would be wise for me to communicate with Bing about. . . . The paintings are not to be sold until Saturday of next week, so I can telegraph Mr. Bing up to Thursday or Friday next.[24]

It was at that sale in February 1903 that Freer acquired a large hanging scroll by Kitagawa Utamaro showing the interior of a teahouse, and a pair of hanging scrolls attributed to Hokusai (see figs. 79 and 80). The quality of the scrolls speaks well of Fenollosa's advice to Freer on ukiyo-e paintings.

Freer expressed gratitude for the assistance Fenollosa gave him and, with most delicate concern for his precarious financial situation, touched on the matter of an honorarium and expenses:

Fig. 92. Katsushika Hokusai (1760–1849), *Country Scenes,* Japan, Edo period. Pair of six-fold screens; ink, gold, and color on paper (each screen 150.9 x 353.1), 02.48–49. When the right-hand screen was exhibited in Tokyo in 1901, Fenollosa wrote in the catalogue about the "extraordinary triumph" of the colors, which include "shaded gold," "pearl blue," and an "idyllic wash of rose" — the "whole passage a mosaic of glows between the extremes of lemon yellow and ultramarine blue."

In asking this favor, I must beg you to let me take care of your traveling expenses and to show some other recognition as well. To be sure, your visit will be largely of a social nature, which I know we will both enjoy. On the other hand, inasmuch as you are sure to be consulted professionally, you will, I trust, accept something more than thanks.[25]

In return for Fenollosa's advice, Freer issued him checks, usually in the amount of two hundred dollars (although there was one payment of five hundred) for his "services as an expert" or "services rendered." Freer also offered to reimburse Fenollosa for any expenses incurred by his missions. The typical courtesy of their relationship is evident in a letter from Fenollosa:

Now, my dear Mr. Freer, I appreciate fully your kind offer, most courteously and delicately made, to pay my expenses in coming to New York; and there might be times when I should feel it quite right to accept such an offer, this is, cases where I had to put myself to considerable and unusual expense. But, in this case, I had already planned to come to New York for purposes of my own, and it only added to my natural pleasure in seeing the kakemonos to know that my doing so might also be of service to you.[26]

Fig. 93. Kanō Hōgai (1828–1888), *Kannon Bosatsu* ("Creation of Man"), Japan, Edo period, completed in 1883. Hanging scroll; ink, gold, and color on silk (165.7 x 84.8), 02.225. Fenollosa wrote to Freer on October 1902: "The Bodhisattva [Kannon] pours in mid air from her crystal water-vase a spray from which is born a little naked babe, typifying man, who, falling through the clouds toward the savage peaks of earth, turns to his spirit-creator as if asking reproachfully if this was the awful world for which had been planned the tragedy of his birth and fate."

Another important object that Freer acquired at Fenollosa's urging is a six-fold screen attributed to Sesshū Tōyō (fig. 95). In October 1904, Fenollosa informed Freer that John Kirby of the American Art Galleries in New York had asked him to prepare a "small special section of the elaborate catalogue" of a sale by the Washington real-estate tycoon Thomas E. Waggaman, scheduled to be held in late January and early February 1905. Fenollosa, who had never before accepted that type of commission, asked Freer's opinion about what a fair fee for his work might be. He also announced, "Of course you know that the Sesshū landscape screen will be the biggest piece in that Waggaman lot."[27]

The Sesshū landscape was well known. In 1894, when Fenollosa organized an exhibition of Japanese painting and metalwork at the Museum of Fine Arts, Boston, the first exhibition of early Japanese painting in the United States, the screen was among the major works.[28] Waggaman acquired the screen after the 1894 exhibition; before the 1905 sale, it was valued at twenty-five-hundred dollars. Freer's initial reaction to the screen was qualified, and his reservations remain valid:

There is a certain hardness of finish in the work and a vast mass of detail which I find objectionable. On the other hand, the distance seems to me very beautiful and the notan [light and shade] in certain parts of the screen remarkable. But perhaps its greatest charm to me, as I now view it, lies in the delightfully inspiring gray tone of the general effect of the screen produced by the quality of the ink, its use and the condition of the paper. At the same time, certain parts of the paper have been so much soiled in handling that the notan is injured thereby.[29]

Nonetheless, spontaneous applause followed when the screen was set up for auction on the evening of 30 January 1905; the bidding started at five hundred dollars but quickly went to thirty-one hundred, when the screen was knocked down to Freer.

When Freer's offer to give his collection to the nation was accepted by the Regents of the Smithsonian Institution in 1906 after lengthy, and occasionally ambivalent, negotiations, Fenollosa was one of the first people Freer notified: "Smithsonian Regents accepted unanimously today," said his terse telegram.[30] The following month Fenollosa was in Detroit to lecture at the University Club on ancient Chinese and Japanese art. For the rest of the ten-day stay, he helped Freer carry out a sweeping review of his Japanese paintings in light of the Smithsonian's decision. Freer wrote to the artist Thomas Wilmer Dewing:

Fig. 94. Lin Tinggui, *Luohan Laundering,* China, Song dynasty, dated 1178. Hanging scroll; ink and color on silk (111.8 x 53.1), 02.224. When Freer purchased this scroll, he believed it was by the twelfth-century master Li Longmian (Jpn.: Ririomin).

Overleaf:
Fig. 95. Sesshū Tōyō (1420–1506), *Landscape,* Japan, Muromachi period. Six-fold screen; ink on paper (156.2 x 357.8), 05.20. Many scholars have commented on the dense, assertive brush strokes and bold outlines that Sesshū used to define the three-dimensional contours of the mountains in this screen. The deep recession into space from the foreground mountain is another notable feature of the composition.

I have been buried to my ears in working with Professor Fenollosa on the Japanese paintings. We are weeding out every specimen that does not seem to be absolutely first-class. All of the poorer ones we have thrown out permanently; and many others which seem doubtful we have put aside for future reference. The result will be that the ones of which the titles are to be transferred to the Smithsonian Institution . . . will be absolutely beyond aesthetic criticism.[31]

Freer's admiration of Fenollosa reached its peak when he was able to compare the

Fig. 96. Tawaraya Sōtatsu (active 1614–ca. 1639), *Waves at Matsushima,* Japan, Edo period. Pair of six-fold screens; ink, color, and gold on paper (each screen 152.0 x 355.7), 06.231–32. These screens are among the finest works accepted as authentic compositions by Japanese master Tawaraya Sōtatsu. The islands, a famous scenic spot in Miyagi Prefecture in northeastern Japan, are portrayed in boldly stylized forms and colors.

profundity and subtlety of Fenollosa's connoisseurship to that of other Asian specialists. In the late summer and fall of 1906, Gaston Migeon, curator at the Louvre and by then a close friend of Freer's, spent several days with Freer and Fenollosa looking at Freer's collection. Migeon, as Freer described him, was an "enthusiastic student of Oriental Art and a very charming man" who "speaks very little English, but is a wonder in expressing his feelings through signs and motions."[32] True to Freer's assessment, Migeon, after studying Freer's Japanese screens, suggested with his appealing Gallic wit that Freer should be referred to as the "Mikado of the Screens."[33] The contrast between Migeon's and Fenollosa's evaluations of objects made a striking impression on Freer, who wrote to his friend and fellow collector Charles J. Morse:

I must tell you how far Fenollosa's knowledge of Chinese and Japanese Art is ahead of Migeon's. The fact is Europeans are really far behind the Americans in their understanding of the finer Arts of China and Japan. I really feel that ignorance rather than dishonesty influenced the writers of the many catalogues which have emanated from Paris and this, I am sure, will be a comforting thought to us both. It is a real comfort to me to feel that Bing was not dishonest in many of his attributions. Now I am wondering how much dependence can really be placed upon the attributions made by Migeon, Koechlin and other Parisian savants on the potteries found throughout Syria and Arabia.[34]

In November 1907, Fenollosa spent a week at Freer's home in Detroit studying the collection. Since Freer did not approve of examining objects under artificial light, all serious inspection was limited to daylight hours, and it is not unusual to find notations in his diaries of guests reaching his home in the early morning. Fenollosa arrived at 8:30 A.M. on Monday, 4 November. During their review, Fenollosa recorded in a notebook his reactions to pieces in Freer's collection as well as comments Freer made about various objects, traditions, and techniques.[35] Since Fenollosa wrote in haste, using abbreviations obviously intended for his own future reference in lectures and in the preparation of a proposed descriptive catalogue of Freer's collection, the notebook entries are difficult to decipher. Indeed, their illegibility may account for the slight attention that scholars have given them. Yet the refreshing directness of his unpolished prose captures his sensitive reactions without the literary excesses found in his volume *Epochs of Chinese and Japanese Art*. The jottings, personal and spontaneous, reveal Fenollosa's direct response to specific works and record the remarks Fenollosa and Freer exchanged as they studied the collections and discussed a wide range of topics. No other record provides so intimate or informative a glimpse of the relationship between teacher and student.

Among the works that merited Fenollosa's comment is *Waves at Matsushima* (fig. 96). The pair of six-fold screens depicting pine-covered islands—one of five sets of

Fig. 97. Ambassador Horace N. Allen (1858–1932), 1904. From Fred Harvey Harrington, *God, Mammon and the Japanese: Dr. Horace N. Allen and Korean-American Relations, 1884–1905* (Madison: University of Wisconsin Press, 1944).

screens by Tawaraya Sōtatsu accepted as authentic by scholars[36]—today is regarded as a masterpiece; certainly it is the finest pair of Japanese screens in the Freer Gallery. Fenollosa noted that the temple in which the screens had been housed for centuries was located in Aki, a city in southeastern Kōchi Prefecture.[37] He cited the relationship between Freer's Sōtatsu screens and Ogata Kōrin's version of the same subject, a work he once owned and now part of the Fenollosa-Weld Collection in the Museum of Fine Arts, Boston.[38] The dealer Kobayashi Bunshichi, from whom Freer acquired the screens in 1906, asserted, "This Sōtatsu screen was a treasure of a Buddhist monastery, which after three years' efforts on my part, I succeeded in legitimately transferring into my collection. I dare say, it is the very best of Sōtatsu. Experts and connoisseurs are of the same opinion."[39] Since Kobayashi regularly offered Freer objects of exceptionally high quality, he was reluctant to agree to the reduced prices that Freer invariably demanded, with the result that the men often negotiated, sometimes acrimoniously, for extended periods. In the case of *Waves at Matsushima,* Freer reported to Fenollosa, "After much dickering of an almost exasperating nature, I bought the pair of six-fold wave screens by Sotatsu. . . . [Kobayashi's] original price for the Sotatsu was ten thousand dollars [but] I cut his prices exactly in half."[40]

According to Fenollosa's notebook, he and Freer also went over the collection of Korean pottery that Freer had purchased several months earlier from Horace N. Allen (fig. 97).[41] Freer had first learned of the availability of the ceramics when, in Japan on his second Asian tour, he saw a catalogue of the collection being offered for sale by Allen, a Presbyterian medical missionary who first went to Korea in 1884. Allen had served for twenty-two years in Korea and China, both as a missionary and for the United States diplomatic service, and was ultimately appointed the American ambassador to Korea. During his stay in East Asia, he developed a keen interest in ceramics; his collection was remarkable for the number of pieces that had been recovered from excavations of tombs of Korean nobility. The outstanding quality of those ceramics, complemented by the fact that they could be dated with precision, made Allen's collection one of particular importance (fig. 98). Although Sir Caspar Purdon Clarke, director of the Metropolitan Museum of Art in New York from 1905 to 1910, had offered to purchase thirty-five pieces from the collection, Allen, who was then retired and living in Toledo, preferred to sell his holdings intact. From Japan, Freer cabled Frank Hecker in Detroit and asked him to act as his agent in purchasing the Allen collection. He subsequently set out the importance of the purchase:

From the descriptions given in the catalogue, I am sure that a large number of the specimens are extremely rare and interesting—some probably unique—the better ones added to the pieces I already have, will place my collection of Corean pottery along with the best in existence. The price of $5,000 for the 80 pieces is really low. All kinds of ancient pottery in Japan are now fearfully dear—old Chinese, old Corean and first-class Japanese has doubled in price within twelve months.[42]

Hecker handled the purchase of Allen's ceramics with the acumen he would have brought to a business merger. To Freer's surprise and delight, Hecker pursued his "old time habit of always getting rock bottom prices" and obtained all eighty pieces for three thousand dollars.[43] Hecker promised Allen that if Freer decided the collection was of "sufficient importance," he would consider increasing the price to thirty-five-hundred dollars.

Going over the ceramics with Fenollosa was Freer's first opportunity to study them closely. After he had examined the collection "both from its aesthetic side and a financial one," Freer agreed, "in view of the fine quality of several of the rarer pieces," to pay the additional five hundred dollars.[44] He could well afford to be generous, for he had acquired a major collection at a minimum price.

Fenollosa's first statement about the Allen ceramics in his notebook is sharply perceptive. He asked himself—and presumably Freer, also—"Can some of them be Chinese?" That question has been raised many times by scholars in ensuing years; today it is generally agreed that some of the pieces are Chinese and date from the Song dynasty. Nonetheless, it is clear from many of Fenollosa's comments that he was recording Freer's opinions and deferring to his wide experience in ceramics from many parts of the ancient world. Some of the statements are cryptic, others simply unfathomable. By contrast, many of Freer's views reflected his belief in cultural relationships that stretched from the Mediterranean across Central Asia to Japan. While most of those diffusionist theories are untenable today, it is obvious that both Freer and Fenollosa were grappling with questions of intercultural influences that preoccupied scholars and connoisseurs in the early twentieth century.

While Fenollosa was visiting Freer in Detroit in November 1907, he published an article on Freer's collection in *Pacific Era*, a Detroit-based journal that was partially supported by Freer. Fenollosa accurately appraised the strengths and weaknesses of Freer's collection at the time and described the three parts of Freer's holdings:

Fig. 98. The Allen ceramic collection with numbers added as references to his catalogue, ca. 1907. Rare Book Collection, Library of Freer Gallery of Art and Arthur M. Sackler Gallery.

First, by far the largest and most representative series of all the pictorial work of James McNeill Whistler that now exists in any group, or that it is physically possible shall ever exist;—second, the most comprehensive and aesthetically valuable collection anywhere known of all the ancient glazed pottery of the world, Egyptian, Babylonian, Persian, Indian, Chinese, Korean, and Japanese:—and third, the finest and best unified group of masterpieces by the greatest Chinese and Japanese painters of all ages that exists outside of Japan, with the possible exception of that in the Boston Art Museum [Museum of Fine Arts].

Having inserted the essential caveat of the East Asian collection in Boston, Fenollosa continued by pinpointing gaps in Freer's holdings:

The limitations in this grouping are obvious at first sight. Sculpture is practically omitted. . . . Metal is excluded from the list of materials. Even in ceramics, the important field of porcelain is not touched; and in the varied lines of Far Eastern pictorial art, the large and popular class of Japanese color prints is not exemplified. This last omission is the more remarkable in that, of the Whistler series, the prints, in all manners, form a conspicuous member.

And he justified the limitations, saying:

But this narrowness, as it may appear to the ordinary student, though deliberately adopted by Mr. Freer, does not imply any arbitrary whim upon his part; rather has it a definite purpose. It is true that he would lay chief claim for the merits of his treasures on the fact that they embody a single, clearly followed taste. But that their vast variety only exemplifies a single set of principles is perhaps the strongest ground of our belief in their future educational value.[45]

Fenollosa's evaluation and criticisms were well taken, and his final emphasis on Freer's belief that the interrelated "manifold meanings" of all the pieces in his collection contain a unique message for the world remains as valid today as it was in 1907. The two men had long discussions about the future of Freer's art holdings, and, it is clear, Freer was pleased to have so distinguished a connoisseur as his "teacher, adviser and inspirer."[46] As early as 1905, Freer wrote to Fenollosa about his hopes with unusual candor:

It is extremely good of you to continue your intelligent interest and assistance in my group of Oriental paintings, and I trust you understand what great assistance you have rendered me in the work. I feel there is a fair hope of eventually making it fully equal, in an artistic way, to the Boston Museum's collection, but I do not care to have it so bulky. I am confident that quality should be the standard, and I know you agree with me in this.[47]

Freer was well aware of Fenollosa's contributions to the Asian holdings at the Museum of Fine Arts; on several occasions when Freer was in Boston he tried to persuade Fenollosa to accompany him to the museum to review its latest acquisitions. For reasons perhaps too personal and painful, Fenollosa always made excuses. There is no mistaking Freer's grudging admiration of the high quality of the Asian collections in Boston. Indeed, during the final years of his life, as he sought a curator for his own museum, it was to the Museum of Fine Arts, specifically to John E. Lodge (fig. 99), that he turned.

Fig. 99. John Ellerton Lodge (1876–1942), ca. 1910. Massachusetts Historical Society, Boston. Following in the footsteps of Ernest Fenollosa and Okakura Kakuzō, Lodge took charge of the Asian collections at the Museum of Fine Arts, Boston, in 1913. He served as the first director of the Freer Gallery from 1920 to 1942.

Such was Freer's regard for Fenollosa's scholarship that he hoped Fenollosa would eventually prepare a descriptive catalogue of his collection. In the notebook Fenollosa compiled during that fruitful visit to Detroit in November 1907, he recorded: "Mr. Freer wishes me to cooperate in final Washington catalogue—also is to refer his executors to me in case of a dispute as to what it was Mr. Freer's intention to include for Washington."[48] That degree of trust in the final disposition of Freer's collection, a subject that dominated every aspect of Freer's life after the Smithsonian Institution's formal acceptance of his gift in 1906, indicates how much he relied on Fenollosa. Had he not died unexpectedly the following year, Fenollosa certainly would have continued to play a major role in the planning of Freer's museum. It is conceivable, moreover, that he might have become its first director. His sudden death of a heart attack in London on 21 September 1908 was a great blow to Freer:

I was dreadfully shocked this morning by the receipt of a telegraphic message announcing the death of my friend Professor Fenollosa in London, day before yesterday. I have no particulars of his sudden going, but fancy it was entirely unexpected. We had planned to do together in the future lots of work in connection with my catalogue, etc. etc. His death prevents this and is a great loss.[49]

As a young man living in Japan, Fenollosa had studied Buddhism at Miidera, a temple in Otsu overlooking Lake Biwa; together with William Sturgis Bigelow, he had

Fig. 100. The Fenollosa memorial at Miidera.

Fig. 101. Freer (seated extreme right) and Hara (seated sixth from right) at the memorial ceremony for Fenollosa at Miidera, September 1909. Participants dressed in a variety of secular and sacred costumes: somber Western attire, traditional Japanese robes, and Buddhist garments resplendent with gold decoration.

received the precepts of the Tendai sect at the temple on 21 September 1885. Fenollosa maintained an attachment to Miidera ever after and requested that his remains be interred there. Although his ashes were temporarily placed in Highgate Cemetery in London, a year later, in keeping with his wishes, they were buried in an ornate, pseudo-Gothic reliquary on the temple grounds at Miidera.

When Freer heard the plans for reburying Fenollosa's ashes in Japan, he arranged for the erection at the site of "an incense burner, a flower vase and two lanterns all to be of stone and to be of the size and kind usual in Japan" (fig. 100), a memorial presentation from friends outside Japan, including Laurence Binyon, keeper in the Department of Prints and Drawings at the British Museum, Gaston Migeon, and the painter Arthur W. Dow.[50] The ashes were interred during a solemn ceremony that Freer attended with his friend Hara Tomitarō (fig. 101). A photograph of Fenollosa wearing his imperial decorations surmounted an elaborate altar in the main hall of the temple. Set in front of the photograph was a tablet bearing Fenollosa's Buddhist posthumous name, with red and white lotus cakes and chrysanthemum blossoms arranged on either side. Following a traditional Buddhist service, several officials spoke about Fenollosa's contributions to Japanese art. The final activity on the program would have pleased Fenollosa: all who attended the memorial service were invited to spend the remainder of the afternoon enjoying a special exhibition of Japanese paintings. ■

CHAPTER SIX

LINDA MERRILL

The American Renaissance

T HE WORLD'S COLUMBIAN EXPOSITION, the commemoration of the four-hundredth anniversary of Columbus's voyage to America, officially opened in Chicago at the beginning of May 1893, exactly thirty years before the inauguration of the Freer Gallery of Art. Although Freer had not yet formulated his gift to the nation, he was profoundly influenced by his experience of the fair, which would affect his scheme of collecting.

On a visit to Chicago in mid-July, Freer admired the gleaming neoclassical buildings and the elaborate system of waterways that linked the islands of the White City, and he recounted to Dwight Tryon the pleasures of "life in the gondolas."[1] He recommended the Columbian Fountain by Frederick MacMonnies and the magnificent Court of Honor, which he found especially agreeable in the early hours of the evening; the Midway, the site of more popular amusements, was notable for the Ferris wheel and the Japanese village, but Freer disdained the dance houses and "theatrical fakes," which he believed were better avoided altogether.[2] His particular reason for going to the fair was to visit the Fine Arts Palace, where eight of the one thousand contemporary American paintings on view were from his own collection. Freer had contributed nearly all the works that adorned his new house in Detroit and he felt their absence acutely, although he knew he would be amply repaid by the pleasure the paintings would give the "large number of intelligent art lovers" who would see them in Chicago.[3] He paid an obligatory visit to the French and Dutch art exhibits and returned to the American department with renewed respect for the few modern artists whose paintings he had chosen to collect, deciding at that moment that their works, more than the others, revealed "refinement, knowledge and soul."[4] Afterward, Freer proclaimed the belief that would underlie his collection of American art: "After careful study at the Fair, I am more thoroughly impressed than ever," he wrote to Thomas Dewing, "that the art of yourself, Tryon, Thayer and Whistler is the most refined in spirit, poetical in design and deepest in artistic

In the days of the early Renaissance in Italy, and still earlier, when the great art of Japan and China was at its best, encouragement and appreciation were supreme: and, of course, under friendly encouragement, the Goddess was more frequent in her visits to the home of the artists.

Freer to Augustus Koopman, 12 December 1901

Fig. 102. Charles Lang Freer at the Villa Castello in Capri, ca. 1901.

truth of this century."[5]

That conviction led to Freer's abiding faith in the talents of the four American artists whose friendship he cultivated and works he collected throughout his career as a connoisseur. Although the paintings he had acquired were few, and most of them were meant to appoint his Detroit home, Freer was already beginning to consider himself a patron of the arts in the tradition of the Medici. Abbott Thayer did what he could to encourage that attitude, reminding Freer in 1893 that the noble patrons of Raphael and Michelangelo, "lacking the painter gift themselves," had made a vital contribution to the Renaissance in Italy by bestowing earthly comforts upon the artists, who then were free to "blossom and bear fruit."[6]

On a trip to Florence the following year, Freer saw those fruits of the Renaissance for himself. He observed that the Medici must have been sympathetic indeed with the art of their time, or they could not have encouraged the production of the many masterpieces that had made their name immortal. After several days of studying the art collections at the Accademia, the Uffizi, and the Palazzo Pitti, Freer enjoyed an intense, revelatory moment at Petraia, one of the Medici villas in the outskirts of the city, which he related impersonally in a letter to Frank Hecker:

As he stands upon the terrace of Petraia and sees Florence five miles distant, at sunset, and listens to the bells of the city, and the gentle wind sighing through the tall cypresses, and thinks of the history of what he has seen and then feels—he must say yes, the Medici were magnificent.[7]

Awed by their achievement, Freer determined to play the part of the Medici himself, to foster creative genius in the period of artistic prosperity known as the American Renaissance.

In Freer's estimation, Whistler occupied a category apart from the other artists of his day: "Whistler, you know, was an accident of our own time."[8] The year before the Columbian Exposition, Freer had heard a rumor that the artist would be commissioned to produce a painting for the fair, presumably because his grandfather was thought to have selected the site of the city of Chicago. Although Freer knew nothing about the commission, he fervently hoped the report would prove true: such a work, he wrote to Mrs. Whistler, would undoubtedly inspire the "countless thousands who are destined to study Art for its real value" and stand as a "lasting monument of the best art of this century—may I add of any century?"[9] The Chicago scheme was never realized, but Freer would himself create a monument around the works of Whistler to benefit the nation.

By the time Freer met him, Whistler was past the point of requiring a patron. Relatively few of the works in Freer's collection were purchased directly from the artist, and only one, *Harmony in Blue and Gold: The Little Blue Girl* (see fig. 33), was painted on commission. But the other artists whom Freer held in high regard, three whose works similarly exemplified the "highest ideals of American art," were considerably younger than Whistler (closer in age to Freer) and more in need of financial support.[10] Tryon, Dewing, and Thayer had all participated in the decoration of Freer's house, a collaborative effort conducted in the spirit of the Renaissance that set the stage for later productions.

Of the painters whose work corresponded with Freer's ideals of American art, Abbott Handerson Thayer (fig. 103) was to Freer the "rare genius."[11] Born in Boston, Thayer began his artistic training in Brooklyn, where he studied with the amateur painter of animals Henry D. Morse. Eventually, after a stint at the National Academy of Design in Manhattan, he went to Paris to study at the Ecole des Beaux Arts with Henri Lehmann and later with Jean-Léon Gérôme, then one of the most celebrated artists in Europe. Upon his return to New York in 1879, Thayer joined the Society of American Artists, a confederation of artists whose European education made their works incompatible with the traditional style of the National Academy, and for many years he maintained a studio in Washington Square. After the untimely death of his wife in 1891 and his precipitant remarriage, Thayer gave up his New York studio and began spending most of his days near Dublin, New Hampshire, where he owned a modest house with a stunning view of Mount Monadnock.[12]

Fig. 103. Abbott Handerson Thayer (1849–1921), ca. 1918.

Freer purchased his first painting by Thayer in April 1890 from Newman E. Montross, a New York art dealer with a consonant taste in American art. *Head* (fig. 104), a half-length figure of a woman in classical drapery, resembles a Roman portrait bust; but the painting was placed in an elaborate architectural frame ornamented with Corinthian pilasters and other Greco-Roman elements, a Renaissance-inspired setting that effectively transformed the classical portrait into a private devotional object. Thayer customarily drew inspiration for his work from both classical and quattrocento sources. *Virgin Enthroned* (fig. 105), a painting of the artist's sixteen-year-old daughter, Mary, flanked by his younger children, Gladys and Gerald, has a composition that recalls a Renaissance altarpiece: Mary sits enthroned before a tapestry separating her from the earthly realm, represented by the background landscape, while her brother and sister play the parts of attendant saints.

Freer encountered *Virgin Enthroned* a year after purchasing Thayer's *Head* and regretted to find that it was already owned by someone else. He may have thought it rem-

Fig. 104. Abbott Handerson Thayer (1849–1921), *Head*, 1888–89. Oil on canvas (76.3 x 51.0), 90.4. Frame designed by Stanford White (1853–1906), 1892.

iniscent of the San Zaccaria altarpiece in Venice, Giovanni Bellini's *Enthroned Madonna with Saints* (1505), which Freer would call "*the* Madonna of Bellini" and count among his favorite works of art.[13] In language that conveys the intensity of his appreciation, Freer wrote Montross his impressions of Thayer's enthroned Madonna: "How tender and yet how strong! How dignified and yet how kind! An emblem of purity; a protest against sin! It speaks in countless ways and sings many unsung songs." Still under the elevating

Fig. 105. Abbott Handerson Thayer (1849–1921), *Virgin Enthroned,* 1891. Oil on canvas (184.3 x 133.2). National Museum of American Art, Smithsonian Institution, Washington, D.C.; Gift of John Gellatly.

influence of the painting, Freer would not allow himself to envy its fortunate owner; but had he seen Thayer's *Virgin Enthroned* in time, he told Montross, "it would have been mine, even had I been compelled to mortgage my few earthly possessions."[14]

The next year, in compensation, Freer bought *A Virgin* (see fig. 1), a comparable depiction of the artist's children. The active pose of the central figure was probably based on the Winged Victory of Samothrace, another masterpiece of European art that Freer admired; when he lent *A Virgin* for exhibition at the University of Michigan in 1910, he ordered a replica of the Victory to display beside the painting. Thayer's inclination to convert the cloud formation in the background into wings was stimulated in part by his "lifelong passion for birds," but more emphatically, the artist explained, by a desire "to symbolize an exalted atmosphere (above the realm of genre painting) where one need not explain the action of his figures."[15] He had painted his first angel, also a picture of his daughter Mary, in the late 1880s and would continue producing monumental portraits of winged young women until the close of his career.

Sympathetic with Thayer's wish to exalt American art above the commonplace, Freer approved of Thayer's idealized por-

Fig. 106. Abbott Handerson Thayer (1849–1921), *Winged Figure Seated upon a Rock*, 1903/16. Oil on canvas (213.5 x 153.0), 15.67.

trayal of women, which conformed with his own ideal of "madonna and saintlike" feminine perfection.[16] He bought three of Thayer's life-size winged figures, perhaps as a public-spirited investment: the artist perceived the works as "things not made to sell but of a pure prophetic quality and of an inestimable value to the nation."[17] For public monuments, however, Thayer's angels and winged victories can be painfully personal. *Winged Figure Seated upon a Rock* (fig. 106), for example, pictures Thayer's younger daughter as a rather sullen, corporeal angel. As a model, Gladys had played supporting roles in both *Virgin Enthroned* and *A Virgin,* but she appears alone in this painting, wearing wings and a halo. Grown up, she resembled her late mother, to whom the canvas is dedicated in a Latin inscription incised into the rock on which the figure sits. A second inscription, added by the artist some years later, stipulates that the painting never be retouched, "not one pin-point," a provision that makes the monument inviolable.

Winged Figure Seated upon a Rock is a variation of Thayer's *Stevenson Memorial* (fig. 107), now in the National Museum of American Art, Smithsonian Institution, which was executed in 1903 as a tribute to the artist's favorite author, Robert Louis Stevenson. Thayer frequently produced series of related works, a practice he compared to Monet's. "This system is a marvel," Thayer wrote to Freer, "each picture raising the standard, so that all that stay in one's shop go on enlightening each other till all are far above what a much fussed over lone one ever can be."[18] *Winged Figure,* begun the same year as *Stevenson Memorial,* was still in Thayer's studio in 1908 when he declared the figure complete except for one leg—probably the right one, which falls at an unlikely angle and appears never to have received the intended finishing touches. Thayer conceded that *Stevenson Memorial* outshone its successor; *Winged Figure* had nonetheless comforted his family when it was brought out for their inspection.[19] Six years later, when Thayer again wrote his beneficent patron about the painting he had come to consider one of his best, Freer answered with an offer to buy it. Thayer was delighted almost beyond expression that his *Winged Figure,* which he called "my heart's legacy to the world," would reside forever in Freer's "noble collection."[20]

More than the other artists whose works Freer collected, Thayer depended on Freer's patronage. Squalor irritated him excessively, and he did not share the "puritanical illusion" that poverty was good for an artist—"except perhaps to work through and emerge from while still in one's prime." The demands of his family were forever in con-

Fig. 107. Thayer with *Stevenson Memorial* (National Museum of American Art, Smithsonian Institution), ca. 1903.

flict with the commands of his muse, and if he were forced to bear "money-anxiety or poverty or ugliness as well as the strain of painting pictures with heart's blood," he said, he would not long remain a painter in his prime.[21] Although Freer did not always give in to Thayer's repetitious requests for money, he did pay high prices for his pictures to keep the artist afloat, as Thayer put it, for the sake of his work. Thayer acknowledged that in Freer he had found "a golden man, a true thing," and his paintings, he knew, would never find a more appreciative possessor. "Hear once more," Thayer wrote Freer, "that I would rather send every single picture as fast as I do them straight to your home than [to] any other private house in this country."[22]

Thayer once confided to Freer, who he felt sure would understand, that he did not invent his paintings so much as write them down "to the dictation of a higher power."[23] Especially attuned to a transcendent realm, Thayer was most at home in the country, communing with nature. He approached the landscape reverentially and customarily fed his soul, he said, by gazing on Mount Monadnock. When development threatened to destroy the purity of the place, he became an ardent and ultimately effective conservationist. "Were that mountainside in my keeping, as it is in yours," he wrote the owners of the property, "I should feel that my only rights were to see that no deterioration of its virginity occurred."[24] From his studio in New Hampshire, Thayer idealized his view of Monadnock as he had his images of women, using snow rather than wings to create an "exalted atmosphere."

Monadnock No. 2 (fig. 108), one of Thayer's many paintings of the mountain, was "really very brilliant," the artist informed Freer, as it presented Monadnock with "up-to-date perceptions."[25] Consistent with other renditions, *Monadnock No. 2* shows the mountain at dawn, distinct against a wintry white sky. But this version captures a particularly vivid perception of the snow-covered mountainside, a natural phenomenon the artist expressed in painter's terms as "burnished silver stabbed vertically in between the purple tree verticals."[26] That course of calligraphic brush strokes perforates the scene's illusion, rendering the painting almost abstract. In style and sensibility, *Monadnock No. 2* may indeed be the most modern, or "up-to-date," work in Freer's American collection.

Dwight William Tryon (fig. 109), a second artist in Freer's American triumvirate, was as attached as Abbott Thayer to the landscape of New England. Tryon, however, preferred simple settings that showed signs of human intervention: without "some association of man," the landscape was too wild and vast, Tryon thought, too disorganized and scattered to offer up scenes for an artist to paint.[27] Tryon was temperamentally opposite to Thayer, and his work is comparatively quiet and composed. While Freer did not regard Tryon, like Thayer, as a genius, he bought a great number of Tryon's works, eventually assembling a group of Tryon paintings second in number only to his Whistler

Fig. 108. Abbott Handerson Thayer (1849–1921), *Monadnock No. 2*, 1913. Oil on canvas (90.2 x 90.2), 13.93.

Fig. 109. Dwight William Tryon, 1912, inscribed, "To my friend Charles L. Freer."

holdings. Freer seems also to have found more to enjoy in Tryon's easygoing nature and undemanding friendship; and Tryon, for his part, appreciated Freer's keen sensitivity to beauty. "Many times of late while walking about the fields I have thought of you," he wrote Freer one spring day when he felt overcome by the glory of the season. Whenever Tryon encountered "specially rare and beautiful things," Freer came to mind as one of the few who possessed "eyes to see."[28]

Tryon was born in Hartford, Connecticut, where he spent several years working in a bookstore before deciding to pursue a career in art. In the year of the Centennial he left America for Paris and enrolled in the atelier of Jacquesson de la Chevreuse. During the summers, Tryon and his wife toured Europe, spending one memorable holiday with the Thayers on the island of Guernsey; and when Tryon grew tired of the academic system, he sought instruction directly from the artists Charles Daubigny and Henri Harpignies. Consequently, the landscapes Tryon produced upon his return to America in 1881 echo the paintings of the Barbizon school. In New York, where the Tryons settled, the artist rented a studio next to Thomas Dewing's. In South Dartmouth, Massachusetts, near New Bedford, they built a summer house they called The Cottage, where they lived happily for six months of every year. An enthusiastic teacher, Tryon accepted a position at Smith College requiring periodic visits to Northampton, Massachusetts, and he remained a respected member of the art faculty for nearly forty years. By the time he met Freer in 1889, Tryon had already earned a number of prestigious awards and secured a reputation as one of the most promising landscape painters in the country.

Tryon focused his artistic vision on the meadows surrounding South Dartmouth, and from the time he designed the decorations for Freer's house, he portrayed those uncomplicated scenes with single-minded devotion. Because he worked primarily in an urban studio, Tryon produced landscape paintings from memory, a practice that cast a spell of wistfulness upon a recurrent row of trees. *Sunrise: April* (fig. 110), for example, executed over the course of two winters in New York, has a surface textured with pigmented glazes that settle over the scene like layers of nostalgia. The painting appears to be an emanation of the artist's mind, a shadowy recollection made visible with paint.

The apparent immateriality of Tryon's landscapes made them particularly attractive to Freer, who customarily sought transcendent beauty in art. The works he appreciated most tended to be the least accessible; Tryon's paintings were so subtle, he thought, that to be understood properly they required continuous acquaintance and constant study. "The self restraint exercised by the painter is of itself a marvellous piece of technic," Freer wrote his business associate William Bixby in explanation of the ineffable charm of a Tryon painting, pointing out the artist's talent for conjuring visions of nature in a "poetic mood."[29] To Freer's mind, Tryon's works evinced the perfect balance of body and soul: in some pastel landscapes he had recently acquired, Freer observed the expression of "charm of the highest order in the most delightfully mysterious way . . . and at

Fig. 110. Dwight William Tryon (1849–1925), *Sunrise: April,* 1897–99. Oil on panel (50.9 x 76.3), 06.79.

the same time brimming with the solidity of old mother earth. I doubt if art can do more."[30]

Tryon himself was anything but ethereal. The reason he confined his painting to the winter months was that he reserved the summers for sailing and fishing, avocations for which he gained distinction among the natives of South Dartmouth. But he also used his holiday to prepare for winter's work. While sailing on the bay (fig. 111), Tryon could observe the countryside from a distance; and while waiting for fish to bite his flies (which he tied himself, in a different form for every day of the season), he could commit to memory the features of the landscape for later translation into art.

Tryon's solitary days on the water gave him an unusually sensitive appreciation of the shifting splendor of the sea. In the autumn of 1906, on his first trip to Ogunquit on the south coast of Maine, Tryon attempted to capture those fleeting effects in pastel. The following February, on a rare winter journey outside Manhattan, Tryon returned to Ogunquit, where he was awestruck by the austerity of the ocean at that time of year. Back in his studio in the city, he recorded the recollection in a monumental marine, *The Sea: Evening* (fig. 112), which he considered the "nearest to a masterpiece" of any work he had ever produced. The painting, as Tryon himself described it, is "apparently very direct and simple," entirely unlike his landscapes, which show signs on their surfaces of repeated reworking. The fluid brushwork of *The Sea: Evening* conveys the clarity of Tryon's impression: begun in February and completed before the third week of April, when he left for the country, it was executed while the memory of the chilly ocean scene remained distinct in his mind. The unusually efficient process of production helped Tryon realize his ambition of preserving the "utmost physical truth, but subject always to the thought or mood of the hour."[31]

Freer instantly recognized the merits of *The Sea: Evening* but spent two full days "soaking in" the marine before expressing his appreciation. "Nothing could be more truthful," he finally concluded, "and, at the same time, so subtle." The directness of the painting called to Freer's mind the works of such fifteenth-century Japanese masters as

Fig. 111. Tryon sailing in Buzzards Bay, ca. 1910. Dwight William Tryon Papers, Freer Gallery of Art and Arthur M. Sackler Gallery Archives.

Fig. 112. Dwight William Tryon (1849–1925), *The Sea: Evening,* 1907. Oil on canvas (76.2 x 121.8), 07.151.

Sesshū Tōyō (see fig. 95) and Sesson Shūkei, and its monumental simplicity corresponded to a Chinese ink painting he had recently seen in Kyoto. "Your Marine," he wrote Tryon, "while totally different in subject, has to me the same big qualities of excellence."[32] In reply, Tryon accounted for the perceived affinity of his own masterpiece to great works of Asian art with the observation that as an artist, he belonged to a timeless community of creative souls.[33]

One kindred spirit was Thomas Wilmer Dewing (fig. 113), whose work was especially compatible with Tryon's. While the artists were together in Detroit decorating Freer's reception rooms in 1892, they agreed to undertake a joint commission for Frank Hecker, who lived in the house next door. The resulting *Seasons Triptych* (The Detroit Institute of Arts, Michigan), in which Tryon's restrained springtime and autumn scenes hang on either side of Dewing's exuberant summer landscape with figures, demonstrates

Fig. 113. Thomas Dewing, ca. 1900, inscribed, "To my friend Freer." Photograph by G. C. Cox.

the sympathy of their artistic styles; Freer noted his own pleasure in the "general harmony of the effect."[34] Perhaps because each artist kept to his chosen subject, they enjoyed mutual admiration untainted by competition. Tryon wrote that a Dewing painting he had received as a gift from Freer was "one of the things that will live for all time with the Elgin marbles, with Tanagra, with all that is beautiful and uplifting. If there are more beautiful pictures being painted today . . . I do not know where."[35]

Two years younger than Tryon and Thayer, Dewing followed the same pattern of beginning his training as an artist at home, at the School of the Museum of Fine Arts in Boston, and continuing his studies abroad. In Paris at the Académie Julian, Dewing worked with Jules Lefébvre and Gustave Boulanger and endured an impoverished, bohemian existence in Montmartre. He returned to America in 1878 and lived briefly in Boston before taking up residence in New York. In 1881, a year after Dewing joined the Society of American Artists, Tryon, who was just back from France and inclined to think that art outside Europe was by definition second rate, saw at the society's exhibition "a fine Dewing" (and a Thayer) that he said outshone everything he had seen in Paris or London.[36] Dewing married Maria Oakey, an artist whose career was further advanced than his own, and joined the faculty of the Art Students' League, where he taught for seven years. From 1887 until 1905 the Dewings spent their summers at Doveridge, a house in the Cornish Hills of New Hampshire, just across the Connecticut River from Windsor, Vermont.

During the 1880s, Dewing drew on his recent acquaintance with contemporary English painting to produce symbolic and classicizing works in the manner of Edward Burne-Jones and Frederic Leighton; but by the time Freer met him in the early 1890s, Dewing seems to have discovered the works of Whistler. *The Piano* (fig. 114), the first Dewing painting that Freer acquired, has a radically simple, asymmetrical composition. As if to illustrate Whistler's vague analogy of painting with music, a woman plays a piano in an ambiguous space enveloped by an opalescent mist. Even the frame, designed by Dewing's friend Stanford White, is covered with a delicate, gauzelike grille that diffuses light, seeming to dematerialize the structure.

The Piano was the first in a succession of images of women in interiors that would

Fig. 114. Thomas Wilmer
Dewing (1851–1938), *The Piano*,
1891. Oil on panel (50.8 x 67.5),
06.66. Frame designed by
Stanford White (1853–1906),
ca. 1891.

join the distinguished company in Freer's collection. Like Thayer, Dewing concentrated on female figures; but even Thayer's angels seem more substantial than Dewing's delicate women, and their existence may be no more improbable, since the inhabitants of Dewing's interiors appear almost like objets d'art. *The Mirror* (fig. 115), which Freer purchased in 1907, allows us to admire the sitter from two points of view: the woman's reflection in the looking glass creates a picture within a picture, reminiscent of works by Vermeer and Velázquez. Nevertheless, the sitter remains as inanimate as the pitcher of flowers that rests on a chair identical to hers. The luminous surface of the vase is a visual rhyme to the lady's bare shoulders, and the blossoms that turn on their stems toward an unseen source of light imitate the head on the slender neck that turns to face the mirror on the wall. Dewing would have been aware of the metaphorical meaning held by flowers and mirrors in the tradition of European painting; it would be difficult to overlook such obvious emblems of *vanitas* even in the interest of art for art's sake. Nevertheless, the formal beauty of the composition was for Dewing more compelling than the symbolism the painting might incidentally contain. Casting the reflected face in shadow may have been the artist's means of stressing the immateriality of the subject.

Perhaps because they appeared to represent a perfectly ordered world remote from the clamor and confusion of the marketplace, Dewing's pictures of refined young women in tasteful interiors appealed to contemporary collectors. His landscapes with figures were less popular. As Dewing's word for them implies, the "decorations" were designed for specific architectural settings. The first Dewing landscape that Freer acquired, *After Sunset,* was intended to hang between the door and the fireplace on the east wall of his parlor, and the artist took the unfinished painting with him to Detroit to tune its colors to its surroundings. Naturally, then, the decorations could not be shown to best advantage apart from their architectural environment, and they sometimes fared poorly in exhibitions. Dewing maintained that the works were simply "above the heads of the public." [37]

The lack of popular appreciation for the decorations only enhanced their aura of refinement. "My decorations belong to the poetic and imaginative world," Dewing wrote Freer in 1901, "where a few choice spirits live." [38] *Before Sunrise* (fig. 116), a pendant to *After Sunset,* pictures two female phantoms in evening dress wafting through a lush green glade at dawn, one of them carrying a Chinese lantern. While working on the painting, Dewing received a package destined for Freer containing three woodblock prints by Kitagawa Utamaro. The elegant women in the prints appeared to the artist to be Japanese counterparts of the rarefied figures floating through the world of his decorations, and he fleetingly considered calling one of his works, probably *Before Sunrise,* "Dedicated to Utamaro." [39]

Fig. 115. Thomas Wilmer
Dewing (1851–1938), *The Mirror,*
ca. 1907. Oil on panel (50.8 x
40.0), 07.168.

Fig. 116. Thomas Wilmer
Dewing (1851–1938), *Before
Sunrise,* 1894–95. Oil on canvas
(106.8 x 137.6), 94.22.

Before Sunrise was begun early in the summer of 1894, temporarily abandoned, and completed in November 1895. The interruption in its progress was caused by a year's sojourn in Europe. Dewing had long cherished the hope of going abroad and exhibiting his works to what he presumed would be more appreciative audiences and also of reviewing his earlier opinion of the "Old Art of the world."[40] In the autumn of 1894 he sailed for England with Freer's blessing and financial support and in November met his patron in Paris. With the sculptor Frederick MacMonnies, Dewing and Freer hosted a party for thirteen American artists, the "cream of the hundreds here," which began at eight o'clock in a ramshackle restaurant in the Latin Quarter and lasted almost till dawn. Whistler, who presided at dinner, Freer considered "simply immense."[41] The next week Dewing and Freer spent an afternoon in Whistler's studio; Freer reported to Tryon afterward that the artists had "got on together famously."[42]

Homesick and tired of Europe, which had not lived up to his expectations, Dewing returned to America that summer. During the next season in Cornish, he embarked on a project that may have been conceived on the rue Notre Dame des Champs. Beside the printing press in Whistler's studio had stood a two-fold Japanese screen with gilded borders, on which the artist had painted a stylized version of Old Battersea Bridge by moonlight (see fig. 117). The screen had been decorated for F. R. Leyland in the 1870s but never relinquished by Whistler, and it had moved with the artist to Paris, where it formed the background for *Harmony in Blue and Gold: The Little Blue Girl* (see fig. 33), the painting Dewing and Freer had seen in progress that memorable afternoon.

Fig. 117. James McNeill Whistler in his studio at 86 rue Notre Dame des Champs, Paris, ca. 1894, with *Blue and Silver: Screen, with Old Battersea Bridge* in the background. Photograph by M. Dornac.

Overleaf:
Fig. 118. Thomas Wilmer Dewing (1851–1938), *The Four Sylvan Sounds,* 1896–97. Pair of two-fold screens; oil on wood panels (each screen 175.7 x 153.0), 06.72–73

One or the other of them may then have decided that Dewing should try his own hand with a folding screen.

At home in New England, the artist toyed for most of the summer with the "old ideas," perhaps devised in Freer's company, before developing a scheme of decoration that gave him tremendous pleasure to paint: "the four forest notes—the Hermit thrush, the sound of running water, the Woodpecker and the wind through the pine trees." The theme of "forest notes" was probably derived from a poem by Ralph Waldo Emerson tellingly titled "Woodnotes," and the number four was undoubtedly determined by the format Dewing and Freer had chosen for the work, a pair of two-fold screens. Dewing began with the thrush, whose song filled the morning air at Cornish: he represented the bird metaphorically as a "figure with a gold and ivory flute."[43]

The Four Sylvan Sounds (fig. 118), as the screens were eventually titled, displays the same conflation of classical and Asian elements that characterizes Whistler's experiments of the 1860s, such as *The White Symphony: Three Girls* (see fig. 23). Like Whistler, Dewing was taken with the beauty of Tanagra figurines, the Greek terra-cottas that were gaining popularity in America during the early 1890s, and their influence probably accounts for the appearance of the personifications of sylvan sounds, women who look like Grecian goddesses; a few years previously, after attending an exhibition of Tanagras on Freer's behalf, Dewing had produced pastel drawings of a model wearing "Greek costume."[44] Yet *The Four Sylvan Sounds* assumes an authentic Japanese form—a pair of two-fold screens—and employs elements of style that counter Western tradition, such as the suspension of figures in fields of foliage without regard for the conventions of linear perspective. Moreover, the variegated fabric of forest leaves and flowers, a design no less compelling than the figures it envelops, suggests the elegant, stylized patterns that decorate a Rimpa screen (see, for example, fig. 165).

In the two years it took Dewing to compose *The Four Sylvan Sounds,* Freer acquired twelve Japanese folding screens; one of the first was by the founder of the Rimpa school, Tawaraya Sōtatsu.[45] Many of Freer's purchases in those early years were made from Yamanaka and Company in New York. Dewing sometimes accompanied the collector on his art-buying missions so that he could act as his agent on other occasions, an indication of the faith that Freer placed in Dewing's judgment. Of his artist companions, Dewing seems to have been Freer's closest friend. They saw each other frequently in the city and occasionally in Cornish, where Freer was permitted to sleep as late as he pleased and encouraged to listen to music and paddle on the water or walk through the woods to recover from his cares—in short, as Dewing said, to take his "choice of idleness."[46] Freer repaid Dewing's hospitality in Detroit and discovered countless other ways of reciprocating his kindness. He acquired extensive holdings of Dewing's work and made substantial loans as advances on paintings, financial support that almost equaled the assistance provided the impecunious Abbott Thayer.

Another measure of Freer's generosity was the frequency with which he allowed works in his collection to travel. The first time Dewing asked Freer to lend a painting for exhibition, his patron readily consented: the two of them, he said, held "joint ownership."[47] Not only did Freer comply with every artist's request, but he himself would not consent to exhibiting any paintings without first securing the artist's express permission. "It seems to me," he wrote the director of fine arts for the Pan-American Exposition in Buffalo, "that the possessor of a work of art by a living artist is practically a caretaker, and in all matters pertaining to exhibitions he should be governed not so much by his own desires as . . . by those of the creator of the work."[48] From Freer's perspective, works of art were not his to keep, but his to care for: he considered himself "simply a guardian."[49] Founded in his friendships with a few American painters, Freer's perception of patronage held important implications for the future of his collection. ■

CHAPTER SEVEN

LINDA MERRILL

Composing the Collection

O N A MORNING in May 1902, when Freer was in London prospecting for paintings, he called at 49 Prince's Gate, a private residence just south of Hyde Park. The Mansion, as the house was known, belonged to Mrs. James Watney; its previous owner had been Frederick R. Leyland, Whistler's most important patron. Mrs. Watney accommodated Freer's wish to see the dining room, which she herself detested and was thinking of having remodeled. Afterward, Freer went to Whistler's Chelsea studio to report his impressions of the Peacock Room. The artist might have been amused, but surely not surprised, to learn that bric-a-brac and dime novels were gathering dust on the shelves he had gilded, years before, to frame individual pieces of Chinese porcelain.[1]

Whistler's involvement with the dining room at Prince's Gate began in the spring of 1876, when Leyland asked him to advise the decorator, Thomas Jeckyll, on a color to paint the shutters and doors. Jeckyll had designed an elaborate setting for the painting by Whistler that would hang above the mantelpiece, *La Princesse du pays de la porcelaine* (fig. 119), and for the distinguished collection of blue-and-white porcelain meant to surround it. The walls were hung with embossed and gilded antique leather decorated with colorful tendrils of flowers, which Leyland had purchased at great expense from a country house near Norwich. On the floor was an oriental carpet with a brilliant red border.

In Whistler's eyes, certain elements of the scheme disturbed the color harmonies of *La Princesse du pays de la porcelaine,* and he received authorization from Leyland, who was on his way out of town, to make minor alterations to the room. First he retouched the red flowers on the leather and cut off the red border of the rug; then he embellished the cornice and ceiling with a profusion of peacock feathers, painted in blue and green over a golden ground and arranged in concentric circles around the pendant lamps. Whistler proceeded to gild the spindle shelving that Jeckyll had designed to hold the porcelain and to paint magnificent golden peacocks on the panels of the shutters, where they

Comparison is the first habit of the real student. What more is needed by the real searcher after truth and beauty?

Freer to John Gellatly,
5 April 1904

Fig. 119. James McNeill Whistler (1834–1903), *La Princesse du pays de la porcelaine,* 1863–64 (199.9 x 116.1), 03.91. Frame designed by the artist. Shown in place on the north wall of Whistler's *Harmony in Blue and Gold: The Peacock Room.*

would glimmer in the gaslight at evening dinner parties.

Leyland returned from Liverpool in mid-October to see the confusion of pattern and color that Whistler had wrought, mostly without permission, on his dining room in London. The two men quarreled over the cost of the project but finally agreed "to bear alike the disaster of the decoration," as Whistler recorded his understanding of the compromise: "I pay my thousand guineas as my share in the dining room, and you pay yours."[2] Leyland made the mistake of paying his part in pounds, the currency of trade. Irreparably insulted, Whistler continued redecorating the dining room without further inhibitions. He coated the valuable leather with prussian blue paint, and on the wall opposite his painting of the princess, he portrayed himself and his patron posturing as peacocks. At the feet of the bird that proudly fanned its feathers (a caricature of Leyland), Whistler strewed the silver shillings he had found lacking from his payment. He called the mural "L'Art et L'argent" (Art and money), and the decoration *Harmony in Blue and Gold: The Peacock Room* (fig. 120).

After leaving The Mansion in early March 1877, presumably at his patron's insistence, Whistler never saw the Peacock Room again. Leyland, to his credit, kept the room intact and continued to use its shelves to display blue-and-white porcelain until his death in 1892. The centerpiece, *La Princesse du pays de la porcelaine,* was later sold to the Glasgow collector William Burrell, who sold it to Charles Freer less than a month after Whistler died in 1903. "It certainly is a great picture, and I am glad to have it under my care," Freer wrote Burrell, confiding that the painting would eventually go to the "American National Museum."[3] Within a year of that purchase, Freer had also acquired the Peacock Room and begun to negotiate the terms of his gift to the nation.

Whistler himself may have planted the notion in Freer's mind of preserving his holdings for posterity. The artist's plan for "*the* collection" of his works, proposed in 1899, would surely have included provisions for its future; and Freer's own equation of patronage with guardianship would have entailed responsibility for the art in his possession beyond his own lifetime. Perhaps Freer and Whistler agreed that nothing should be done toward safeguarding the collection while the artist was alive, for the sequence of events leading to Freer's munificent offer seems to have been set in motion by Whistler's death in July 1903. The second incentive came six months later, when Gustav Mayer, an art dealer with the London firm Obach and Company, offered Freer first option to buy the Peacock Room.

The acquisition was not made without misgivings. Relying mainly on a receding recollection of his visit to Mrs. Watney's house two years before, Freer replied to Mayer that although he did not care to own the entire room, he would "greatly love" to have the peacock shutters and mural. To Rosalind Birnie Philip, Whistler's executor (see fig.

38), Freer explained that he felt obliged to "save the most valuable parts" if he could, "and reunite them with the 'Princess of Porcelain.' "[4] But Miss Philip entreated Freer to buy the rest of the decorations as well, even offering to subsidize the purchase herself. Her sister Ethel Whibley suggested that the room be "re-erected in the wonderful new Museum," an idea that ultimately changed Freer's mind on the matter. Until then, he had not been able to conceive of a practical purpose for Whistler's whimsical Peacock Room.[5]

In May, Freer sailed from New York and, soon after landing in England, quietly purchased the Peacock Room. News of the sale spread rapidly on both sides of the Atlantic (see fig. 121), but no one could confirm the name of the owner, widely believed to be J. Pierpont Morgan. Months went by and the decorations were crated and shipped to Detroit before Freer would publicly acknowledge ownership of what had become the single most famous work in his collection; in spite of his efforts, he became renowned by association. Freer's only intention in acquiring the celebrated dining-room decoration, an extravagant frame for a painting in his possession, had been to honor Whistler's wish to provide an appropriate setting for a great work of art.

But in the addition to the house on Ferry Avenue where the Peacock Room came temporarily to rest, Freer cultivated a new appreciation for Whistler's decoration, which he referred to as the Blue Room. His own collection did not include the Chinese porcelain intended for the shelves, so Freer substituted "beautiful pieces of Oriental or other harmonizing pottery" with iridescent glazes that glowed against the peacock-colored walls.[6] With his own ceramics installed on the shelves (fig. 122), he began to enjoy architectural features of the room that he had formerly disdained. Freer also reappraised the golden peacocks, writing to Richard Canfield, a fellow collector of Whistler's works:

I have been making some quiet comparisons of the large decorations of the room with the most successful things of a similar nature of fifteenth and sixteenth century work in the Orient. It will please you to know that Whistler's things, in bigness of feeling, strength of line, use of space and general aesthetic accomplishment, hold their own with the very best.

Before making those comparisons, Freer said, he could never have placed the Peacock Room "on as high a pedestal as it deserved."[7] In the context of his collections, the work assumed new importance.

Relating the decorations of the Peacock Room to works of art that Whistler never saw, Freer sought evidence of aesthetic affinity rather than signs of artistic influence. For him, the practice of comparison was the exercise of taste. "Of course, I make no pretence to art knowledge," he wrote Dwight Tryon, "nor do I think it necessary to ana-

Overleaf:
Fig. 120. James McNeill Whistler (1834–1903), *Harmony in Blue and Gold: The Peacock Room,* 1876–77, detail showing south wall. Resin/oil paint and gold- and metal-leaf on leather, wood, and canvas (425.8 x 1010.9 x 608.3), 04.61.

Fig. 121. *New York Herald,*
17 July 1904. Whistler press-
cutting book 2.

lyze art, but I do believe that one's appreciation of beauty, in any form, can be strengthened, deepened and broadened by intelligent comparative study."[8] Employing Whistler's method of selecting compatible elements and arranging them into aesthetic unity, Freer worked like an artist to compose his collection, gathering "objects of art covering various periods of production," as he explained his method to Miss Philip, "all of which are harmonious and allied in many ways."[9] His intention was to create a legacy possessing "the power to broaden esthetic culture and the grace to elevate the human mind."[10]

Freer had long admired the barons of the Gilded Age who used their wealth in the service of humanity, such as Andrew Carnegie, whose "great generosity and untiring interest in fine arts" was an example, he said, that "should not go unheeded by anyone interested in these matters."[11] Carnegie had established an art gallery in Pittsburgh, the city where he earned his fortune, and Freer might have been expected to do the same for Detroit. His decision to place his collection instead in Washington, D.C., was predicated in part on his conviction that it was of national importance, but he was further influenced by the fact that Detroit had recently let him down. In 1899, motivated by civic pride, Freer had organized a committee of prominent American artists, including Dwight Tryon and Thomas Dewing, to assist the architect Stanford White with designs for a monument commemorating the bicentennial of the founding of Detroit (fig. 123). Conceived in the spirit of Chicago's White City, the scheme was envisioned to include a marble colonnade extending all the way across Belle Isle and a two-hundred-foot fluted column rising from the Detroit River, with a tower on top to afford a panoramic view of the city.[12] But funding for the project could not be found among the citizens of Detroit, and Freer took the failure as a sign of the city's insensitivity to beauty. "When one thinks of the vast accumulations of wealth and the many ways of misapplying it," Tryon wrote in commiseration, "the need of education in taste is apparent."[13]

The idea of presenting his collections to the Smithsonian Institution came in 1902 from Charles Moore, a historian who had recently returned to Detroit after serving in Washington as Senator James McMillan's administrative assistant.[14] McMillan, lately deceased, had been the chairman of the Michigan-Peninsular Car Company and a good friend of Freer's; as senator from Michigan, he had initiated a plan for beautifying the capital that included a scheme for improving the National Mall, where the Smithsonian was situated. When Freer first discussed the probable terms of his legacy with Moore, the interests of the Smithsonian Institution remained strongly scientific; its secretary, Samuel P. Langley, was an astronomer and aeronautic engineer. Moore insisted, however, that Langley was sympathetic to art and that the Smithsonian, dedicated to the increase and diffusion of knowledge, would be the ideal repository for Freer's collections. Freer accordingly promised to study the history of the institution, and in August

Fig. 122. Whistler's Peacock Room in Freer's Detroit residence, 1908. Detail showing north wall and *La Princesse du pays de la porcelaine*.

1903, just back from Whistler's funeral, he wrote to Moore that he was ready to discuss more fully the "matter we have under consideration."[15]

The following spring, after helping install the Whistler Memorial Exhibition in Boston, Freer went to Washington to spend an afternoon with Secretary Langley going over the contents of his collection and the provisions for its care. In December 1904 he communicated the terms of his gift in writing for consideration by the executive committee of the Smithsonian's Board of Regents. At that time Freer's holdings consisted of an impressive collection of works by Whistler (160 paintings and drawings, more than seven hundred prints, and the Peacock Room) and a group of about fifty contemporary paintings and pastel drawings by the American artists Tryon, Dewing, and Thayer. The Asian collections were much larger, with approximately four hundred hanging scrolls, eighty screens, and thirty panel paintings "by various masters of Chinese and Japanese schools of painting, beginning with the tenth century and ending with the nineteenth century." In addition, there were nearly one thousand ceramics "by various potters of the Far East and Central Asia" and an assortment of East Asian bronzes, lacquers, and wood carvings. Freer explained in his letter to Langley that "these several collections include specimens of very widely separated periods of artistic development," connected by a common quality of "spiritual and physical suggestion."[16]

Whistler stood at the heart of Freer's enterprise as the modern artist whose work most clearly manifested, or suggested, the aesthetic qualities detectable in the art of other, earlier cultures. In January 1904, while the purchase of the Peacock Room was under consideration, Freer wrote Gustav Mayer of his conviction that the world would begin to acknowledge the universality of Whistler's work when the "intelligent few" could compare certain of his paintings and prints with "the best specimens of Babylonian pottery, Greek and Egyptian sculpture and the paintings of the masters of the Sung [Song] period."[17] Freer was constructing his own collections to afford such comparisons, which he believed would lead not only to a heightened appreciation of Whistler's achievement but also to a more refined American sense of beauty. Especially during 1904, the year he was framing the terms of his gift to the nation,

Fig. 123. Stanford White (1853–1906), rendering of proposed monument to commemorate the bicentenary of Detroit, 1899. From *The Evening News* (Detroit), 23 February 1900.

Freer looked for telling correspondences. In both the drypoint *Whistler's Mother* and the oil painting *Arrangement in White and Black* (figs. 124 and 125), for example, he detected aesthetic affinities with the "accomplishments of the masters of the Sung period," works of Chinese art that the American artist could never have known. "The more I see of the best art of the universe," Freer wrote Richard Canfield, "the more universal Whistler's work seems to me."[18]

Before attempting to expound his theory to Secretary Langley, Freer had related his ideas about universal beauty to only a few trusted friends. In February 1903 he introduced Whistler's work to Ernest Fenollosa, the authority on Asian art who had a "remarkable appreciation of beauty," and together they seem to have practiced the art of comparison.[19] That December, in an appreciation of Whistler's work published in a memorial issue of *Lotus*, Fenollosa alluded to the most abstract of the Six Projects, *Symphony in Green and Violet* (fig. 126), pointing out the resemblance of Whistler's sweeping brush strokes to the "broad blunt line" that characterized the work of the fifteenth-century Japanese artist Sesshū Tōyō (see fig. 95).[20] A few months later, when the collector John Gellatly wrote to Freer about his own admiration for Whistler's *Symphony*, Freer replied that Gellatly's taste for that particular painting marked him destined to become "sympathetic" to masterpieces of Asian art.[21] As Fenollosa would later explain in an article summarizing the scheme of the collections, it was Whistler's "modern centrality" that accounted for his supreme importance to Freer: "In the wide play of experimenting with absolute beauty, he struck again and again, without consciousness of imitation, and often in complete ignorance, the characteristic beauties of the most remote masters, both Western and Eastern."[22]

Leila Mechlin, another writer who interpreted the collections for the public, compared Freer's practice of gathering works of art from diverse cultures to weaving a beautiful pattern from the "loose and broken threads of a great embroidery."[23] Yet in 1904, as the stipulations placed on his proposed gift to the nation imply, Freer's artful design remained an unfinished work. He insisted on retaining the collections during his lifetime, partly because he could not bear to part with them but primarily because he wished to make further improvements. "Believing that good models only should be used in artistic instruction," Freer explained, "I wish to continue my censorship, aided by the best expert advice, and remove every undesirable article, and add in the future whatever I can obtain of like harmonious standard quality." Upon his death, when its composition would be finally complete, the collection would become the property of the United States and be housed in a building constructed with funds from his bequest. The gallery would frame his composition, ensuring "the protection of this unity and the exhibition of every object in the collections in a proper and attractive manner."[24]

Fig. 124. James McNeill Whistler (1834–1903), *Whistler's Mother*, 1870–73. Drypoint, first state (25.2 x 15.3), 03.252.

Fig. 125. James McNeill Whistler (1834–1903), *Arrangement in White and Black*, ca. 1873. Oil on canvas (191.4 x 90.9), 04.78.

The most controversial of the conditions that Freer imposed on the gift reflected his conception of the collection as a coherent, aesthetic unity with artistic integrity of its own. He stipulated that works in the collection never be exhibited outside the building, that no other works be exhibited there, and that after his death nothing be added to (or taken away from) the collection. The purpose of those strictures, he explained to Tryon, was "to maintain the harmony of the collections to which I have given so much attention."[25] Langley was especially troubled by the clause prohibiting future acquisitions, but Freer could not countenance an amendment to the proposal. "I regard my collections as constituting a harmonious whole," he explained. "They are not made up of isolated objects, each object having an individual merit only, but they constitute in a sense a connected series, each having a bearing upon the others that precede or that follow it in point of time." The collection embodied a theory that later additions might not uphold; to modify the stipulation, Freer said, could "lead to results so serious as to defeat the main purpose that induces me to make my offer to the institution."[26] That purpose was to illustrate the "most conspicuous fact in the history of art," as Fenollosa said, "that the two great streams of European and Asiatic practice, held apart for so many thousand years, have, at the close of the nineteenth century, been brought together in a fertile and final union."[27]

To Freer's annoyance, word of his proposal leaked to the Associated Press and was announced in newspapers all over the country; most of the articles focused on Freer's holdings of works by Whistler, many prominently featuring the Peacock Room (fig. 127), and "scattered a rather garbled report on the matter much earlier" than Freer thought proper.[28] "Nothing has been determined by the Institution," he wrote to his friend Charles J. Morse, "except to send a committee here to view the collections, and what an 'expert' committee it is!"[29] Freer himself had suggested the committee, envisioning a group of leading art authorities reviewing his collections and making a report to the Smithsonian. The Board of Regents, however, was content to appoint Secretary Langley and three of its own members as delegates to Detroit: James B. Angell, president of the University of Michigan; John B. Henderson, a former U.S. senator; and

Alexander Graham Bell, the inventor of the telephone and president of the National Geographic Society. "The four Regents are men of broad education, wide experience and of unquestioned judgment," Freer wrote Morse, "but what they do not know about art would fill many volumes."[30]

The committee's visit to Freer's house at the end of February was, as Freer had predicted, "rather a weird experience" for everyone. The delegates were shown the collection one object at a time and, according to Charles Moore, by the end of four interminable days in Detroit were "puzzled to know whether they were crazy or Mr. Freer was."[31] In an effort to relieve some of the restrictions on the gift, they had made the unwelcome suggestion that Freer move with his collection to Washington, where he could participate in the organization of a national art gallery. "Think of trying to convince the politicians of America," Freer wrote to Rosalind Philip, "that the fine arts have any virtue."[32]

In Washington, action on Freer's offer was postponed for several months, but the collector was willing to allow the matter to "simmer along" for a while. He was beginning to fear it would prove impossible "to harmonize all of the questions and conditions involved,"[33] and he confided to Fenollosa that he doubted the Smithsonian would ever accept his gift with all of its strings attached. To his friend Thomas Jerome, Freer cast a different interpretation on the problem, explaining that many in Washington thought it wiser "to keep the Institution nailed firmly to matters of purely scientific interest."[34] Finally in November 1905, when all negotiations appeared to have reached a standstill, Moore wrote a letter to the president of the United States, who had reportedly

shown interest in the fate of Freer's collection, urging immediate acceptance of the gift. Theodore Roosevelt replied directly to Freer: "Can't you come down here and spend a night at the White House next week? . . . I desire to speak to you about the magnificent gift you desire to make to the Government and which I wish to see accepted without haggling or quibbling."[35]

In preparation for the meeting Roosevelt so casually arranged, Freer composed a formal letter reprising for the president the offer he had made to Secretary Langley the previous year. Although the terms remained essentially unchanged, Freer appended a promise to deliver a descriptive inventory of the collections by the first day of April, when the deed of gift would be ready to execute—a provision recommended, not unreasonably, by the president himself.[36] On December 18, Freer dined at the White House with the Roosevelts, Justice Oliver Wendell Holmes, Senator Henry Cabot Lodge (whose son [see fig. 99] would become the Freer Gallery's first director), and other distinguished company whom Freer considered the "better class citizens of Washington." Afterward, he returned to Detroit to await a decision. "It is too early to prophesy what will happen," he wrote to Tom Jerome, "but I shall be surprised if the President does not eventually carry the day and bring about an acceptance of my offer."[37]

Indeed, Roosevelt had dispatched a "strong letter" to Melville W. Fuller, chief justice of the United States and chancellor of the Smithsonian Institution, which Freer felt sure would "wake up some of the sleepy ones connected with the Smithsonian."[38] Alexander Bell, undoubtedly motivated by the president's endorsement, led the campaign to secure Freer's collection for the Smithsonian and proposed the resolution of acceptance that the Regents unanimously adopted on 24 January 1906. Bell's daughter, Marian Fairchild, who had accompanied the delegation to Detroit, was the first to send Freer the "glorious news," but telegrams came and went all afternoon.[39] Roosevelt's said, "I need not say how pleased I am at what has been done." Freer replied, "Without your good influence it could not have been accomplished." As the president had written to Chief Justice Fuller, Freer's was "one of the most valuable collections which any private citizen has ever given to any people."[40]

Acknowledging the importance of Theodore Roosevelt's intervention, Freer commissioned Gari Melchers to paint a portrait of the president to take a permanent place in his collection. Melchers, a native of Detroit, had come to know Freer during the late 1880s, when they had worked together on exhibitions for the Detroit Club. In Freer's estimation, Melchers's sincere and direct style of painting made him the perfect match for Roosevelt, whose character seemed

Fig. 127. "Charles L. Freer's Gift to the Smithsonian Institution." From an unidentified newspaper, 3 February 1905, Detroit. Press-cutting book 3.

equally authentic. It was agreed that the president would pose in his riding costume, and Freer and Melchers spent an entire afternoon at the White House deciding the details, while Roosevelt obligingly changed his clothes several times. Melchers, who feared he would not be given sufficient sittings to produce the masterpiece that Freer had in mind, wrote to his wife in a state of apprehension that "this painting the President is rather anxious business."[41] But he completed the portrait on schedule, in less than a fortnight, and it was instantly declared a tremendous success (fig. 128). Roosevelt considered it the best that had ever been done—exceeding in his estimate even the portrait by John Singer Sargent[42]—and Freer predicted that Melchers's work would always be regarded as the one that captured the "real dignity, force and character" of the man. "Art is a language," he wrote to the artist, "and your portrait will talk to the people through coming centuries."[43]

Assured that his holdings would have a permanent home in Washington, Freer

Fig. 128. Gari Melchers (1860–1932), *Portrait of President Theodore Roosevelt,* 1908. Oil on canvas (214.4 x 112.5), 08.17. Frame designed by Hermann Dudley Murphy (1867–1945).

reconsidered them in view of posterity: anything that might not communicate with future generations could not remain a part of the gift. He spent most of 1906 "weeding and comparing," a process set in motion by the need to inventory the more than two thousand objects he had promised the Smithsonian.[44] In a matter of months he culled a collection he had taken twenty years to assemble, employing the comparative method to test every object's aesthetic quality and remaining ever mindful of the "very important consideration of harmony." Whistler's *Venus Rising from the Sea,* for instance, could stand beside a glazed earthenware jar he believed to be Babylonian (fig. 129). Fenollosa, writing under Freer's influence, had mentioned the kinship between Whistler's paintings and "warmly glazed ceramics," and Leila Mechlin had observed that certain of Whistler's canvases looked as though they had been "dipped, like a piece of pottery, in translucent glaze."[45]

As he worked his way through the collection, exercising his faculties of appreciation, Freer developed an interest in chronology, the history of art. He acknowledged, first of all, that it was necessary to classify his holdings for the convenience of the scholars who would someday study them in Washington. But he also began to wonder whether the aesthetic affinities he detected among certain objects might be evidence of direct artistic influence. Doubts had arisen as to the age of Rakka ware, for example, and although Freer maintained that the value of the pottery lay in its beauty rather than its date of origin, he was curious to know whether the West Asian ceramics had influenced, or been influenced by, early Chinese wares. Having studied the ancient art collections in the Louvre and the British Museum, Freer determined to strengthen his own holdings with "articles of beauty and sympathy of earlier or earliest origin." Among the Egyptian antiquities he acquired were the bronze statuettes flanking a tiny Whistler pastel in a portrait that illustrates Freer's concept of art history (fig. 130). He knew that Whistler's *Resting* had been modeled on Greek Tanagra figurines, and he believed that the Tanagras had been influ-

Fig. 129. Freer comparing Whistler's *Venus Rising from the Sea* (03.174) to an Islamic glazed ceramic pot (05.61), 1909. Photograph by Alvin Langdon Coburn (1882–1966).

Fig. 130. Freer with Whistler's *Resting* (02.176) and a pair of bronze statuettes, probably ancient Egyptian (on the right, 07.1; on the left, unidentified), 1909. Autochrome by Alvin Langdon Coburn (1882–1966).

enced by Egyptian statuettes: the beauty of Greece, he maintained, owed everything to Egypt. Whistler was thus Egypt's heir, the modern exemplar of the "greatest art in the world."[46]

The objects in Freer's collection, then, were related to each other either by shared artistic ancestry or by close harmonic connections that suggested a common lineage. Works by certain living American artists were linked to early Asian paintings, Freer believed, by a "certain harmony of composition, color and other technical qualities."[47] Tryon, Dewing, and Thayer—like Whistler, and "equally independently and unintentionally"—were the American "continuers of the early Oriental ideal."[48] Freer intended to assemble collections that represented the range of their achievements, both historically and aesthetically, and he continued to add examples of their current work until the end of his life.

Although his deed of gift had specified an American collection limited to the work of four modern painters, Freer gradually loosened his restriction to make occasional purchases of paintings by a select group of their compatriots. Eventually the works of those artists, whom he referred to as "miscellaneous Americans," coalesced into a collection that Freer regarded as aesthetically related to his holdings of Asian art. Although it contained paintings by many acknowledged masters of late nineteenth-century American art, his miscellany was never meant to survey the field, and Freer found it necessary to explain that his collection differed in scale, scope, and intention from the "broadly selected group" of 150 paintings by 105 American artists that William T. Evans, following Freer's example, presented to the Smithsonian in installments beginning in 1907.[49] Freer acquired no more than twenty-three oil and watercolor paintings by eleven American artists between 1903, when he won a work by John Henry Twachtman in a drawing, and 1918, when he purchased a landscape by Charles Platt while the artist-architect was supervising the construction of the Freer Gallery of Art.

Among the first acquisitions for Freer's miscellaneous American collection was Winslow Homer's *Early Evening* (fig. 131). Begun in 1881 in Cullercoats, a village on the coast of England near Tynemouth, the painting had remained in the artist's hands until November 1907, when the canvas was cut down and the background altered to represent a twilight scene. Freer had long desired a "characteristic Marine" by Homer but could not resist buying *Early Evening* in 1908 because he thought the figures so beautifully painted.[50] The two stalwart women standing on the cliffs with their knitting, apparently impervious to the coastal gale, appear to be composed of the same domesticated supernaturalism that distinguishes the winged figures by Abbott Thayer; their striking silhouettes against the evening sky may also have reminded Freer of elements of Japanese design.

A few months later, when he was at Cottier and Company in New York buying a Persian ceramic bowl, Freer picked up a dark, indistinct barnyard scene called *The Red Cow* (fig. 132), one of the earliest extant paintings of Albert Pinkham Ryder.[51] Although Ryder's reputation was on the rise in 1908, his paintings were not yet in great demand, and Freer bought *The Red Cow* at a fraction of the cost he customarily paid for American works. His purchase may have been influenced by his friend John Gellatly, who possessed a parallel taste in American art and a collection that grew to include fifteen Ryder paintings in addition to a large number of works by Dewing and Thayer. Freer himself knew practically nothing about Ryder's work—he told the dealer he felt more confident about West Asian pottery—and because he remained uncertain whether *The Red Cow*, like the Persian bowl, should occupy a permanent place in his collection, he took it "on probation."[52] There is nothing to suggest, however, that Freer ever considered parting with the painting. Seeing it at home with his collection, he may have found its warm colors and densely painted, crackled surface comparable to his glazed ceramic pots, or its

Fig. 131. Winslow Homer
(1836–1910), *Early Evening,*
1881/1907. Oil on canvas
(83.8 x 98.5), 08.14.

dreamlike atmosphere relevant to other of his American paintings that were drawn in the same way from shadowy recollections.

In some cases, the connections between Freer's new American paintings and objects already in the collection are obvious. Childe Hassam's *Chinese Merchants* (fig. 133), which Freer purchased in 1910, has an Asian subject in an American setting—the Chinese Quarter of Portland, Oregon—portrayed in a style that distinctly recalls Whistler's street scenes of the early 1880s such as *Chelsea Shops* (fig. 134). Hassam had also adopted Whistler's practice of decorating the frame to complement the picture, placing a Chinese character in each corner. Indeed, most of the paintings in the American collection appear more closely related to the work of Whistler than to Asian art objects, which were often, at best, distant relations. According to Agnes Meyer, Freer repeatedly stated that he would acquire nothing that did not relate in some way to Whistler's achievement, a requirement that maintained harmony among his heterogeneous holdings. Both the Asian and American collections were meant to be an "extension" of Freer's Whistler collection, Mrs. Meyer said, "an amplification of the spirit and intentions and artistic expression of his great friend."[53]

Some American paintings that bear aesthetic affinity to Whistler's works seem to have been inspired less by the artist himself than by the sources that provided him with inspiration, making them related through common influence. John Singer Sargent, for instance, was, like Whistler, deeply indebted to the art of Velázquez. Even if the influence had not been readily apparent, Freer would have known about it, since he once encountered the artist copying paintings by Velázquez in the Prado.[54] *The Weavers* (fig. 135), one of a pair of paintings by Sargent that Freer bought ten years after their meeting in Madrid, may owe its inspiration to Velázquez's *Hilanderas* (The Spinners), part of the Prado collection. Sargent's work was probably also produced in Spain, where the artist spent the autumn of 1912; the scene is a somber workshop punctuated by brilliant bolts of light, with skeins of yarn hanging in the sunshine to dry. Freer must have admired Sargent's virtuosic handling

Fig. 132. Albert Pinkham Ryder (1847–1917), *The Red Cow,* early 1870s. Oil on panel (29.0 x 30.5), 08.25.

Fig. 133. Childe Hassam
(1859–1935), *The Chinese
Merchants,* 1909. Oil on canvas
(50.4 x 91.3), 10.22. Frame
probably designed by the artist
and made by Hermann Dudley
Murphy (1867–1945).

of light and shade and would have considered the dark palette of the picture, composed mostly of browns and blacks, compatible with a number of nearly monochromatic paintings by Whistler.

Aware that many contemporary artists were eager to be represented in what would be the first national art gallery, Freer was especially careful in choosing works for the miscellaneous collection. After he bought a summer landscape by Willard Leroy Metcalf from the Panama-Pacific Exposition in San Francisco, Metcalf wrote to the collector directly, offering to sell another of the exhibited paintings. Freer tactfully declined to consider the work that Metcalf proposed, explaining that he had selected *Blossom Time* precisely because in comparison with the exhibits it seemed "in greater harmony with the ideals on which the entire collection is based."[55]

Eventually, Freer bought two more works by Metcalf, a winter and an autumn scene, which he intended to hang with *Blossom Time* as a triptych. But the artist felt that the group still lacked one note to be "perfect and unique," and he suggested that Freer acquire one of his "moonlights," romantic paintings of New England houses at night. Because of the difficulty in obtaining the desired results, Metcalf said, the moonlights were rare; but he had one, completed only that season though started several years before, of an "old house partly in shadow, with white lilacs in bloom."[56] Thematically related to Whistler's Nocturnes, *The White Lilacs* (fig. 136) arrived in Detroit in November 1918, in the last year of Freer's life. Surrounded by works of Egyptian, Mesopotamian, and Chinese art, it appeared "perfectly at home," Freer said, "in the midst of old time influences."[57]

As long as his strength would allow, Freer continued working on the collection, judiciously adding works of art that rounded out his holdings and eliminating each discordant note. He completed the Whistler collection shortly before his death with the purchase of an exceptionally somber, abstract evocation of Cremorne Gardens (fig. 137). He had first attempted to buy *Nocturne: Cremorne Gardens, No. 3* ten years earlier and was especially pleased to finally obtain it because, as the dealer pointed out, it was one of the last important Whistler Nocturnes that would ever come onto the market.[58] By then, Freer had spent the better part of thirty years assembling beautiful objects and disposing them in harmonious arrangements, and his composition was virtually complete.

But four months before he died, Freer made a decision that would irrevocably alter

Fig. 134. James McNeill Whistler (1834–1903), *Chelsea Shops,* early 1880s. Oil on panel (13.5 x 23.4), 02.149.

the collection and eventually obscure the aesthetic principle that underlay its structure. After falling seriously ill at Christmas, Freer had moved in February 1919 from Detroit to New York City for medical treatment; he took up residence in the Gotham Hotel, where he was attended by Agnes Meyer, Louisine Havemeyer, and his "co-laborer in the collection," Katharine Nash Rhoades. Despite increasing physical limitations, and with the assistance and encouragement of his friends and physician, Freer devoted several hours of every day to his collection of Chinese art, which was "steadily growing," he wrote to Rosalind Philip, "in both variety and quality."[59] Indeed, during the final three years of his life, Freer acquired 150 Chinese paintings, some two hundred jade objects, and a number of bronzes and stone sculptures.

That surge in collecting at a time when his own life was drawing to a close seems to have caused Freer to reconsider his gift to the nation in the belief, as Agnes Meyer phrased it, that there existed "new and, he hoped, as yet unheard-of Chinese wonderworks that would reveal even more fully the genius of that superb civilization."[60] In

Fig. 136. Willard Leroy Metcalf
(1858–1925), *The White Lilacs*,
1912/18. Oil on canvas (73.8 x
83.8), 18.157.

Fig. 137. James McNeill
Whistler (1834–1903), *Nocturne:
Cremorne Gardens, No. 3,*
ca. 1875. Oil on canvas
(44.9 x 63.1), 19.12.

May, Freer appended a codicil to his will providing the Smithsonian with a bequest "for the promotion of high ideals of beauty," to be achieved with "occasional purchases . . . of very fine examples of Oriental, Egyptian, and Near Eastern fine arts."[61] Miss Rhoades, Mrs. Havemeyer, and Mrs. Meyer were appointed to approve the new acquisitions, which suggests their participation in Freer's decision to modify the stipulation he had considered inviolable in 1905; he had then asserted that additions made after his death would not only destroy the harmony of the collections but might even be considered more valuable or important than his own treasures and could crowd them out of favorable places, if not altogether out of sight.[62] In the end, the prospect of future discoveries in Asian art seems to have superseded Freer's desire to leave a legacy indelibly imprinted with his own aesthetic ideals.

Yet Freer's radical, last-minute reversal did not encompass American art. Having seen signs of the direction that modern art was taking, Freer concluded that his assembly of American paintings, unlike the Asian collections, could probably not be improved over time. The standing prohibition against future acquisitions was not, therefore, meant to imply that the American collection was less important, only that it was already complete; and it remains today as Freer left it, an unalterable testament to the collector's taste.   ∎

CHAPTER EIGHT

THOMAS LAWTON

The Late Years

I N MAY 1911, one month after Freer returned to Detroit from his fifth Asian trip, he fell seriously ill. According to his own account, Freer suffered an attack of ptomaine poisoning and shortly afterward was stricken with what his doctors described as a comparatively mild form of "cerebral effusion" that affected his right side.[1] Apparently Freer had a stroke. For several months he lost the use of his right leg and had difficulty raising his right arm. Following intensive therapy Freer's condition improved, but for the remainder of his life he always favored his right leg.[2] Freer had greatly enjoyed the excitement and rewards of foreign travel, and the gradual realization that he would never again be able to go abroad marked a critical turning point in his collecting activities.

Throughout the remaining eight years of his life Freer was forced to conserve his strength; he experienced long periods when the slightest physical or mental effort proved to be completely debilitating. Seeking relief from the illness that confined him physically and mentally, he experimented with the potential beneficial effects of the warm climate of California and the clear mountain air of Vermont, but neither environment provided a lasting cure. Eventually, as Freer found congenial medical assistance in New York City, he spent more and more time there, occupying a suite at one of the more comfortable hotels such as the Plaza or the Gotham.

While in New York, Freer took advantage of opportunities to visit the East Asian art dealers who maintained shops in the city. Unable to travel to Europe and Asia to study collections or make additions to his holdings, Freer also depended on those dealers who were willing to journey to the United States or to ship antiquities to him for approval. After 1911, Freer concentrated on acquiring Chinese art and, by maintaining contacts with dealers he had met on earlier trips to the East, made a number of outstanding purchases, even during World War I, when international traffic was precarious.

Fig. 138. Charles Lang Freer, ca. 1915–16. Detail of a photograph by Edward Steichen (1879–1973). Collection of George Eastman House, International Museum of Photography, Rochester, New York.

It was in the area of archaic Chinese jades in particular that Freer demonstrated his individual taste and the level of his connoisseurship. Western collectors were slow to appreciate archaic Chinese jades, whose subtle colors and sparse, enigmatic decoration contrasted markedly with the elaborate Qing dynasty overglaze porcelains that were popular at the turn of the century. The highly colored and technically immaculate ceramics did not appeal to Freer. Rather, he turned his attention to a group of objects made from a material that was equally, if not more, technically demanding but with an entirely different aesthetic appeal. That Qing porcelain was much sought after by wealthy Western collectors while the taste for early jades was limited is evident in the dramatic contrasts in value when examples of archaic jades first appeared on the antique market. In 1914, an outstanding jade tiger plaque from the Han dynasty sold in Paris for 320 francs—the equivalent of sixty dollars—at a time when Western collectors of Chinese porcelain, including J. Pierpont Morgan and Henry O. Havemeyer, frequently paid between twenty-five and fifty thousand dollars for a Qing dynasty polychrome porcelain vase.[3]

Freer, who had purchased his first Chinese jade in 1907, became seriously interested in the material four years later, during his second visit to China. There he began to collect in earnest, buying large numbers of jades, most of them from antique and curio dealers in Beijing, Shanghai, and Kaifeng. He also purchased a few from Japanese dealers, including Yamanaka Sadajirō, who maintained a shop on Fifth Avenue.

At the time Freer was assembling a particularly impressive group of the archaic jades, little was known about their original ritual functions. Their descriptions in Chinese textual sources were based on obscure statements that had been written centuries after the pieces were made. The dating, too, was extremely imprecise; Chinese archaic jades were assigned vaguely to the Zhou and Han dynasties, from the mid-eleventh century B.C. to the third century A.D.[4] Only in the 1970s, when archaeological excavations uncovered large numbers of jades from Late Neolithic (ca. 3000–2000 B.C.) sites in China, was the importance of Freer's purchases fully appreciated: stylistic comparison with archaeologically attested jades proved that many of Freer's pieces were actually from the Late Neolithic period. Moreover, a large number of the Neolithic jades in the Freer collection can now be identified as having been made by specific cultures located in widely separate areas of ancient China. The most impressive are those from the Liangzhu culture of southeastern China dating to approximately 3000 to 2500 B.C. Their outstanding workmanship and sophisticated decoration—the same features that had prompted earlier specialists to propose the conservative Zhou and Han dynasty attributions—are now recognized as being characteristic of that surprisingly refined Late Neolithic culture.

Freer purchased most of his Liangzhu jades from Chinese dealers active in

Shanghai, which is now known to have been a major center of the Liangzhu culture. On the invoice for a small plaque decorated with an elaborate mask dominated by large eyes, nose, and mouth (fig. 139), the dealer Seaouke Yue (You Xiaoqi) stated that the jade had been found at Xiaqi, Zhejiang Province, and, with seemingly prophetic insight, gave its date as the Xia dynasty (2d millennium B.C.).

A finely worked jade *cong* that Freer purchased in 1916 (fig. 140) also has emphatic round eyes modeled in relief. The sturdy prisms known as *cong,* which are square in cross section and perforated longitudinally with a circular opening, remain the most enigmatic of all Chinese archaic jades. Scholars traditionally have described them as symbols of the earth, but a number of ingenious interpretations have been proposed, the most fanciful of which is that they originally formed part of a stargazing instrument. Placement of the forceful masks around the four corners of the Freer Gallery *cong* lends them an assertive three-dimensionality. Comparable decoration on excavated Liangzhu jades leaves no doubt that the piece was made in southeastern China and dates from the Late Neolithic period.[5]

Among the most spectacular of the jades that Freer purchased from Seaouke Yue—who met Freer in 1917 and continued to offer him many antiquities until Freer's death—are three large blades formerly owned by the late Qing dynasty official and connoisseur Duanfang (see fig. 61). One of the blades (fig. 141, *top*), a dagger ax based on a lethal

Left:
Fig. 139. Plaque, China, Liangzhu culture, Late Neolithic period, ca. 3000–2500 B.C. Jade (6.9 x 8.1), 16.511. While the function of the jade plaque remains unknown, pairs of holes on the back suggest that it might have been attached to clothing or a headdress, perhaps of a tribal leader or a shaman.

Right:
Fig. 140. *Cong* prism, China, Liangzhu culture, Late Neolithic period, ca. 3000–2500 B.C. Jade (4.5 x 7.3), 16.118.

Fig. 141. *Top, Ge* blade with engraved inscription, China, Western Zhou dynasty, ca. 1050–1000 B.C. Jade (length 67.4), 19.13. *Center,* "Red Sword" blade, China, Shang dynasty, ca. 1500–1200 B.C. Nephrite (length 84.1), 17.396. *Bottom,* Blade, China, Longshan culture, Late Neolithic–early Shang period, ca. 2000–1500 B.C. Jade (72.0 x 18.3), 18.1. The blade at the bottom is especially striking for the stylized mask with an elaborate headdress worked in raised relief at one end. Masks of this type are associated with the Late Neolithic Longshan culture centered in the area of modern Shandong Province.

bronze prototype but manifestly made for ceremonial purposes, has achieved special distinction for the inscription, engraved horizontally across the butt end, that refers to military activity at the beginning of the Zhou dynasty.[6] Duanfang nicknamed another of his jade blades "Red Sword" (fig. 141, *center*). Only random flecks of reddish pigment remain on the jade surface today, but it is conceivable that the dagger ax, said to have been unearthed in 1903, may have retained considerably more of the cinnabar applied in antiquity before the piece was buried.[7] Judging from its scale and elegant finish, "Red Sword" was made for a royal patron and dates from the mid to late Shang dynasty (ca. 1500–1200 B.C.). Its length remained unchallenged until 1976, when a slightly longer jade dagger ax was unearthed in a mid-Shang dynasty tomb.[8] The last of the three blades from Duanfang's collection (fig. 141, *bottom*) is admired for its decoration and distinctive mottling, which Seaouke Yue described as "streaked red giving the beautiful appearance of sunset clouds."[9] The carefully articulated serrated projections that enliven the silhouette of the jade are related to decoration on excavated examples of the Late Neolithic to early Shang period (ca. 2000–ca. 1500 B.C.).

The First Public Exhibitions, 1897

Freer was extremely generous in permitting people to study his collections at his home in Detroit and equally so in lending pieces to exhibitions. Most of the loans were from his American collection, but requests were also made for his Asian objects, to which he liberally acceded. Some Asian exhibitions were drawn solely from Freer's holdings; for others, he collaborated with fellow collectors. That Freer's participation was actively sought and prominence was given to his loans reflect his considerable reputation as a connoisseur. During the last years of his life, the opportunity to participate in exhibitions and innovative projects, even indirectly, offered welcome relief from the tedium of the sickbed.

The earliest instance in which Freer loaned his Asian paintings for public exhibition appears to have been in 1897, five years after he seriously began collecting Japanese scrolls.[10] At the behest of Dwight Tryon, Freer agreed to lend thirty of his Japanese paintings to the Hillyer Art Gallery at Smith College in Northampton, Massachusetts, where the artist had taught studio classes since 1886. The spacious, high-ceilinged room normally used by the students as a painting studio provided the exhibition area: twenty-six hanging scrolls were displayed on two walls, above four folding screens. Tryon was enthusiastic about the paintings, all of which were recent acquisitions, and described *Carp* (fig. 142) by Kuroda Tōkō as "out of sight."[11] The exhibition received such favorable publicity that Richard A. Rice, professor of the history of art and civilization at Williams College in Williamstown, Massachusetts, asked Freer whether he would be willing to send the Japanese paintings to Williamstown for display there; Freer consented, and the paintings traveled to Williams that year.

Four years later Tryon again approached Freer, and as a result, thirty-five Japanese hanging scrolls went on display at the Hillyer Art Gallery in March 1901. For the earlier exhibition Freer had chosen works by artists from several schools; in the latter he concentrated on ukiyo-e paintings, believing they would give the students "keener pleasure and more direct knowledge of the aims and methods of the principal masters of the school which was first to break away from academic practices."[12] Once again the selected scrolls were recent acquisitions, most of them purchased from Edward S. Hull, Jr., the lawyer who had negotiated the sale of Ernest Fenollosa's Japanese prints and paintings following the Fenollosa divorce in 1895. When Fenollosa presented three lectures at the Detroit Museum of Arts (now The Detroit Institute of Arts) in December 1901, he selected one hundred Japanese prints from Freer's collection to be displayed there at the same time; many of the prints, in fact, had originally belonged to Fenollosa. Their quality demonstrates the importance of Freer's purchases from Fenollosa in establishing the basis for the Freer Gallery's present holdings of ukiyo-e paintings (fig. 143). Initially enriched by his purchases from Fenollosa, that area of Freer's collections continued to grow, so that his final gift to the nation included an extraordinary number of works by Japanese artists of the ukiyo-e school.

In 1905, Freer made a second loan to Williams College, this time of his Hokusai scrolls. Again, most of the pieces, which included *Boy and Mount Fuji* and *Thunder God* (see figs. 90 and 91), had passed through Fenollosa's hands. With the paintings, Freer sent Professor Rice a copy of Fenollosa's catalogue of the first exhibition of Hokusai's work, held in Tokyo in January 1900.[13] He consented, moreover, to Rice's request that the exhibition travel to the Albany Institute and Historical Society but required that Rice explain to officials there how East Asian scrolls should be handled.

To coincide with Fenollosa's lecture, "Ancient Chinese and Japanese Art," presented to members of the University Club in Detroit in February 1906, Freer arranged to have twenty of his Japanese paintings shown in the same building. Although he described the exhibition as being "hastily prepared" and "altogether inadequate," Freer was pleased that the members of the club were interested in his scrolls and enthusiastic about Fenollosa's talk.[14]

Fig. 142. Kuroda Tōkō (1785–1846), *Carp*, Japan, Edo period. Hanging scroll; ink and color on silk (44.9 x 85.8), 96.92.

University of Michigan, 1910

Those early loans from Freer's collections were relatively informal, quickly organized, and not documented by scholarly catalogues. More wide-ranging in scope was the loan exhibition of American and Asian art from Freer's collections held in 1910 at the University of Michigan, Ann Arbor, to mark the opening of the University's Alumni Memorial Hall, dedicated to alumni killed in the Spanish-American War (fig. 144). The exhibition was an ambitious undertaking, complete with an elaborate installation and catalogue.[15]

The Asian section comprised many important Japanese screens, two Chinese paintings, Japanese and West Asian pottery, and Japanese lacquer. Comments about East Asian art and about objects in the catalogue were based on the writings of contemporary scholars, such as Fenollosa and the English specialists Dr. William Anderson, Laurence Binyon, and Herbert A. Giles, and included selections from the Japanese art journal *Kokka.*

The upstairs gallery in Memorial Hall, where Freer's Japanese screens were displayed, was similar to the exhibition space in Freer's home on Ferry Avenue in Detroit and, later, to the galleries at the Freer Gallery: natural light came from overhead and a simple cove molding rose from a heavy horizontal cornice. No daises or platforms were used, nor was there an attempt to display the screens as traditionally placed in Japanese interiors; all of the screens were placed flat atop the wainscoting and butted one against another, recalling Fenollosa's description of Japanese artists "who girdled the lofty walls of Hideyoshi's palaces with painted panoramas of Chinese court-scenes, enamelled in deep glowing pigment upon colossal gilded backgrounds."[16]

The six-fold Sesshū landscape screen that Freer had acquired in 1905 from the Waggaman sale (see fig. 95) provided the frontispiece of the University of Michigan catalogue; its description was taken verbatim from Fenollosa's long statement in the auction catalogue. Freer had received several congratulatory messages after purchasing the screen, and he took great pride in the painting. Another six-fold screen in the exhibition was *Pine Trees in the Snow*, then attributed to the sixteenth-century artist Kanō Eitoku, which Freer had acquired from Matsuki Bunkyō in 1898 (fig. 145). Executed in ink and color on a gold-leaf ground, the panels originally served as *fusuma*, or sliding doors, in a Japanese interior. For this screen, the catalogue borrowed a quotation from Binyon's *Painting in the Far East*, a passage that epitomizes the author's effusive literary style:

A noble example. How simple are the elements that compose this picture; but what a sense of vastness, of majesty, of solitude! A certain solidity of effect allies such work as this to the masterpieces of Europe; and in its own kind I do not know where we shall find painting to surpass it, whether in Japan or in the West.[17]

Fig. 144. Upstairs gallery, Memorial Hall, University of Michigan, 1910. From *Exhibition of Oriental and American Art* (Ann Arbor: Alumni Memorial Committee and Ann Arbor Art Association, 1910).

A pair of six-fold screens depicting events from the life of the Chinese Tang dynasty emperor Xuanzong and his favorite concubine, Yang Guifei, was also exhibited (fig. 146). Freer had purchased the screens in 1901 from Fenollosa, who had acquired them several years earlier in Japan from the collection of Count Inoue Kaoru. To Freer's credit, he also included *Geese Flying over a Beach* by Maruyama Ōkyo, the four-panel screen he had acquired from Matsuki in 1898 (see fig. 68). Another work was *Mount Fuji and Enoshima* by

by five works, Tawaraya Sōtatsu by three (including *Waves at Matsushima,* fig. 96), and Ogata Kenzan by two; Ogata Kōrin, Kanō Eitoku, and Mori Sōsen were each limited to a single example. The catalogue made Laufer's personal inclination toward Chinese art obvious: the Chinese section opened with a chronology of the various dynasties—a nicety not observed for Japan—and then noted the names of the artists, many of whom are among the greatest in China's long history. Laufer included biographical information about the artists, most of which was taken from the publications of the English scholar Herbert A. Giles and the German-born sinologist Friedrich Hirth, and from *Kokka.*[20] The paintings were then listed according to format.

The final portion of the exhibition was assembled under the general rubric "Miscellaneous Oriental Objects." A case contained nine Chinese Buddhist bronze "statuettes" and six bronze mirrors dated "T'ang [Tang] and earlier," as well as an ancient bronze ritual vessel and an "arrow-vase for the game of pitchpot." Freer had also loaned four examples of Chinese sculpture, which he dated to the Northern Wei and Tang dynasties. Other cases held Chinese, Korean, Persian, and "Mesopotamian" ceramics. Four of Freer's Persian and Indo-Persian illuminations were displayed in another case, while seven pieces from his large collection of Egyptian glass were shown separately.

The examples Freer selected for the Smithsonian exhibition were, in his view, of

Fig. 147. Katsushika Hokusai (1760–1849), *Mount Fuji and Enoshima,* Japan, Edo period. Pair of two-fold screens; ink and color on paper (each screen 163.2 x 157.0), 04.175-176. Hokusai's interest in Western perspective is apparent in the bold diagonals leading into the composition from Sagami Bay in the foreground, past a small village on Enoshima Island, to the muted silhouette of Mount Fuji in the distance.

singular importance and intended to indicate the richness of his gift to the nation. Few of the Chinese and Japanese paintings, however, retain their original attributions. He included, for instance, the long handscroll attributed to Ma Yuan now assigned to an anonymous Ming dynasty artist (see fig. 55). The figural handscroll *Admonishing in Chains* (fig. 65) was shown as a genuine work by Yan Liben of the seventh century; although that attribution is no longer accepted, the painting remains one of the most impressive figure compositions in the Freer collection. *Wang Wei's Villa at Wangquan* (fig. 59), originally attributed to the fourteenth-century Yuan dynasty artist Wang Meng, currently is

attributed to Song Xu of the Ming dynasty. Song Xu's reference to Wang Meng's brush-work is clearly apparent, but the loose undulating lines and the delicate color reflect later developments in Chinese painting. Perhaps nostalgically, Freer loaned the fan then attributed to Kōrin, his earliest Japanese acquisition (see fig. 41). Although the Kōrin attribution is no longer accepted, the *Waves at Matsushima* screens remain among the most famous Japanese screens in the Freer Gallery, still regarded internationally as one of the finest examples of Sōtatsu's work.

A review of the 1912 Smithsonian exhibition in the *Philadelphia Enquirer* mentioned

Fig. 148. Artist unknown,
Phoenixes, Rocks, and Flowers,
Korea, Yi dynasty, 18th century.
Pair of hanging scrolls; ink and
color on silk (155.0 x 103.3),
05.15-16.

that the Freer collection was shown in the new National Gallery (now the National Museum of Natural History) in a large hall

intended for the display of natural history objects, including the Roosevelt Collection of stuffed animals, the results of his slaughter of the innocents in Africa. . . . The hall, which is very handsome and well lighted, is nevertheless by common consent agreed to be the most inappropriate place for the setting forth of a collection such as Mr. Freer's, a fact which emphasizes the wisdom of the provisions of his gift to the nation, that a separate building shall be erected for the installation of his collection exclusively.[21]

Innovations, 1914

As an honorary vice president of the Japan Society, Freer participated in a pioneering exhibition of Chinese, Korean, and Japanese ceramics in 1914. Shown under the auspices of the Japan Society at the Knoedler Galleries, 556 Fifth Avenue,[22] it was the first exhibition of its kind held in New York, although the Burlington Fine Arts Club in London had installed a major exhibition of East Asian ceramics as early as 1910. The principal lenders of the ceramics shown in the Knoedler Galleries were Freer; Samuel T. Peters, a businessman, collector, and trustee of the Metropolitan Museum of Art; and Howard Mansfield.

R. L. Hobson, the legendary ceramics specialist from the British Museum, authenticated the Chinese and Korean pieces and wrote a short prefatory note, "Chinese and Corean Potteries." Considerably more detailed and scholarly was the long essay by Rose Sickler Williams, "A Report on Early Chinese Potteries, Compiled from Original Sources." Mrs. Williams, wife of Edward Thomas Williams, a missionary who subsequently served in the American legation in Beijing, had lived in China for many years. She had been commissioned by the Asiatic Institute to prepare a report on Chinese and foreign sources of Chinese ceramics; her essay for the exhibition catalogue was an effort to combine traditional Chinese connoisseurship with information then becoming available on Song dynasty ceramics. Edward Sylvester Morse of the Museum of Fine Arts, Boston, wrote a brief, characteristically gruff introductory statement about the Japanese pottery, in which he applauded Western collectors for their ability to appreciate the subtleties of Japan's glazed wares:

Few, if any, would have appreciated such a collection thirty-five years ago, when the auction-rooms were filled with stuff made for foreign trade and repeatedly marked "Corean," and with gaudily decorated pieces in gold and colour supposed to represent Satsuma. In other words, our collectors are now appreciating those kinds of pottery that the Japanese most admire.[23]

Notwithstanding flagging catalogue sales and the forbidding installation in the Knoedler Galleries (fig. 149), the 1914 exhibition was successful. Visitors saw a wide range of wares, and some of the eighty-four ceramics Freer loaned to the exhibition were of truly impressive quality. They included the Song dynasty Guan ware vase with a lustrous bluish gray crackled glaze probably made for imperial use at the Phoenix Hill kiln in Hangzhou, which Freer had acquired in Beijing in 1911 (fig. 150, *right*), and the large Jun ware flowerpot with thick, opaque, evenly fired glaze with subtle variations in blue tonality *(center)* purchased in China in 1907. Another piece was a tea bowl *(left)*, whose unusually large size and flaring silhouette set it apart from other examples of this sturdy, black-glazed ware made in the Jian ware kilns in Fujian Province.

The Japanese ceramics included a small square plate by Kenzan (fig. 151) from a set of twelve, with decoration based on imagery from a set of poems for the twelve months by the twelfth- to thirteenth-century poet Fujiwara Teika. Inscribed on the back of the plate are two poems, "Early Plum" and "Water Birds," themes that Kenzan combined in his painted decoration:

> It is that time when snow buries the colors
> of the hedge,
> Yet a branch of plum is blooming, on "this side"
> of the New Year.
>
> The snow falls on the ice of the pond on which I gaze,
> Piling up as does this passing year
> on all those past
> And on the feathered coat of the mandarin duck,
> the "bird of regret." [24]

Fig. 149. Knoedler Galleries exhibition gallery, New York, 1914. From a portfolio of thirty-nine plates by Lawrence X. Champeau, Champeau Studio, *Chinese, Corean, and Japanese Potteries* (New York: Japan Society, 1914).

Freer loaned twenty-nine Korean ceramics to the exhibition, not a surprising number in light of his rich holdings, which were made up of his 1907 acquisition of the Allen collection and subsequent purchases, particularly an important group of thirty-four pieces from Yamanaka Sadajirō in March 1909. An outstanding item that was part of the Allen acquisition was the thirteenth-century lobed ewer of the Koryŏ dynasty (fig. 152). A large thirteenth-century *maebyŏng* vase notable for its somewhat unusual decoration (fig. 153, *right*) was among the ceramics Freer purchased from Yamanaka. The beauty and versatility of the Korean celadon glaze may be fully appreciated on another *maebyŏng* that was in the exhibition (fig. 153, *left*). Dating from the twelfth century and probably made for the royal court, it remains one of the finest Korean pieces in the Freer collection.

At the Metropolitan Museum of Art, 1916

In 1916, Sigisbert Chrétien Bosch-Reitz, the newly appointed curator of the Department of Far Eastern Art at the Metropolitan Museum of Art in New York, organized an exhibition of early Chinese pottery and sculpture (fig. 155). For the pottery section, he leaned heavily on the Japan Society show of two years earlier, even reprinting the essays by R. L. Hobson and Rose Sickler Williams in his catalogue.[25] Samuel Peters, Howard Mansfield, Freer's assistant Katharine Rhoades, Agnes and Eugene Meyer, Jr., and Grenville Lindall Winthrop, a New York lawyer, banker, and collector, all loaned objects from their collections, and Freer loaned several pieces of Chinese sculpture. One was a white marble figure of a bodhisattva seated beneath a tree (fig. 154), the style of

Fig. 150. *Right,* Vase, Guan ware, China, Song dynasty, 12th century. Glazed clay (23.2 x 14.1), 11.338. *Center,* Flowerpot, Jun ware, China, Yuan dynasty, 13th–14th century. Glazed clay (25.6 27.2), 07.38. *Left,* Tea bowl, Jian ware, China, Song dynasty, 12th century. Glazed clay (8.8 x 19.2), 09.369. Called Temmoku, tea bowls with purple-black glaze and irregular silvery patterns were highly prized in Japan for use in tea ceremonies.

Fig. 151. Ogata Kenzan (1663–1743), plate, Japan, Edo period, ca. 1702–03. Glazed clay (2.4 x 16.9 x 16.8), 05.58. The gray body of this plate has an iridescent transparent lead glaze over white slip and a decoration of underglaze enamels.

Fig. 152. Ewer, Korea, Koryŏ period, 13th century. Glazed clay (27.1 x 15.3), 07.286. This ewer, based on metalwork prototypes, is unusual for its intricately shaped lid, which is rendered as tiered petals with a bird at the top.

Fig. 153. *Right, Maebyŏng* vase, Korea, Koryŏ period, 1st half 13th century. Glazed clay (34.4 x 20.3), 09.31. The contrasting ginseng leaves, first incised and then filled with white slip, stand in striking contrast to the black tone of the body, which was produced by an ash mixture applied over an undercoating of iron-rich slip; a transparent celadon glaze covers the entire vessel. Korean *maebyŏng* are distinguished from their Chinese prototypes, *mei ping,* by their elongated waist and high, broad shoulders. *Left, Maebyŏng* vase, Korea, Koryŏ period, 12th century. Glazed clay (28.5 x 18.8), 12.96. The glaze enriches the sculptural effect of the allover bird-and-flower design, intensifying with its greenish blue color areas where elements have been carved to greater depth.

which is now widely recognized as being typical of the Northern Qi period, some half-century later than the Wei dynasty date given in the catalogue.[26] Freer also loaned the horizontal section of a gray limestone funerary base; its bas-relief decoration combines Chinese and Central Asian elements (fig. 156). The stone base is said to have been found in Hebei Province, near the site of Ye, an important Buddhist center and the capital of Northern Qi.

Although the 1916 exhibition at the Metropolitan Museum was intended to be a display of Chinese pottery and sculpture, a group of ancient Chinese ritual bronzes was added at the last moment. The bronzes comprised objects owned jointly by Freer and Agnes and Eugene Meyer, Jr. Freer and the Meyers, who often visited art dealers together, had from time to time made joint purchases since they met in 1913. The Meyers would insist that Freer have the first choice since his collection was intended for a national museum, but they assured Freer that they intended to bequeath their Asian art collection to his museum, a promise they faithfully kept. When, in 1915, the choice collection of early Chinese bronzes assembled by Marcel Bing was offered to Freer for one hundred thousand dollars, Freer discussed the collection with the Meyers. Recognizing the outstanding quality of the bronzes, they decided to make the purchase together. Shortly after the bronzes arrived in the United States in 1916, the owners agreed to lend them to the Metropolitan Museum's exhibition.

The earliest of the bronzes was a large ritual pouring vessel remarkable for its size and fantastic hybrid imagery (fig. 157). Recent archaeological finds have enabled scholars to date the bronze to the Shang dynasty around 1100–1050 B.C. and to place its startling decoration within the context of southern Chinese regional

Fig. 154. Seated Bodhisattva, China, Northern Qi dynasty, ca. A.D. 575. Stone (height 33.0), 11.411. Knowledge of Northern Qi Buddhist sculpture of this type improved dramatically with the discovery in 1953 of large numbers of white marble sculptures by a Chinese farmer who was digging a pit to store sweet potatoes at the site of what had been, in antiquity, a famous Buddhist temple. Of the more than twenty-two hundred pieces unearthed at the site, some 250 were inscribed.

style. The most appealing in the group was the bird-shaped ritual wine container that embodies both the technical skill and the elegance of Chinese bronze casters (fig. 158). At the time of the 1915 purchase, the bronze was dated to the Zhou dynasty and said to have been found near Taiyuan in Shanxi Province. A fifth-century B.C. tomb recently excavated in the area of Taiyuan yielded a similar bird-shaped bronze wine container (fig. 159), confirming the traditional attribution of the vessel.[27]

Perhaps the most extraordinary of the bronzes lent to the exhibition is the Taibao *gui,* a large ritual food container said to have been found in northeastern China in the 1850s (fig. 160). Bold monster masks and large assertive handles give the vessel a sculptural monumentality. On the basis of style alone it would be possible to date the bronze to the eleventh century B.C. The inscription cast inside the bronze, which refers to the period shortly after the Zhou conquest of the Shang around the mid-eleventh century B.C., proved to be important for the study of ancient Chinese history. After the 1916 exhibition, the Meyers took the bronze vessel to their country estate in Mount Kisco, New York, where it remained on the piano in their music room for more than fifty years. After Mrs. Meyer's death in 1970, the bronze was packed in a plain wooden box labeled simply "Chinese bronze" and shipped to the Freer Gallery with the rest of the Meyer bequest. When the box was opened, the historic vessel became accessible once again to study by scholars.

Fig. 155. Far Eastern (East Asian) ceramic exhibition at the Metropolitan Museum of Art, New York, 1916. From *Bulletin of the Metropolitan Museum of Art* 11, no. 1 (January 1916): 75.

Fig. 156. Funerary base, China, Northern Qi dynasty, A.D. 550–77. Stone (60.0 x 234.0 x 23.5), 15.110. The elaborate incense burner and figures at the center of the composition are executed in typical Northern Qi style, while the musicians and dancers reflect Central Asian influence.

Fig. 157. Ritual vessel *(gong)*, China, Shang dynasty, ca. 1100–1050 B.C. Bronze (31.4 x 14.2). Gift of Eugene and Agnes E. Meyer, 61.33.

The display of Chinese ritual bronzes loaned by Freer and the Meyers had little relevance to the other objects in the exhibition. Presented as an afterthought, the Chinese bronzes nonetheless marked the first time that ancient ritual vessels of such quality had ever been shown in the United States. Their exhibition was a milestone in the beginning of Western understanding of Chinese culture.

An Exhibition in Chicago, 1917

In 1917, Charles L. Hutchinson, president of the Art Institute of Chicago, asked Freer whether he would be willing to lend some of his Chinese pieces for display at the same time Dikran Kelekian's Chinese ceramics were to be shown there (fig. 161). Freer agreed. From 15 November to 8 December visitors to the Art Institute—to Freer, "people of the right sort"[28]—were able to see some of Freer's Chinese jades, paintings, and sculpture together with Kelekian's Chinese ceramics. The task of selecting objects and preparing the catalogue was handled mainly by Frederick W. Gookin, curator of the

Fig. 158. Bird-shaped ritual vessel, China, Eastern Zhou dynasty, ca. 500 B.C. Bronze with gold inlay (height 26.5). Gift of Eugene and Agnes E. Meyer, 61.30.

Fig. 159. Line drawing of bird-shaped bronze ritual vessel unearthed at Taiyuan, Shanxi Province, China, in 1987. From *Wenwu* 9 (1989): 72, fig. 21.

Buckingham collection of Japanese prints at the Art Institute, with the aid of Katharine Rhoades and Berthold Laufer.[29] Many of the painting attributions would be questioned by contemporary scholars, but Gookin did provide a brief biography of each artist and cite inscriptions and seals. Laufer selected thirty-four Chinese jades from Freer's collection for what was to be the first time any of them were shown publicly. Significantly, he chose few of the genuinely outstanding ones Freer was acquiring during those years; his failure to include the jade plaque (see fig. 139) that today is recognized as one of the finest Late Neolithic Liangzhu pieces in the Freer Gallery is especially surprising. An impressive white jade disk that Laufer catalogued as Tang dynasty (fig. 162) has been reattributed to the Eastern Han period, based on stylistic features such as the abstract nipple pattern and serpentine ornaments. Freer had purchased the jade from C. T. Loo in 1916, and Laufer may have based his attribution on information in Loo's invoice. In addition to preparing the notes concerning jades and stone sculpture, Laufer urged that Chinese characters be included in the exhibition catalogue, a feature that advanced the development of scholarly catalogues of Asian art exhibitions in the United States.

Because of his interest in museum installations, Freer requested detailed information on how the objects would be placed in the exhibition halls at the Art Institute. He visited the museum in advance to see the space, and afterward proposed that the walls be covered with cream-colored fabric and made many suggestions about the placement and juxtaposition of objects. His sensitivity to subtle gradations of ink and tone, no doubt the influence of Whistler, prompted him to request that several ink paintings—the "Black and White" group—be placed in a small separate room. Freer had definite ideas on the display of his Chinese jades. He wanted certain pieces to be shown lying flat on a silver-gray ground, some on a black ground, and others left in their boxes, which were lined with white fabric.

It was Laufer who persuaded Freer to lend the *Nymph of the Luo River* handscroll (see fig. 62), which Freer had not intended to show publicly until his museum in Washington was completed. But Freer yielded to Laufer's argument that the scroll would "give largely increased interest" to the Chicago exhibition, and it proved to be unquestionably the finest painting in the show. The validity of the scroll's traditional attribution to Gu Kaizhi has always been a source of debate among connoisseurs: the entry in the 1917 catalogue notes that Freer, cautiously optimistic, regarded the painting "as more probably a copy made after [Gu Kaizhi's] original design by some painter of the T'ang [Tang] dynasty who fully carried out the style of the early master."[30] Today the painting is assigned to the Song dynasty.

Many of the Chinese paintings included in the 1917 exhibition at the Chicago Art Institute had already been shown at the Smithsonian Institution. But Miss Rhoades,

Fig. 160. Taibao *gui* (ritual food container), China, Early Western Zhou dynasty, 11th century B.C. Bronze (23.5 x 37.5). Gift of Eugene and Agnes E. Meyer, 68.29. The thirty-four character inscription cast inside this ritual food container mentions the Taibao, or "Grand Protector," a title bestowed on the powerful Duke of Shao at the beginning of the Western Zhou dynasty.

Laufer, and Gookin, with some assistance from Freer, also selected the majestic hanging scroll associated with Mi Fu (see fig. 53) and two album leaves, *Crab Apples and Gardenias* (fig. 163), by the early Yuan dynasty master Qian Xuan. Freer had just acquired the leaves from Seaouke Yue and Pang Yuanji, another Shanghai collector-connoisseur, and was justifiably pleased with them. Aside from the artist's seals that appear on each painting, a short inscription by the celebrated scholar-official-calligrapher-painter Zhao Mengfu written directly on the silk mounting at the end of the scroll supports the Qian Xuan attribution. Recognized today as an important early example of Zhao Mengfu's calligraphy, the inscription evoked little comment from Freer and his contemporaries; appreciation for Chinese calligraphy has only recently developed among Western specialists.

Korean painting was not well understood during Freer's lifetime, so it is not surprising that in 1917 one of Freer's landscapes executed in ink was attributed to an anonymous Chinese artist, even though no signature or seals appear on the coarse silk ground (fig. 164). The dramatic contrast in the composition between the foreground trees and mountains and the distant space is characteristic of traditions formulated by Chinese artists of the Zhe school during the fifteenth and sixteenth centuries. Only in the past few decades has research on Korean painting enabled specialists to reattribute the painting to the Yi dynasty of the sixteenth or seventeenth century.

Even though a few of the dates have been modified, the attributions of all of the Chinese sculpture exhibited in 1917 remain unchallenged today. Freer's success, even daring, in assembling an imposing collection of Chinese sculpture at a time when Westerners were reluctant to buy stone carvings is especially remarkable. The works shown at the Art Institute represented the aspect of East Asian art that absorbed almost all of Freer's interest during his final years. Considering how little was known about Chinese art at that time, problems of attribution and provenance may be less significant than Freer's eagerness to explore relatively unstudied areas of Chinese culture. That inquiring spirit enabled the collector to enrich his appreciation of Chinese art and further expand his already substantial holdings.

Fig. 161. Freer's paintings displayed at the Art Institute of Chicago, 1917. From *Bulletin of the Art Institute of Chicago* 12, no. 1 (January 1918): 7.

Fig. 162. *Bi* disk, China, Eastern Han dynasty, 2d century A.D. Jade (21.8 x 15.2), 16.155. Standing atop the disk are an intertwined dragon and feline enframed by curvilinear appendages. The flamboyant asymmetry of the fantastic animals contrasts with the geometric, granular pattern that embellishes the surface of the disk.

Fig. 163. *Crab Apples and Gardenias,* painting by Qian Xuan (ca. 1235–after 1300), calligraphy by Zhao Mengfu (1254–1322), China, Yuan dynasty. Album leaves mounted as handscroll (29.2 x 78.3), 17.183. Originally part of a larger album, these two meticulously painted floral studies were later put together to form a short handscroll. The delicate colors and finely drawn outlines capture the transient beauty of newly opened blossoms.

The Metropolitan Museum, 1917

Freer's residence in New York made him particularly amenable when Sigisbert Chrétien Bosch-Reitz again asked him to loan objects from his collection for a special exhibition of the Kōrin school at the Metropolitan Museum of Art. The exhibition of Japanese screens and paintings was arranged to coincide with the visit of Viscount Ishii Kikujirō and the Japanese Commission in 1917.[31] Freer generously agreed to loan fourteen screens and ten panels, including such famous pieces as the Sesshū landscape screen and Sōtatsu's *Waves at Matsushima* (see figs. 95 and 96). Freer also loaned several works believed to be by Kōetsu, including a pair of two-fold screens, *Coxcombs, Maize, and Morning Glories* (later reattributed to an anonymous artist of the Momoyama period), which in Freer's day exemplified the bold, decorative compositions of the Rimpa school (fig. 165).

AT HOME IN Detroit on Christmas Eve, 1918, Freer became seriously ill. By New Year's Day, he was strong enough to sit up in bed and shave himself, and when, several days later, he was able to walk from his bed to a chair, he believed he would soon recover. Freer's doctor tried to determine the cause of the illness, recommending a strict regime of rest and massage that brought Freer some relief but no lasting change in his condition. By February 1919 he was well enough to travel to New York City for a week of extensive tests and therapy at a sanatorium. He then moved to a suite in the Gotham Hotel, where he could continue his medical treatment in comfortable surroundings suitable for entertaining friends and colleagues.

For most of the remaining months of his life, Freer experienced chronic physical weakness and mental depression, with intermittent outbursts of violent temper. While he occasionally felt strong enough to take short rides in an automobile or spend a few hours studying objects in his collections, Freer slowly but irreversibly succumbed to a disease that his doctors could never precisely identify.

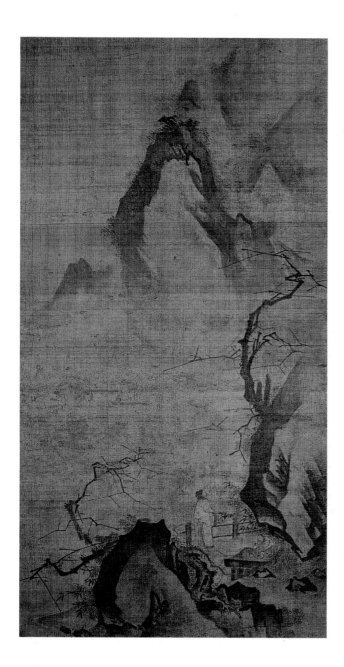

Fig. 164. Artist unknown, *Landscape,* Korea, Yi dynasty, 16th–17th century. Hanging scroll; ink on silk (102.4 x 54.6), 07.143.

Entries in Freer's pocket diary for 1919 serve as a barometer of his fluctuating condition. Most entries begin tersely, "ill," followed by "all day in room." Once, in tremulous script, Freer referred to an illusion of a "great fire" during the night, which suggests that he sometimes had troubled dreams. Occasional gaps in the diary beginning in May mark the days Freer felt too weak or too depressed to record the monotonous minutiae of his narrowing existence. Whenever his condition improved, his handwriting would become firm and steady, manifesting a brief resurgence of strength.

Visits from friends such as Agnes and Eugene Meyer and Louisine Havemeyer helped to relieve the tedious passage of the days. Freer, who retained some of his zest for negotiating with art dealers, continued to purchase objects throughout the summer. Always punctual with his correspondence, he managed to reply to letters promptly in spite of his condition, and although he was unable to move about freely, he experienced no pain during the last weeks of his life. On 25 September, in his suite at the Gotham Hotel, surrounded by a selection of his favorite art treasures, Freer died. Katharine Rhoades, who was with him throughout most of his illness, sketched Freer on his deathbed and arranged to have a death mask made. His body was buried in Kingston, New York. ∎

Fig. 165. Artist unknown, *Coxcombs, Maize, and Morning Glories,* Japan, Momoyama period, 17th century. One of a pair of two-fold screens; color, gold, and silver on paper (144.2 x 174.5), 01.99. Lush red coxcombs against broad-leaved maize create a dynamic composition.

CHAPTER NINE

LINDA MERRILL

The Washington Building

WHEN THE Freer Gallery of Art opened to the public in 1923, there was no name inscribed above the portals. The founder had worked out virtually every detail of the building except the "modest and appropriate form" the title his gift to the nation would take. The museum, to him, had always been simply the "Washington building." Inside, there were no portraits of Freer on display or any other indications that the new gallery on the National Mall had been conceived, constructed, furnished, and endowed by a single benefactor whose lifelong ambition was realized in the collections and embodied in the building. Yet even in the absence of his name at the entrance, the Freer Gallery of Art was so thoroughly imbued with the spirit of the founder that one acquaintance was inspired to call it "Mr. Freer's Autobiography."[1]

Freer had not established a national gallery of art to fulfill a dream of personal glory. In fact, when he pledged a half-million dollars in 1904 to erect a "fireproof building connected with the National Museum" for housing his collections, he intended the gallery to be built only after his death.[2] The "delayed delivery" of Freer's gift had occasioned some concern; as Freer explained to his friend Alfred Chapman, the Smithsonian Regents regarded him as

still a young man, and one possessed of fairly good health, and they fear that it will be many years before the treasures come into their hands; that, in fact, the present Board of Regents will probably have gone over to the large majority before the Collections reach their Institution.

Freer, who was fifty-two in 1906, argued that he was already as old as Methuselah and that art, in any event, would outlive them all; and the Smithsonian eventually accepted his gift with the troublesome provision intact.[3]

Scarcely two years had passed, however, before certain officials in Washington

The longer the investigation lasts, the simpler my opinions become of how the building should be constructed. The art objects should, in my mind, have first consideration.

Freer to Abbott Thayer, 12 August 1912

Fig. 166. Peacock in the Freer Gallery courtyard, 1923. Photograph by Arnold Genthe (1869–1942).

Fig. 167. Augustus Saint-Gaudens, inscribed to Freer by Augusta Saint-Gaudens in December 1907. Photograph by De W. C. Ward, 1903.

began agitating to begin immediate construction of the promised museum. At first Freer contended that it would be "impracticable" to build the gallery during his lifetime.[4] Nevertheless, he went to Washington twice in the early months of 1908 to meet with President Theodore Roosevelt and the new secretary of the Smithsonian, Charles D. Walcott, presumably to discuss his objections; in April, Walcott paid a visit to Detroit in an attempt to resolve the difficulty, which was ostensibly financial. Upon his return, the secretary proposed obtaining a federal appropriation to cover the cost of the museum's construction and converting the funds Freer had promised for that purpose to an endowment for maintaining the building and caring for the collections.[5]

The principal advantage of Walcott's plan, as Freer's attorney advised him, was that it would permit Freer to supervise personally the building's design and construction and to oversee the placement of objects within it. At length, and "with no little personal regret," Freer consented to the scheme: "Perhaps the time has come when I ought to make some self denial in order that students, art lovers, and the general public may have such access to these works of art as can be afforded by their permanent housing and exhibition at the National Capital."[6] As it happened, Walcott failed in his effort—the appropriations bill was defeated in the House of Representatives—but by then Freer had become determined to proceed, even at his own expense. He hoped to live to see the building materialize, even as he dreaded the distant prospect of parting with his collections.

Freer had said nothing in his initial proposal to the Smithsonian about the architectural style he envisioned for the museum. In January 1906 he informed Wilson Eyre—who, as the architect of Freer's Detroit house, took a particular interest in knowing what his patron had in mind—that he would not "take any steps concerning the building" until the Smithsonian had concluded its deliberation.[7] Privately, however, Freer seems to have conveyed his own vision to the historian Charles Moore, who had assisted in framing the McMillan Plan for the nation's capital. Moore was enthusiastic about the architectural renaissance under way in Washington, which recalled, he said, "the beginning of the building that marked the end of the Middle Ages." In a letter to President Roosevelt, he mentioned that Freer had conceived a "beautiful, small building by Stanford White, . . . a very great ornament to Washington," a work of art in itself.[8]

Stanford White, one of the leading architects of the American Renaissance, had long been a member of Freer's circle. He had designed exquisite, distinctive frames for many paintings in the collection, and his recent participation in the grand but ill-fated scheme to erect a neoclassical bicentenary monument in Detroit (see fig. 123) must have further convinced Freer of the consonance of their aesthetic sensibilities. Although Freer may never have approached White directly with a commission, his earliest ideas about the Washington building were wholly shaped by the architect's style.

Even before the Smithsonian Institution had decided to accept his gift, Freer commissioned the sculptor Augustus Saint-Gaudens (fig. 167), one of Stanford White's closest friends and artistic collaborators, to produce a work for the proposed museum: a classical stele with a life-size female figure in bas-relief representing the art of painting. Freer wrote to Saint-Gaudens in February 1906 that he intended to ask White to design the building, and that they would together decide where to place the stele, once the architect was well started on the plans.[9] Saint-Gaudens may have mentioned Freer's scheme on the morning of 25 June 1906, when he and White met in New York to confer on another project commissioned by Freer, a memorial to James McNeill Whistler for the library at West Point. But that evening White was fatally shot in Madison Square Garden. Freer wired his condolences to the architect's partner, Charles McKim: "The terrible deed of the vile miscreant," he said, "causes gloom throughout Detroit."[10]

Saint-Gaudens, stricken with grief and mortally ill, completed the West Point monument with the assistance of Henry Bacon, one of White's students; but when the sculptor died the next summer, Freer's *Art of Painting* remained incomplete. Years later Freer would purchase two groups of allegorical figures by Saint-Gaudens (see fig. 168): posthu-

Fig. 168. Augustus Saint-Gaudens (1848–1907), *Labor Supported by Science and Art,* one of a pair of models for the Boston Public Library Groups, 1892–1907, cast in 1915. Bronze (82.5 x 154.8 x 57.2), 15.68.

mous bronzes cast from unfinished, half-size plaster models of works intended for another monument of the American Renaissance, the Boston Public Library, designed by McKim. But the bronzes could not substitute for the sculpture Freer had first envisioned, which would have been an integral part of the architectural program of the museum.

In the years following White's death, as Freer later confided to Abbott Thayer, he "refrained from discussing professionally the matter with any architect."[11] On his own, however, he proceeded to refine his conception of the Washington building, unrealizable in its original form. In 1907, Freer presented a "prospective plan" to Ernest Fenollosa, describing a simple, two-story structure with exhibition rooms on the upper level; a rough sketch of the plan in Fenollosa's notebook indicates a large room for storage at the center of the building.[12] The next year, responding to Walcott's request for an estimate of the space the structure might require, Freer wrote that he envisaged a three-story building with exhibition rooms radiating from a central hall. Eight skylit galleries on the top floor would be devoted to American art and four exhibition rooms below to Asian works; study rooms, offices, a library, and Whistler's Peacock Room would be located on the first floor, with storage space assigned to the basement. Freer's vision of the skylit rooms was probably founded in his new picture gallery in the house on Ferry Avenue (see fig. 16), which was somewhat smaller than the galleries he proposed but identically proportioned.[13]

Just as Freer had searched the neighborhoods of American cities for houses that might be models for his own, he started to pay particular attention to the American museums he visited, hoping to find exemplary floor plans and architectural styles for the Washington building. Among the first to make an important impression was a gallery in Buffalo, now the Albright-Knox Art Gallery, which had been presented to the city by the philanthropist John J. Albright. A marble building with caryatids commissioned from Saint-Gaudens, the Albright Art Gallery was modeled on the Erechtheum in Athens. Freer received photographs of the work in progress in 1902 (fig. 169) and wrote to Albright that the building already appeared a "most delightful monument, and one which will grow in excellence and value as the years come and go." After a visit to Buffalo three years later, Freer concluded that the new art gallery was almost ideal, "charming in every way" and exceeding every museum he knew in "cleanliness, light, and comfort."[14]

Freer subsequently embarked upon an international investigation of art museums. The survey began in earnest in 1909, when he toured Europe with the goal of visiting virtually every important museum building and noting the "different methods of heating, ventilating, lighting, size of rooms and other practical items."[15] Systematically, he inspected the major art galleries and museums of Paris, London, Brussels, Ghent, Bruges,

Antwerp, Dresden, Berlin, and Rome, making observations along the way that turned his previously vague impressions of museum mechanics into "concrete notions."[16] In Germany, a country Freer perceived as striding forward "materialistically and in many ways artistically," he found much to admire; he was especially taken with a group of small exhibition rooms on the top floor of the Kaiser Friedrich Museum in Berlin, which were amply lit with skylights and windows.[17]

Fig. 169. The Albright Art Gallery (later the Albright-Knox Art Gallery), Buffalo, New York, under construction in 1902. Edward B. Green, architect. Photograph by Dressel.

For the most part, however, European museums showed Freer more to avoid than to emulate. "The great aim over here seems to be pretentiousness, confusion and ugliness," he wrote to Frank Hecker in Detroit:

The majority of the interiors are dungeon-like and mere tombs for the treasure they overshadow. If the artists whose work is so shockingly treated have any influence with the devil the souls of the architects are surely being well roasted below. I would like to shovel on some fuel myself.[18]

Freer's aesthetic sensibilities were especially offended in London, where he attended the royal opening of the new building of the Victoria and Albert Museum (formerly the South Kensington Museum). The building was a model, he thought, of what not to do in Washington: "I intend to better it from every point," he declared.[19] Years later, outlining the design of the Freer Gallery in a letter and realizing that his description made the scheme sound "over large and confusing," he would assure his correspondent in London that his museum was not by any means a "miniature South Kensington."[20]

While British museums proved disappointing, the country itself disclosed for Freer unanticipated charms. The contempt for the English he had sometimes expressed on previous trips, echoing Whistler's sentiments, all but disappeared in 1909, when he showed a lively appreciation for all that Britain had to offer. At the Bodleian Library in Oxford, Freer was accorded special privileges because of the publication in progress of the Washington Manuscripts, the biblical texts he had purchased in Egypt two years before (see fig. 46); Freer reported with satisfied surprise that elsewhere in England doors were wide open to welcome him.[21] That warm reception from a conventionally cool country may have influenced Freer's new attachment to late medieval English architecture, documented in photographs he collected of the crenellated buildings of Saint John's College, Oxford, and the fortresslike facade of Haddon Hall in Derbyshire (fig. 170). To

Fig. 170. Haddon Hall,
Derbyshire, England, ca. 1909.

Hecker, he confided that he had begun to consider "Tudor-Gothic architecture" for the museum in Washington, a radical departure from his original conception of a modest Renaissance structure in the Stanford White style.[22]

As Freer mulled over possibilities for the building's architectural design, he gave serious thought to the organization of its interior spaces. The theory of aesthetic correspondences informing his collections would be most cogently expressed in the floor plan, and Freer made numerous attempts to devise a logical arrangement of exhibition galleries and study rooms. Scores of pencil sketches representing a variety of possible plans testify to Freer's efforts: all include several galleries for works by Whistler and a place for the Peacock Room; one gallery each for the paintings of Tryon, Dewing, Thayer, and the "miscellaneous Americans"; and separate blocks of the building for the arts of China and Japan. Several drawings show all the rooms on one level; others indicate a lower level for study and storage, suggesting that Freer had abandoned his idea of a three-story building, probably because it would have been difficult to illuminate the lower floors with natural light. One of the more prevalent plans, repeated with several variations (see fig. 171), shows American art galleries in a rectangular hall connected to outlying wings for Asian art by light-filled corridors lined with cases of ceramics.

Freer's apparent preference for a five-part plan may have originated in his admiration for Albright's art gallery in Buffalo. The photographs Freer assembled of other nineteenth-century Greek-revival buildings—the University, the Academy of Science, the National Library, and the National Archaeological Museum in Athens—imply a corresponding interior plan. But the more immediate inspiration may have been the "Tudor-Gothic" manor house, for scattered among his sketches are manuscript notes on an illustrated volume, Alfred Henry Malan's *More Famous Homes of Great Britain* (1900), keyed to pictures of pertinent architectural details. Perhaps part of the appeal of the style was its emphasis on interiors: Tudor buildings often surround courtyards, as did the museum that now lived in Freer's imagination.

At home in Detroit, Freer had discovered the benefits of moving directly from his art gallery to his garden, cultivated as carefully as the collections, where he could meditate in peace upon works of art he had studied indoors. As part of his survey of

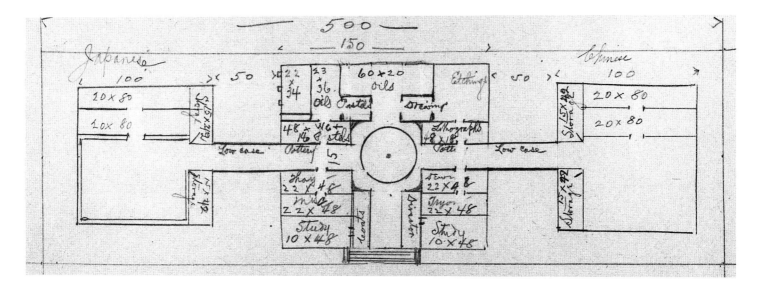

European architecture, therefore, he collected images of open courtyards that might provide a prototype for the open-air garden surrounded by loggias he was envisioning at the heart of the Washington building; one that he particularly admired was the atrium of the Renaissance monastery of San Martino (fig. 172), which he visited in Naples in July 1909. Freer's taste for the Italian style undoubtedly emerged on his 1894–95 tour, when he set out to receive "impressions of Italy and her gardens fresh, direct without guide books." He had been blessed with perfect weather, which permitted him to visit every villa on his list. The memory of those happy Italian hours may account for his purchase, years afterward, of John Singer Sargent's *Breakfast in the Loggia* (fig. 173). Painted at a Florentine villa on a bright autumn morning in 1910, the picture shows two women conversing in a sun-dappled arcade; a marble statue of Venus, the embodiment of beauty, presides over one of the most agreeable scenes in Western art.

Freer's Italian itinerary had been provided by Charles Adams Platt (fig. 174), an artist and architect whom Freer considered a "charming man in every way."[23] The list of Renaissance villas that Platt had advised Freer to see in Italy corresponded to the tour Platt himself had taken two years previously; Platt's impressions were published in 1893 in *Harper's Monthly* and again the next year in his book *Italian Gardens*, which influenced a late nineteenth-century American revival of formal garden design. The point of Platt's study, and the theme of all his future work in architecture, was that buildings should be fully integrated with their grounds:

The evident harmony of arrangement between the house and the surrounding landscape is what first strikes one in Italian landscape architecture—the design as a whole, including gardens, terraces,

Fig. 172. Atrio di San Martino, Naples, Italy, ca. 1909.

groves, and their necessary surroundings and embellishments, it being clear that no one of these component parts was ever considered independently, the architect of the house being also the architect of the garden and the rest of the villa.[24]

In Platt's devotion to aesthetic unity, Freer would have recognized a philosophy of beauty consistent with his own ideals, which would materialize one day in the harmony of elements that distinguishes the Freer Gallery of Art.

Charles Platt, like the other American artists Freer admired, had trained as a painter in Paris. He returned to New York in 1887 and two years later accepted an invitation from a fellow artist, Henry O. Walker, to visit Cornish, New Hampshire, where Augustus Saint-Gaudens and Thomas Dewing had lately begun to spend their summers. The Cornish countryside, dominated by the stately Mount Ascutney in nearby Vermont, provided an inspiring subject for Platt to paint (fig. 175). Though inexperienced as an architect, he proceeded to design a house for Walker, then one for himself on the neighboring lot; encouraged by those successes and appealing to White for architectural advice, he built a stunning hilltop estate called High Court for his friend Annie Lazarus, which led to commissions for other Italianate villas for the summer residents of the community. Building on his experience as a painter, Platt arranged his architecture around prospects of Ascutney, so that from the porches and terraces of Cornish, landscape views were framed like paintings, with classical columns and Tuscan arches.[25]

Charles Freer may have met Charles Platt in Cornish, possibly in late July 1892, when the collector paid a brief visit to the Dewings at their summer home. Platt would then have been newly returned from his Italian tour, and tales of his travels may well have motivated Freer to make his own expedition two years later. From that time forward Freer regarded Platt as his mentor in the field of landscape design, and he warmly recommended his services at every opportunity. Frank Hecker, on Freer's advice, hired Platt to plan a garden community in the outskirts of Detroit, and under Platt's direction, Freer said, the suburb promised to be "one of the best designed and most artistically considered resident tracts" in America.[26] Because of an economic recession the scheme was never realized, but in 1898, Hecker invited Platt to collaborate with White on the family mausoleum. A few years later Freer selected Platt to design an Italian garden for the Yondotega clubhouse, home to an association of one hundred Detroit gentlemen dedicated to the pursuit of "Frivolity and Alcohol." In 1908, again on Freer's recommendation, Platt was appointed landscape architect for a proposed park in Washington, D.C., dedicated to the memory of Senator James McMillan.[27]

Platt, then, had participated in a number of important projects under Freer's discerning eye, but always as a designer of gardens and landscapes. He had long practiced domestic architecture, but his single museum-related commission had been the design in

Fig. 173. John Singer Sargent (1856–1925), *Breakfast in the Loggia*, 1910. Oil on canvas (51.5 x 71.0), 17.182.

1905 of a gallery and stairwell for the Museum of Art at the Rhode Island School of Design in Providence. Freer, therefore, may not have considered Platt in connection with the Washington building much before October 1912, when he called at the architect's New York office to discuss with him "quite fully" his own ideas about the museum.[28] During the preceding months, confined to his house while recovering from a stroke, Freer had found "plenty of time for reflection" in which to give concentrated thought to the building and the architect who might best design it.[29]

Freer spent many of the hours of his recuperation in the new art gallery in his home (see fig. 17), where he created aesthetically illuminating arrangements of objects and attempted to determine the ideal conditions for exhibiting works of art. His intention, as described to Thayer, was "to plan various rooms to suit the objects to be shown therein" before engaging an architect, who would be given Freer's sketches, then left alone to design a "simple, harmonious and suitable building." By then, Freer's scattered preferences and impressions were coalescing into a cogent mental image of the building:

Fig. 174. Thomas W. Dewing (1851–1938), *Portrait of Charles A. Platt,* 1893. Oil on canvas (30.5 x 35.5). Collection of the Platt Family.

"It will probably be two stories, quadrangular with an inner court, no dome, no big, showy halls or rooms of any kind, but with a slight preference for the best English Tudor style. However, the Italian Renaissance style of most simple lines may eventually be adopted."[30] As Freer was evidently beginning to acknowledge, the Italian Renaissance style was better suited than the Tudor to the modest museum he had in mind and more appropriate to express his aesthetic philosophy. Renaissance buildings, scaled to human proportions, are distinguished by a coherence of elements: none of their components can be added or taken away without disturbing the inherent harmony of the design.

By the beginning of the new year, Platt was already at work on preliminary designs for a building in the "Italian Renaissance style of most simple lines." In mid-January 1913 he sent Freer a floor plan showing the features of an Italian villa: a front terrace, an open courtyard, and lateral wings enclosed by gardens on two sides (fig. 176). Although Platt expressed some dissatisfaction with his work, Freer examined the sketch "with great pleasure" and took it with him to New York for further discussion.[31] On 23 April 1913, Freer and Platt met at the Plaza Hotel to revise the plan to suit the deeper lot that Platt preferred; Freer rendered their ideas on a piece of hotel stationery, specifying a two-story building with exhibition galleries on the first floor and study and storage rooms below (fig. 177). The Plaza scheme retained the lateral wings for Asian art but compressed the components of the building into the shape of a Greek cross, roughly square and centrally planned, with the courtyard visible from every point of view.

That autumn, Platt went to Detroit to review the collections, an exercise Freer considered essential to formulating final plans for the Washington building. In early November the architect could estimate the cost of the proposed museum and garden at one million dollars, twice the amount Freer had pledged for the purpose in 1904; Platt justified the expense with the explanation that although the building would not be "elaborate in detail," it would possess a "very large amount of foundation and roof in proportion to the central cube."[32] In December, motivated by the need for working plans to assist the Smithsonian in determining the site, Platt presented Freer with an elevation of what he called "The Freer Museum" (fig. 178). The drawing shows the triple-arched portico, high basement, and balustraded parapet that would remain parts of the final design; the elements Platt later rejected—the pilasters on the facade, for instance, and the ornamental festoons— were closely associated with the Renaissance-revival buildings of McKim, Mead and

Fig. 175. Charles Adams Platt (1861–1933), *The Mountain*, ca. 1900. Oil on canvas (107.0 x 137.3), 18.155.

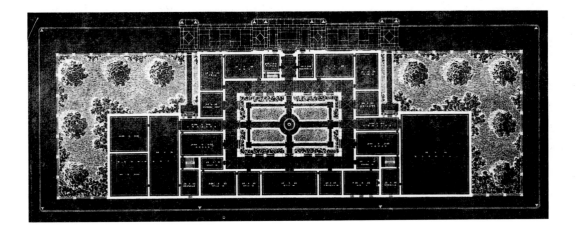

Fig. 176. "Preliminary Sketch for Mr. Freer's Museum," 18 January 1913. Charles Adams Platt (1861–1933), architect. Freer Gallery of Art Building Records.

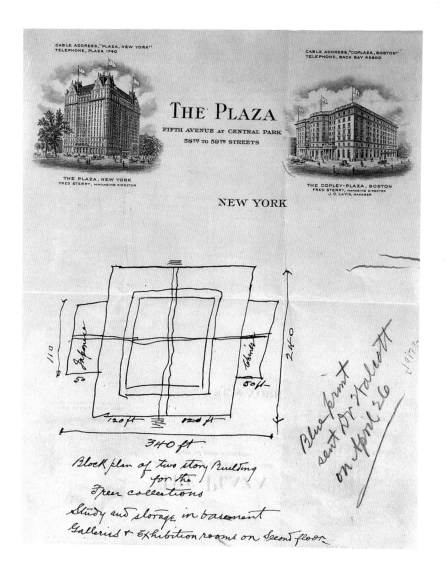

The Plaza

FIFTH AVENUE AT CENTRAL PARK
58ᵀᴴ TO 59ᵀᴴ STREETS

NEW YORK

Block plan of two story Building
for the
Freer collections
Study and storage in basement
Galleries & Exhibition rooms on Second floor

Fig. 177. Freer's plan for a
two-story building for the
collections, 1913.

White. It is safe to assume that Freer had informed Platt that his first choice of architect had been White; with that in mind, Platt may at first have deliberately designed a building that could have been the work of White himself.

The first sites considered for the museum were north of the Mall near the National Museum (now the National Museum of Natural History), but in January 1915 the Smithsonian Regents proposed an alternative location: the grounds southwest of the picturesque Smithsonian building, called the Castle, which Platt was given to understand would ultimately "be taken down."[33] Both Freer and Platt were delighted with the site, even though it meant reducing the size of the building. While Freer worked with Eugene Meyer to secure liquid assets to commit to the construction, Platt remodeled his plans to suit the new location and to incorporate the changes that Freer wanted made to the galleries, presumably to accommodate recent acquisitions. Freer had also requested that Platt render the study rooms "more important, and possibly better lighted," guidelines consistent with his original idea of a museum that showed "special regard for the convenience of students and others desirous of an opportunity for uninterrupted study."[34]

Sometime during the year it took for the Mall site to be formally approved, Platt sent Freer a new elevation of the north facade (fig. 179). The building itself appeared substantially unchanged except for the projection of the porch, expanded to include niches for sculpture on either side of the entrance, and additional basement windows, enlarged to better illuminate the study rooms on the lower level. The style of the facade had undergone a more significant transformation. For this weighty, impenetrable fortress of art designed to hold its own between the turreted Smithsonian Castle and the massive, marmoreal Department of Agriculture building to the west, Platt found inspiration in the work of Michele Sanmicheli, an architect active in northern Italy during the second quarter of the sixteenth century. Sanmicheli had worked primarily in Verona—a city much admired by Freer, who had spent a "red letter day" there on Platt's recommendation in 1894—and his fortified gateway, the Porta Nuova, was the model for the mannerist style of Platt's modified elevation.[35] To impart the appearance of strength and stability to a small and comparatively unassuming building, the architect had extended the rustication of the blocks on the facade from the basement to the frieze, using ornament to hint at the world of art protected within the walls.

Platt's drawings were complete by the third week of May 1916, when they were approved by the Smithsonian Regents and the Commission of Fine Arts, which held responsibility for developing Washington's public spaces. The final design (fig. 180) combined the graceful lines of the first elevation with the powerful mass of the second: Platt simplified the parapet above the portico, which he distinguished from the other features of the facade with an ashlar surface to create a more inviting entrance to the museum. The niches were empty of allegorical figures, and the remaining ornament was spare and elegant. A string course defined the division between floors, and the motifs of the metopes were emblems of the range of cultures represented by the collections. Blind arcades echoing the portico were superimposed on three sides of the building, with Tuscan columns suggested in the piers. Cornerstones were arranged to resemble pilasters, with acanthus capitals displaced capriciously in the frieze. The architecture was sophisti-

Fig. 178. Proposed elevation of the "Freer Museum," 15 December 1913. Charles Adams Platt (1861–1933), architect. Freer Gallery of Art Building Records.

cated and original, a modern translation of the Italian mannerist style that in effect marked the end of the American Renaissance.

In plan (fig. 181) the building reflected Freer's belief that the appreciation of beauty would be enhanced by "lack of confusion, sympathetic surroundings, and perfect opportunity to observe or study the exhibits in a proper way."[36] On the main floor were eighteen galleries and the Peacock Room, linked to one another by four connecting corridors and disposed around an open court. As Freer had envisioned, Japanese and Chinese works occupied rooms on opposite sides of the building, and roughly half the exhibition space was devoted to American art, with a sequence of rooms on the south side given entirely to works by Whistler. The galleries assigned to American art were octagonal, with ornamental cornices meant to be delicately gilded to harmonize with the picture frames; the galleries for Asian art were rectangular and unadorned.

The courtyard (fig. 182), approximately sixty feet square, was the most compelling feature of Platt's design. The architect had planned the main entrance of the museum to afford visitors a fine view of the fountain from the door, and the rooms on the gallery level were arranged so that the court would always be easily accessible. As the critic Royal Cortissoz explained, one could proceed from gallery to garden free from the distraction of intervening works of art: "If he has been absorbed in Chinese pottery, for

Fig. 179. Proposed north elevation of the "Building for the Freer Collections," ca. 1915. Charles Adams Platt (1861–1933), architect. Freer Gallery of Art Building Records.

example, and wants to go off and restfully think about it, he need not glance on his way at Egyptian glass or American painting. He can give himself up to the mood if he wants to."[37] Another hallmark of Platt's plan, which further alleviated museum fatigue, was the considerate size of the galleries. Recognizing that it would be not only impossible but "in fact, opposed to Mr. Freer's ideas, to exhibit all the Gallery's possessions at one time," Platt had designed comfortably small exhibition rooms for a limited number of objects. Serious scholars "with proper credentials" could examine works of art in the commodious study rooms downstairs.[38]

The small exhibition galleries were also proportionally narrow, demonstrating Platt's belief that "for light to fall at the proper angle the distance from the skylight to the object displayed must not be too great."[39] To test his theory, the architect had erected a full-scale model of a typical exhibition room on the roof of his Park Avenue office building, in which he placed a Chinese painting from Freer's collection. Platt shared Freer's conviction that art was best shown by natural light, and he devised a system of skylights featuring movable canvas louvers above the diffusing glass so that the amount of daylight entering each gallery could be adjusted to suit the objects on display.[40]

Ground was broken for the building in September 1916, with the hope of completing the foundation before cold weather set in. Ten days later a steam shovel began exca-

Fig. 180. Sketch of the Freer Gallery, 1920. Charles A. Platt (1861–1933), architect. U.S. Commission of Fine Arts, Washington, D.C.

Fig. 181. First-floor plan,
"Building for the Freer
Collections," ca. 1916. Freer
Gallery of Art Building Records.

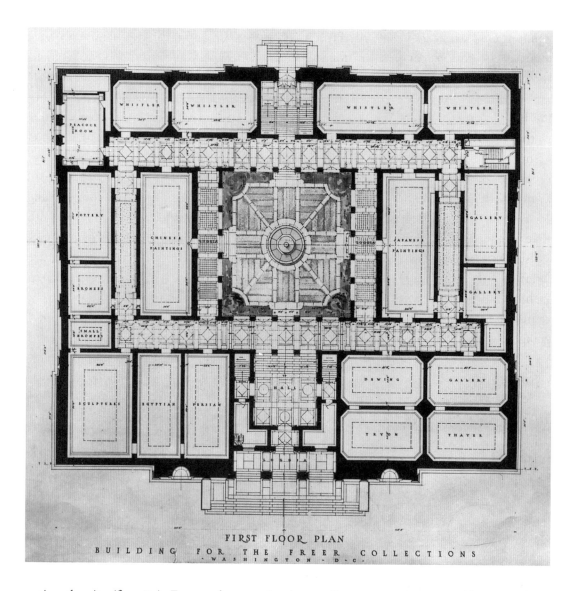

FIRST FLOOR PLAN
BUILDING FOR THE FREER COLLECTIONS
·WASHINGTON·D·C·

vating the site (fig. 183). Freer, who remained unwell, was not present at either occasion. He could not have borne with equanimity the inevitable complications involved in a major construction project, and his doctors advised him not to go to Washington until the building was complete. Perhaps as a diversion, Freer commissioned Platt to design a "summer play residence" in Great Barrington, Massachusetts, not far from his family in Kingston yet "fully twenty miles away from the fashionable center of the Berkshires and outside of all social connections of a disturbing or over-active nature." Freer's summer retreat would be built on a rocky, pine-covered promontory with a commanding view of the Berkshire hills and valleys; the fireproof "bungalow" would be equipped with safe, temporary storage for objects Freer might wish to have there for research and cataloguing, his personal preparation for the long-impending transfer of the collections to the care of the Smithsonian.[41]

From the distance of Great Barrington, Detroit, or New York, Freer kept track of the building under way in Washington. His friends faithfully reported their impressions of the work in progress, and Freer managed to maintain a surprising degree of detachment. When his physician George Draper commented on the large size of the building, Freer counseled him to "concentrate on what it will some day hold and what influence from the things within will eventually emanate," advice he seems to have taken to his own heart.[42] He did, however, direct considerable attention to certain details, such as the style of the display cases and the arrangement of objects for exhibition and storage. In consultation with the architect he decided on gallery furnishings and materials for the interior: solid oak benches, plaster walls, and floors of black and gray marble terrazzo, "which shows spots of dullness like bronze earth encrustation in small white specks."[43] On the whole, Freer deferred to Platt's preferences, writing to Agnes Meyer, "One likes being bossed by a wide-visioned master."[44]

Scarcely six months after the construction began, the United States declared war on Germany. Before long the delivery of materials—most critically the Milford granite for the exterior walls—became practically impossible: Platt wrote to Freer that there was "an

Fig. 182. Sketch of the court of the Freer Gallery, 1920. Charles Adams Platt (1861–1933), architect. U.S. Commission of Fine Arts, Washington, D.C.

absolute cordon around Washington," impeding the entry of any but war-related supplies. By the beginning of 1918, work had come to a virtual standstill.[45] That summer in Great Barrington, Freer was informed that construction was proceeding despite delays, but in September, Platt proposed stopping altogether until conditions became more favorable. Happily, that turn of events occurred with the armistice in November, and work resumed in Washington during the halcyon days of June 1919. By autumn the roof was on the building, the flooring was down, and the walls were plastered and ready for paint. But Freer, by then, was gravely ill. There was never any hope that he would make the promised trip to Washington, where the museum was standing intact on the Mall when he died in September.

The Freer Gallery of Art finally opened to the public at the beginning of May 1923 (fig. 184). A few critics objected to its Italianate style as unpatriotic, but the building's architecture was generally considered "eminently suitable" for a museum of its kind, recalling "other Lorenzos and Florentine patrons who had the touch of Maecenas."[46] The interior was widely admired for its tasteful simplicity: "The exhibits are the thing,"

Fig. 183. Steam shovel beginning excavation for the Freer Gallery, 2 October 1916. Freer Gallery of Art Building Records.

Fig. 184. The Freer Gallery of Art, ca. 1923. Freer Gallery of Art Building Records.

Cortissoz observed, "there is nothing to distract attention from them."[47] The unconventional assembly of American paintings and Asian antiquities may have mystified casual observers—as Louisine Havemeyer remarked, "It is a long step from the stone statues of the early Chinese Dynasties to the art of the nineteenth century"—but visitors more sensitive to aesthetics recognized the reasoning behind the arrangement: "One passes from the Whistler rooms with their faint suggestion of Japanese fantasy into the deeper realms of real Japanese art."[48]

It would have been difficult to ignore Whistler's importance in the scheme of the Freer Gallery. Four rooms devoted exclusively to his works made a comprehensive showing of his artistic achievement, and the celebrated Peacock Room, available for the first time to the American public, was generally regarded as the centerpiece of the museum. Indeed, Whistler's influence was so pervasive that critics named him the "high priest" of the Freer Gallery of Art, "the deity of the whole show."[49] The peacocks that paraded in the courtyard were accordingly taken as tributes to Whistler, living allusions to the gorgeous, golden birds that graced the shutters and the walls of the Peacock Room. But as symbols with a meaning more universally understood, the peacocks at the Freer represented pride in beauty. ■

Chronology, Charles Lang Freer

1854
Born in Kingston, New York, 25 February.

1873
Appointed accountant and paymaster of New York, Kingston and Syracuse Railroad by Frank J. Hecker (1846–1927).

1876
Moves to Indiana to work, with Hecker, for the Detroit and Eel River and Illinois Railroad.

1880
Moves to Detroit; with Hecker, participates in organization of the Peninsular Car Works.

1883
Becomes vice president and secretary when Peninsular Car Works is succeeded by Peninsular Car Company. Begins collecting European prints.

1884
Peninsular Car Company constructs plant on Ferry Avenue.

1887
Meets Howard Mansfield (1849–1938). Buys land on Ferry Avenue.

1889
Meets Frederick Stuart Church (1826–1900) and Dwight William Tryon (1849–1925) in New York.

1890
Commissions Wilson Eyre (1858–1944) to design house on Ferry Avenue. On first trip to London, meets James McNeill Whistler (1834–1903).

1892
Moves into Ferry Avenue house. Tryon and Thomas Wilmer Dewing (1851–1938) undertake decoration of reception rooms.

1893
Lends several American paintings to World's Columbian Exposition in Chicago. United States economic depression begins.

1894
Begins yearlong trip around the world, which includes visit to the Whistlers in Paris and first trip to Asia.

1896
Meets Matsuki Bunkyō (1867–1940) in Boston.

1899
Takes part in consolidation of railroad-car building companies, then retires from active business.

1900
Attends Exposition Internationale Universelle in Paris. Buys villa in Capri with Thomas S. Jerome.

1901
Meets Siegfried Bing (1838–1905) in Paris and Ernest Fenollosa (1853–1908), who visits Freer in Detroit.

1902
Meets Dikran Kelekian (1868–1951). Spends summer in Britain building Whistler collection; sees Whistler's *Harmony in Blue and Gold: The Peacock Room* (fig. 120).

1904
Purchases Whistler's Peacock Room. Offers to the Smithsonian Institution his art collections and funds to build a museum in which to house them.

1905
Smithsonian committee visits Freer in Detroit.

1906
Smithsonian Institution accepts Freer's gift.

1907
On second tour of Asia, meets Hara Tomitarō (1868–1939) in Yokohama, Japan.

1908
Takes third trip to Asia, specifically to West Asia to study Rakka ware.

1909
Tours Europe to study art museums. On fourth trip to Asia, attends memorial ceremony for Fenollosa (died September 1908) at Miidera, Japan, and meets Duanfang (1861–1911) in China.

1910
On last trip to Asia, visits Longmen Buddhist caves in China.

1911
Suffers stroke.

1912
Lends selection of objects for exhibition at Smithsonian Institution.

1913
Meets Eugene (1875–1957) and Agnes E. (1887–1970) Meyer. Commissions Charles Adams Platt (1861–1933) to design museum building in Washington.

1914
Meets Katharine Nash Rhoades (1885–1965) in Detroit.

1915
Settles in New York City. Site of future Freer Gallery of Art is determined.

On a rainy day in May 1930, the mayor of Kyoto and a group of distinguished guests gathered in the garden of the Kōetsu Temple to dedicate a memorial to Charles Lang Freer. Beside the rough-hewn stone that served as Freer's monument, Japanese officials placed an offering of tea and champagne.

1916
Platt's plans for Freer Gallery are approved by Smithsonian Regents and Commission of Fine Arts; ground is broken in September.

1917
United States enters World War I.

1918
After falling ill in Detroit, Freer travels to New York for treatment. Work on the museum building is delayed by the war.

1919
Freer appends codicil to will permitting acquisitions of Asian, Egyptian, and Near Eastern (West Asian) art. Dies in New York City on 25 September; is buried in Kingston. Construction of Freer Gallery is completed.

1920
John Ellerton Lodge (1876–1942) is appointed director of Freer Gallery.

1923
Freer Gallery opens to public on 2 May.

1930
Memorial ceremony for Freer is held at Kōetsu Temple, Kyoto.

Notes

Chapter One

1. Alfred Chapman to Freer, 20 October 1915.

2. Frank J. Hecker, *Activities of a Lifetime, 1864–1923* (Detroit: Privately printed, 1923), 23–26.

3. Agnes E. Meyer, "The Charles L. Freer Collection," *Arts* 12, no. 2 (August 1927): 80.

4. Freer to Dwight W. Tryon, 7 July 1907, typescript, Henry C. White Papers, Archives of American Art, Smithsonian Institution, Washington, D.C.

5. Freer to Charles J. Morse, 4 February 1903.

6. Richard Ellmann, *Oscar Wilde* (New York: Knopf, 1988), 150–211.

7. Susan Hobbs, "Detroit and Its Development in the Arts, 1824–1924," in *Artists of Michigan from the Nineteenth Century,* exhib. cat. (Michigan: Muskegon Museum of Art, 1987), 79.

8. Joseph Maberly, *The Print Collector: An Introduction to the Knowledge Necessary for Forming a Collection of Ancient Prints,* edited by Robert Hoe, Jr. (London, 1844; reprint, New York: Dodd, Mead, 1880), 13–14.

9. Howard Mansfield, "Charles Lang Freer," *Parnassus* 7, no. 5 (October 1935): 16.

10. Carel Nicolaas Storm van 's Gravesande to Freer, 29 March 1887.

11. Freer to Mansfield, 20 August 1903.

12. Freer to William K. Bixby, 7 February 1902.

13. Frederick S. Church to Freer, 15 June 1889.

14. Freer to Frank J. Hecker, 22 October 1892.

15. Tryon to Freer, 19 May 1889.

16. Freer to R. Swain Gifford, 18 April 1893.

17. Agnes E. Meyer, *Charles Lang Freer and His Gallery* (Washington, D.C.: Freer Gallery of Art, 1970), 18.

18. Freer to Tryon, 7 July 1907, typescript, Nelson C. White Papers, Archives of American Art.

19. Julia M. Angell, "Mr. Freer among His Whistlers," *Christian Science Monitor* [latter part of 1922], Freer Gallery press-cutting book 2: 30. See also Betsy Fahlman, "Wilson Eyre in Detroit: The Charles Lang Freer House," *Winterthur Portfolio* 15 (Autumn 1980): 258–59, and Thomas Brunk, " 'The House That Freer Built,' " *Dichotomy* (University of Detroit School of Architecture, Michigan) 3 (Spring 1981): 5–53.

20. Freer to William G. Mather, 28 June 1898.

21. Freer to Bixby, 10 August 1900.

22. Leila Mechlin, "The Freer Collection of Art: Mr. Charles L. Freer's Gift to the Nation, to Be Installed at Washington," *Century Magazine* 73 (January 1907): 367.

23. Freer to W. F. Lord of A. H. Davenport, 20 September 1892; to A. H. Davenport, 22 December 1895.

24. Freer to Morse, 19 August 1904.

25. Tryon to Freer, 5 March 1891.

26. Ibid., 17 April 1892.

27. Thomas W. Dewing to Freer, 15 February [1892].

28. Henry C. White, *The Life and Art of Dwight William Tryon* (Boston: Houghton Mifflin, 1930), 81.

29. Abbott H. Thayer to Freer, 29 May [1893].

30. Freer to Mansfield, 3 March 1893.

31. Thayer to Freer, 24 April 1893 (postmark) and 20 May [1893].

32. Ibid., 26 September 1893 (postmark) and 1 December 1895 (postmark).

33. Ibid., 3 May [1896].

34. J. Gray Sweeney, "Frederick Stuart Church (1842–1924)," in *Artists of Michigan,* 178.

35. Freer to Wilson Eyre, 30 December 1902.

36. Freer to Morse, 31 July 1906.

37. Annie Nathan Meyer, "Charles L. Freer, Art Collector," *New York Evening Post,* 29 September 1919, Freer Gallery press-cutting book 2: 26.

38. Freer to Tryon, 9 December 1894, typescript, Nelson C. White Papers, Archives of American Art.

39. Freer to Tryon, 20 October 1911. The Freer house now belongs to Wayne State University.

Chapter Two

1. "A Day with Whistler," *Detroit Free Press,* 30

March 1890, Whistler press-cutting book 1: 2.

2. Freer to James McNeill Whistler, 9 January 1894, Whistler F438, Glasgow University Library, Scotland.

3. "A Day with Whistler."

4. Whistler, "Mr. Whistler's 'Ten O'Clock,' " in *The Gentle Art of Making Enemies* (London: Heinemann, 1890), 144.

5. "A Day with Whistler."

6. Freer to Frank J. Hecker, from Venice, 9 October 1894.

7. Freer to H. H. Benedict, 26 November 1901.

8. "A Chat with Mr. Whistler," *Pall Mall Budget*, 13 March 1890, Whistler press-cutting book 2: 21, Glasgow University Library. The article is a reprint of "Mr. Whistler's New Etchings: A Chat with the Master," *Pall Mall Gazette*, 4 March 1890, quoted in Katharine A. Lochnan, *The Etchings of James McNeill Whistler* (New Haven: Yale University Press, 1984), 254.

9. Lochnan, *Etchings of Whistler*, 251.

10. "A Chat with Mr. Whistler."

11. Freer to Whistler, 28 April 1890, Whistler F433, Glasgow University Library.

12. William Bell (Whistler's secretary) to Freer, 6 June 1891.

13. Freer to Beatrix Whistler, 29 February 1892, Whistler F435, Glasgow University Library.

14. Freer to Thomas W. Dewing, 11 March 1903.

15. The collection of 745 etchings and 196 lithographs and lithotints includes at least one impression of all but thirty-nine of the Whistler etchings and eleven of the lithographs catalogued by E. G. Kennedy. One of the missing color lithographs, *Lady and Child* (K. 157), was acquired in 1990 for the Freer Study Collection.

16. Freer to Whistler, 31 March 1890, Whistler F432, Glasgow University Library; Freer to Beatrix Whistler, 6 May 1892, Whistler F436, Glasgow University Library.

17. Freer to Howard Mansfield, 20 September 1892.

18. Whistler to E. G. Kennedy, 10 June 1892, Edward Guthrie Kennedy Papers, Rare Books and Manuscripts Division, The New York Public Library.

19. Anna McNeill Whistler to Mr. Gamble, 10 February 1864, Whistler W516, Glasgow University Library.

20. Freer to Beatrix Whistler, 6 May 1892, Whistler F436, Glasgow University Library.

21. Whistler to Freer, 18 July 1894 (postmark).

22. Freer to Whistler, 23 September 1895, Whistler F444, Glasgow University Library.

23. Whistler to Freer, 24 March 1897 (postmark).

24. Freer to John Gellatly, 30 March 1904.

25. Freer to Emma Palmer, 17 February 1905.

26. Freer to Alfred H. Granger, 14 May 1900.

27. Freer to Mary Park, 22 March 1905. Freer's afternoon with Whistler is described in "A Day with Whistler."

28. Whistler to Freer, 29 July 1899.

29. Ibid., from Paris, 4 August 1899.

30. Whistler to Murray Marks, ca. 1872–76, Reserve Collection (Q 4, 5), Victoria and Albert Museum, London; Whistler to John J. Cowan, 6 January 1900, Whistler C240, Glasgow University Library.

31. Whistler to Freer, 29 July 1899.

32. Ibid., 10 July 1901 (postmark).

33. Ibid. (dictated to Rosalind Birnie Philip), 25 October 1901.

34. Freer to Cowan, 19 December 1901.

35. Ibid., 18 November 1901.

36. Freer to Hecker, from London, 6 May 1902.

37. Ibid., 30 May 1902.

38. Ibid., 13 June 1902.

39. Freer to Hecker, from The Hague, 17 July 1902.

40. Freer to William K. Bixby, 7 November 1900.

41. Freer to Hecker, from London, 6 May 1902.

42. Ibid., 13 June 1902.

43. Ibid., 30 May 1902.

44. Ibid., 3 June 1902.

45. Ibid., 20 June 1902.

46. Ibid., 30 May 1902.

47. Ibid., from The Hague, 4 July 1902.

48. Ibid., 30 June and 11 July 1902.

49. Telegram from Whistler to Freer, 31 July 1902.

50. Freer to Hecker, from London, 12 July 1903.

51. Ibid., 18 July 1903.

52. Ibid., 12 July 1903.

53. Freer to Cowan, 13 October 1902.

54. Freer to Alfred Chapman, 7 September 1901.

55. Cowan to Freer, 27 September 1902.

56. Freer to Cowan, 13 October 1902.

57. Freer to Whistler, 9 January 1894, Whistler F438, Glasgow University Library.

58. Freer to Gustav Mayer, 30 December 1907.

59. Freer to Frederick Keppel, 23 December 1901.

60. Royal Cortissoz, "Freer Museum Soon to Be Built in Washington," *New York Tribune*, 15 December 1915, Freer Gallery press-cutting book 3: 19.

61. Freer to August Jaccaci, 4 April 1904, August F. Jaccaci Papers, Archives of American Art, Smithsonian Institution, Washington, D.C.; Freer's diary for 1902.

62. Freer to Mrs. Herod, 3 October 1908.

63. Agnes E. Meyer, *Charles Lang Freer and His Gallery* (Washington, D.C.: Freer Gallery of Art, 1970), 5.

Chapter Three

1. In spite of his sophistication, Freer evidently retained some remnants of a provincial American accent. See Helen Nebeker Tomlinson, "Charles Lang Freer: Pioneer Collector of Oriental Art" (Ph.D. diss., Case Western Reserve University, Cleveland, 1979), vol. 4, 635.

2. Freer to Frederick Keppel, 17 September 1894.

3. *A Handbook for Travellers in India and Pakistan, Burma and Ceylon, Including the Portuguese and French Possessions and the Indian States* (London: John Murray, 1898), 471. Freer stayed at the Grand Oriental Hotel—usually referred to as the "G.O.H." by seasoned travelers—located close

to the jetty and considered one of the best, if not the best, hotels in the East.

4. Freer to Frank J. Hecker, 20 December 1894.

5. *Handbook for Travellers in India and Pakistan,* 446.

6. Freer to Hecker, 15 March 1895; Freer's diary, 23 January 1895.

7. Freer to Hecker, 5 February 1895.

8. Ibid., 18 February 1895.

9. Ibid., 30 March 1895.

10. Freer embarked on the S.S. *Chusan,* a Pacific and Orient Line Steamer bound for Colombo, then transferred to the S.S. *Preussen* for Singapore. Assuming the tone of a seasoned traveler in Asia, Freer later pronounced the ship to be "one of the 'crack' steamers of the North-German Lloyd." He was further impressed by how clean, roomy, and handsome the *Preussen* was, understandable in a ship that was making its first trip after having been rebuilt (Freer to Hecker, 15 March 1895).

11. Freer to Hecker, 20 April 1895.

12. Ibid., 28 April 1895.

13. Basil Hill Chamberlin and W. B. Mason, *A Handbook for Travellers in Japan* (London: John Murray, 1891).

14. The Golden Pavilion was destroyed by fire in 1950.

15. Gaston Migeon, *Le Caire, Le Nil et Memphis* (Paris: Librairie Renouard, 1906).

16. Freer to Hecker, 19 December 1906.

17. The covers are dated considerably later than the manuscripts, none of which antedates the late fourth or fifth century. After extensive conservation in which the leaves were separated, and subsequent preservation in a special environment of constant temperature and humidity, the parchment became more pliable.

Freer supported the publication of a series of scholarly volumes, facsimiles, and collations in the University of Michigan Studies, Humanistic Series, that established the importance of his acquisition in biblical studies. Henry A. Sanders, *The Old Testament Manuscripts in the Freer Collection,* Part 1, *The Washington Manuscript of Deuteronomy and Joshua* (New York: Macmillan, 1910), provides an excellent introduction to the manuscripts.

18. Freer to Hecker, 3 February 1907.

19. Ibid.

20. Ibid., 20 January 1907.

21. Ibid., 5 February 1907.

22. S. M. Burrows, *The Buried Cities of Ceylon: A Guide Book to Anuradhapura and Polonaruwa with Chapters on Dambulla, Kalavewa, Minintale and Sigiri* (Colombo: Ferguson, 1905). Rodrigo's dedication on the flyleaf of Freer's copy reads, "Guide Philosopher & friend to Mr. Freer. Febry 7th 1907."

23. Freer's notes in *The Buried Cities,* 31.

24. Freer to Hecker, 2 March 1907.

25. George M. Reith, *A Padre in Partibus: Being Notes and Impressions of a Brief Holiday Tour through Java, the Eastern Archipelago and Siam* (Singapore: Kelly and Walsh, 1897).

26. Isaäc Groneman, *The Hindu Ruins in the Plain of Parambanan.* Translated from the Dutch by A. Dolk (Semarang-Soerabaia: Van Dorp, 1901). For a more recent discussion of the temples at Prambanan, see A. J. Bernet Kempers, *Ancient Indonesian Art* (Cambridge: Harvard University Press, 1959), 58–62.

27. Reith, *A Padre in Partibus,* 131.

28. Isaäc Groneman, *The Tyandi-Barabudur in Central Java.* Translated from the Dutch by A. Dolk. 2d ed. (Semarang-Soerabaia: Van Dorp, 1906).

29. Freer's diary, 8 March 1907.

30. Among them, an agent of the British and Foreign Bible Society reflected, in schoolboy handwriting, "It testifies to the capabilities of the Javanese people, and if belief in such a noble man causes them to rear such edifices to his glory, what would true belief in the true Christ cause them to do for His Glory?," and an unimpressed visitor from Melbourne had written, "Loss of time. Damned monkey!" (Reith, *A Padre in Partibus,* 123–24).

31. Freer to Hecker, 11 April 1907.

32. Ibid.

33. Ernest Fenollosa to Freer, 12 March 1907.

34. Hara Tomitarō was himself an amateur artist and became an art patron. See *Kindai Nihonga no akebonoten* (Exhibition of the dawn of modern Japanese painting) (Japan, 1987), catalogue of an exhibition held on the anniversary of Hara's 120th birthday, in which some paintings and a self-portrait by Hara are illustrated.

35. For a discussion of the relationship between Freer and Hara, see Christine Guth, "A Tale of Two Collectors: Hara Tomitarō and Charles Lang Freer," *Asian Art* 4, no. 4 (Fall 1991): 29–49.

36. Freer to Hecker, 23 April 1907.

37. Ibid.

38. For information about Masuda, see Christine Guth, "Masuda Don'o: Tea and Art Collecting in the Meiji Era," *Chanoyu Quarterly: Tea and the Arts of Japan,* no. 53 (1988): 7–34. See also Guth, "Tale of Two Collectors."

39. Freer to Hecker, 6 May 1907.

40. Ibid., 30 May 1907.

41. Langdon Warner relates the story of Freer's encounter with unscrupulous Japanese dealers in his article, "The Freer Gift of Eastern Art to America," *Asia* 23, no. 8 (August 1923): 590–91.

42. Freer to Hecker, 4 and 6 May 1907.

43. Ibid., 26 May 1908.

44. Ibid., 16 May 1908. Other stories about Freer's gifts of gold watches can be found in Freer to Francis W. Kelsey, 23 May 1908; to Ali Arabi, 30 January 1909; to Ibrahim Aly, 30 January 1909.

45. Freer to Hecker, 16 May 1908.

46. Ibid., 11 June 1908.

47. The discussion of the Rakka ware collection in the Freer Gallery is based on research by Jonathan Max Bloom, " 'Raqqa' Ceramics in the Freer Gallery of Art, Washington, D.C." (Master's thesis, University of Michigan, Ann Arbor, August 1975).

48. Freer to Hecker, 3 July 1908.

49. John A. Pope, *Fourteenth-Century Blue-and-White: A Group of Chinese Porcelains in the Topkapu Sarayi Müzesi, Istanbul* (Washington, D.C.: Freer Gallery of Art, 1952).

50. Freer to Hecker, 31 July 1908.

51. Freer to Mary Fenollosa, 7 April 1909.

52. Marcel Proust, *Lettres à une amie* (Manchester, England: Editions du Calame, 1942); see also Denys Sutton, "The Lure of the Golden Bowl,"

Apollo 118, no. 258 (August 1983): 121–23.53.
Laurence Binyon, *Ma Yüan's Landscape Roll in the Freer Collection* (New York: Privately printed, 1916).

54. Freer to Hecker, 4 June 1909. For an account of Stein's career, see Jeannette Mirsky, *Sir Aurel Stein: A Biography* (Chicago: University of Chicago Press, 1977).

55. Freer to Hecker, 25 June 1909.

56. Ibid., 13 July 1909. The Sarre collection was badly damaged during the bombing of Berlin in World War II.

57. Le Coq and Grünwedel had been on three of the four German expeditions when Freer visited them in Berlin. For an excellent account of those expeditions, see Herbert Härtel, *Along the Ancient Silk Routes: Central Asian Art from the West Berlin State Museums* (New York: Metropolitan Museum of Art, 1982).

58. Freer to Migeon, 26 October 1908.

59. The contents of the collection are listed in Susan Auth, "Ancient Egyptian Glass from the Dattari Collection," *Apollo* 118, no. 258 (August 1983): 160–63. The best-known objects in the former Dattari collection are the Alexandrian coins (Giovanni Dattari, *Monete imperiali greche: Numi Augg. Alexandrini catalogo della collezione G. Dattari* [Imperial Greek coins: Coins of the Augusti in Alexandria, catalogue of the G. Dattari collection] [Cairo: Tip. dell'instituto Francese d'archeologia orientale, 1901]).

60. Cable from Walter Dennison to Freer, 1909.

61. Shortly before his death, Dennison completed the text for a monograph, *A Gold Treasure of the Late Roman Period* (New York: Macmillan, 1918); see also Thomas Lawton, "The Gold Treasure," *Apollo* 118, no. 258 (August 1983): 180–82.

62. During Freer's July meeting with Nahman in Cairo, the dealer startled Freer by offering him two thousand pounds to buy back the eight gold pieces. Nahman explained that he was trying to reassemble the Gold Treasure at the behest of a Parisian dealer who had acquired the pieces that Freer had rejected; the French dealer hoped to obtain the entire collection, which he believed to be "surely unequalled in the world." Even though Nahman's offer would have permitted Freer to recoup his original expenditure and still retain other pieces he had purchased from Nahman, at no cost, he politely declined (Freer

to Hecker, 28 July 1909).

The remaining pieces from the Gold Treasure eventually were dispersed. They were acquired by J. Pierpont Morgan, Mrs. Walter Burns, and Friedrich von Gans, whose portions are now in, respectively, the Metropolitan Museum of Art, New York; the British Museum, London; and the Antikenabteilung of the Staatliche Museen Preussischen Kulturbesitz, Berlin.

63. Freer to Hecker, 17 September 1909. For a vivid account of Nan Mingyuan and Freer's search for antiquities in Beijing, see Warner, "Freer Gift of Eastern Art to America," 590–94, 612–13.

64. In a letter to Freer from Beijing in 1913, Langdon Warner, who later became professor of Asian art history at Harvard, gave a witty account of his meeting with Nan:

There are countless people here who want to be remembered to you and anxiously ask for news of your health. Your man Nan eagerly saluted military fashion and asked, "How Misser Fleer sick?" He was delighted when I told him of your gain. He seems to be in great demand among the European dealers here, no less than three of them have introduced him to me as "my man Nan who used to be with Mr. Freer" (Warner to Freer, 24 September 1913).

65. Freer to Hecker, 17 September 1909.

66. Ibid., 19 September 1909.

67. Ibid., 27 September 1909.

68. Ibid., 11 October 1909.

69. Ibid., 18 December 1909.

70. Freer paid a portion of the costs of shipping Fenollosa's remains to Japan. See Freer to Ushikubō Daijirō, 28 December 1909.

71. Freer to Hamilton Butler, 26 May 1910.

72. Freer to Hecker, 13 October 1910.

73. In a letter of 26 May 1910, Freer had mentioned his plans to Butler, who was in the American Consular Service in Tianjin. While warning Freer of the hazards of travel to the interior of China, Butler sent him a copy of the 1909 *Journal of the North China Branch of the Royal Asiatic Society*, vol. 40, which contained a short article, "Archaeological Survey of the Environs of China's Ancient Capitals" (pp. 1–9), by Professor Vassile Alexeieff of the University of Saint Petersburg. It gives a summary archaeological survey of the country around Luoyang and

Xi'an. Freer read it carefully, making notes in the margins where points of special interest are mentioned.

74. Freer to Hecker, 23 November 1910.

75. Ibid., 18 October 1910.

76. Ibid., 24 October 1910.

77. Chavannes visited the Buddhist caves at Gong Xian on 21 July 1907; he published the photographs in 1909 (*Mission archéologique dans la Chine septentrionale,* vol. 1, pt. 1 [Paris: Ernst Leroux], nos. 399–416). Chavannes's discussion of the site and the inscriptions was published as part of the same series in 1915 (nos. 562–73). A Chinese monograph on Gong Xian, *Gong Xian shikusi* (The cave temple of Gong Xian), was published in 1963 by the Henan Province Cultural Relics Bureau (Beijing: Wenwu chubanshe, 1963).

78. Freer's Longmen notebook, 38.

79. Freer remained in good health and kept regular hours, going to bed every evening at eight-thirty and rising at five (Freer to Hecker, 21 November 1910).

80. Utai claimed that he had accompanied Chavannes to the caves in 1907 (Freer to Hecker, 24 October 1910). Chavannes makes only one reference to a Chinese photographer in the introduction to his study *Mission archéologique dans la Chine septentrionale,* vol. 1, 1913, p. 2: "Mon brave photographe Chinois, Tcheou, qui a pris sous ma direction les photographies de grand format." Chavannes refers to the photographer by his surname, Tcheou (i.e., Zhou), while Freer uses only "Utai," a rough approximation of his given name. Judging from the excellent quality of the photographs included in Chavannes's publication and those preserved in the Freer Archives, it is reasonable to assume that they were indeed taken by the same person.

81. Freer's Longmen notebook, 60; Freer to Hecker, 21 November 1910.

82. Freer to Hecker, 25 December 1910.

83. Ibid., 23 February 1911.

84. Ibid., 26 March 1911.

Chapter Four

1. For biographical information on Matsuki, see

Murakata Akiko, "Nichibi-hosi—Matsuki Bunkyō—no koto" (Bunkio Matsuki: The connoisseur priest who dedicated his life to introducing Japanese art in America), *Ukiyo-e Art* 66 (1980): 3–17.

2. Dorothy Wayman, *Edward Sylvester Morse: A Biography* (Cambridge: Harvard University Press, 1942); Peter Fetchko and Money Hickman, *Japan Day by Day: An Exhibition in Honor of Edward Sylvester Morse* (Salem: Peabody Museum of Salem, 1977).

3. Freer to Francis W. Kelsey, 8 April 1897.

4. Freer to Matsuki Bunkyō, 27 July 1897.

5. Ibid., 29 December 1898.

6. For a discussion of the importance of the "Eight Views" theme in Japan, see Richard Stanley-Baker, "Gakuō's Eight Views of Hsiao and Hsiang," *Oriental Art* 20, no. 3 (Autumn 1974): 284–303.

7. Matsuki to Freer, 17 October 1898.

8. Freer to Matsuki, 18 October 1902. Freer also wrote to Ushikubō Daijirō at Yamanaka's in New York requesting the same information. See Freer to Ushikubō, 18 and 23 October 1902.

9. Freer to Matsuki, 15 December 1904.

10. Cable from Matsuki to Freer, 17 September 1906.

11. Freer to Ernest Fenollosa, 27 September 1906.

12. Fenollosa to Freer, 19 September 1906.

13. Ibid., 25 September 1906.

14. Morse's comments are noted in folder sheets in the Freer Gallery's registrar's files.

15. Freer to Matsuki, 26 October 1908.

16. Ibid., 19 March 1909.

17. The exchange of cables is summarized in Freer to Matsuki, 25 April 1909. The disposition of the various related Tang figures is discussed in Matsuki to Freer, 26 March 1909. The comment about the sculptures' being in Hayasaki's garden is found in Osvald Sirén, *Chinese Sculpture from the Fifth to the Fourteenth Century,* vol. 1 (London: Ernest Benn, 1925), 105.

18. In 1914, Freer acquired another standing Guanyin (14.55) from the same Tower of Seven Jewels group from Edgar Worch in New York.

19. For biographical information on Kelekian, see Richard Beer, "As They Are, 'Namesake of Tigranes,'" *Art News* 32, no. 20 (17 February 1934): 11, 15; and the entry in *Les donateurs du Louvre* (Paris: Musée du Louvre, 1989), 240.

20. Beer, "As They Are," 11.

21. Dikran Kelekian to Freer, 3 February 1905.

22. Ibid., 28 March 1905.

23. Ibid., 21 May 1914.

24. Ibid., 6 April 1916.

25. Kelekian published a catalogue of his Chinese ceramics, *The Kelekian Collection of Ancient Chinese Potteries* (Chicago: Art Institute, 1917), most of which had been exhibited at the Musée des Arts Décoratifs in Paris in 1914. On the copy of the catalogue that Kelekian presented to Freer, he added an inscription, "The great Benefactor and Instructor of this Wonderful Art Charles L. Freer Esq. Respectfully Dikran Khan Kelekian Detroit November 18th 1917."

26. Freer to Frederick W. Gookin, 24 August 1917.

27. Kelekian to Freer, 20 November 1917.

28. Freer to Kelekian, 28 November 1917.

29. Frank Crowninshield, foreword, *Kelekian As the Artist Sees Him* (New York: Durand-Ruel Galleries, 1944).

30. For a detailed study of Siegfried Bing and his career, see Gabriel P. Weisberg, *Art Nouveau Bing: Paris Style 1900* (New York: Abrams, 1986).

31. For information on that circle in Paris, see Glenn D. Lowry with Susan Nemazee, *A Jeweler's Eye: Islamic Arts of the Book from the Vever Collection* (Washington, D.C.: Arthur M. Sackler Gallery in association with University of Washington Press, 1988).

32. *Objets d'art Japonais et Chinois peintures, estampes composant la collection des Goncourt* (Paris: May and Motteroz, 1897).

33. The "very old" celadon bowl (97.11), now believed to be Japanese and ascribed to Aoki Mokubei (1767–1833), is illustrated in John A. Pope, ed., *Oriental Ceramics: The World's Great Collections* (Tokyo: Kodansha, 1975), fig. 206; the unillustrated nineteenth-century Japanese piece is a Kyoto ware tea bowl (97.12).

34. *Red and White Poppies* (fig. 78) was later published in Ernest Fenollosa, *Epochs of Chinese and Japanese Art,* vol. 2 (London: Heinemann, 1912), facing 114.

35. *Objets d'art et peintures de la Chine et du Japon réunis par T. Hayashi ancien Commissaire Général du Japon a l'Exposition Universelle de 1900* (Paris, February 1903), pt. 2, lots 1585 and 1667.

36. Freer to Bing, 31 March 1903.

37. Freer to Hecker, 24 June 1903.

38. Ibid., 22 June 1903.

39. Freer to Bing, 26 August 1903.

40. *Collection Ch. Gillot, arts d'Extrême-Orient: Objets d'art et peintures du Japon et de la Chine* (Paris: Durand-Ruel Galleries, 1904).

41. Freer to Bing, 18 February 1904.

42. Ibid., 4 April 1904.

43. Gaston Migeon, *Chefs-d'oeuvre d'art Japonaise* (Paris: D. A. Longuet, 1905).

44. Freer to Bing, 20 August 1904.

45. Ibid., 14 December 1904.

46. Freer to Margaret Watson, 9 March 1905.

47. Freer to Hecker, 23 May 1905.

48. R. C. "The Passing of Siegfried Bing," *Brush and Pencil,* November 1905, 161–64.

49. Freer had acquired only one Indian painting (07.155) before he purchased Colonel Hanna's collection. That single earlier purchase, made from the New York branch of Dikran Kelekian a few weeks before Freer left the United States to begin serious negotiations with Hanna, was believed to be Persian. The painting, which depicts a Madonna and Child, is illustrated and discussed by Milo Cleveland Beach in *The Imperial Image: Paintings for the Mughal Court* (Washington, D.C.: Freer Gallery of Art, 1981), 211.

50. Henry Bathhurst Hanna, *Catalogue of Indo-Persian Pictures and Manuscripts, Principally of the Fifteenth, Sixteenth, and Seventeenth Centuries by Mughal Artists, Collected by Colonel H. B. Hanna* (London: Dowdeswell and Dowdeswells, 1890), 5.

51. Milo Cleveland Beach, "Colonel Hanna's Indian Paintings," *Apollo* 118, no. 258 (August 1983): 154–59; and Beach, *The Adventures of Rama* (Washington, D.C.: Freer Gallery of Art, 1983).

52. Hanna, *Catalogue of Indo-Persian Pictures and Manuscripts,* 5.

53. Freer to Hanna, 30 May 1907.

54. Ibid., 24 September 1907.

55. Hanna to Freer, 26 September 1907.

56. Freer to Hecker, 26 September 1907.

57. Hanna to Freer, 3 October 1907.

58. Ibid., 4 October 1907.

Chapter Five

1. Basic studies of Ernest F. Fenollosa include Van Wyck Brooks, *Fenollosa and His Circle* (New York: Dutton, 1962); Lawrence W. Chisolm, *The Far East and American Culture* (New Haven: Yale University Press, 1963); Hisatomi Mitsugu, *Fenrosa: Nihon bijutsu ni sasageita tamashii no kiroku* (Fenollosa: A record of a life devoted to Japanese art) (Tokyo: Risōsha, 1957); Yamaguchi Seiichi, *Fenrosa: Nippon bunka no senyō ni sasageita isshō (Ernest Francisco Fenollosa: A Life Devoted to the Advocacy of Japanese Culture)* (Tokyo: Sanseido, 1982).

2. Ernest Fenollosa to Edward Sylvester Morse, 27 September 1884, collection of the Phillips Library, Peabody Museum of Salem, Massachusetts.

3. Langdon Warner, "The Weld Bequest: Paintings," *Museum of Fine Arts Bulletin* 11, no. 52 (August 1911): 34-36.

4. In *The Far East and American Culture,* 170, Lawrence Chisolm states that Freer met Fenollosa in the early 1890s; in *The Proud Possessors: The Lives, Times and Tastes of Some Adventurous American Art Collectors* (New York: Random House, 1958), 135, Aline Saarinen writes that they met in 1900.

5. Freer to Howard Mansfield, 1 February 1898. Three days later, again writing to Mansfield, Freer spoke of wanting to see all of the Fenollosa collection.

6. Freer to Edward S. Hull, Jr., 26 May 1898.

7. Ibid., 3 September 1898.

8. Ibid., 30 June 1900.

9. Ernest F. Fenollosa, *Catalogue of the Exhibition of Paintings of Hokusai, Held at the Japan Fine Art Association, Ueno Park, Tokyo, from 13th to 30th January, 1900* (Tokyo: Privately printed, 1901), entry 212.

10. Freer to Hull, 31 October 1900. Once Fenollosa returned to the United States from Japan in September 1901, all correspondence between Freer and Hull ceased.

11. Fenollosa to Freer, 4 March 1901.

12. Freer to Matsuki Bunkyō, 2 March 1901.

13. Freer to Fenollosa, 23 September 1904.

14. The screen is illustrated and discussed by Fenollosa in *Catalogue of the Exhibition of Paintings of Hokusai,* 131-33.

15. Freer to Fenollosa, 11, 21, 25 February and 5 April 1902.

16. Fenollosa to Freer, 13 September 1902.

17. Ibid., 12 October 1902.

18. Ibid.

19. Ibid.

20. In 1907, in Tokyo, Freer acquired another of the paintings from the same set, *The Rock Bridge at Tiantai Mountain* (07.139). For an excellent discussion of problems relating to the entire set of paintings, see Wen Fong, *The Lohans and a Bridge to Heaven* (Washington, D.C.: Freer Gallery of Art, 1958).

21. Freer to Dwight W. Tryon, 10 February 1903.

22. An exchange of letters and telegrams in 1903 between Freer and Fenollosa regarding some Japanese paintings being offered by Matsuki and by Yamanaka and Company gives an idea of the relationship between the two men. See Seiichi. Yamaguchi, "Unpublished Letters of Ernest Francisco Fenollosa to Charles Lang Freer," *Journal of Saitama University* 13 (1979): 101-6; 15 (1981): 29-44.

23. Hayashi Tadamasa, *Collection Hayashi: Objets d'art* (Paris: Privately printed, 1903).

24. Freer to Fenollosa, 12 February 1903.

25. Ibid., 29 August 1903.

26. Fenollosa to Freer, 9 March 1903.

27. Ibid., 27 October 1904.

28. *An Exhibition of Japanese Paintings and Metalwork Lent by Mr. F. Shirasu, of Tokio, Japan, Catalogue* (Boston: Museum of Fine Arts, 1894), 10-11.

29. Freer to Charles J. Morse, 2 February 1905.

30. Telegram from Freer to Fenollosa, 24 January 1906.

31. Freer to Thomas W. Dewing, 6 February 1906.

32. Freer to Fenollosa, 6 July 1906.

33. Freer to Gaston Migeon, 17 October 1906.

34. Freer to Charles J. Morse, 7 September 1906.

35. The notebook, "Notes Taken before Mr. Freer's Collection in Detroit," is in the Rare Book Collection of the Library of the Freer Gallery of Art and Arthur M. Sackler Gallery.

36. Yoshiaki Shimizu, "An Individual Taste for Japanese Painting," *Apollo* 118, no. 258 (August 1983): 149, lists the five sets of screens.

37. In *Epochs of Chinese and Japanese Art* (London: Heinemann, 1912), vol. 2, 135, Fenollosa states that the screens were "formerly in a private collection in Sakai," a port city now located within Osaka Prefecture.

38. Fenollosa is believed to have acquired the Kōrin screens during his first visit to Kyoto in 1880 (*Asiatic Art in the Museum of Fine Arts Boston* [Boston: Museum of Fine Arts, 1982], 57).

39. Kobayashi Bunshichi to Freer, 28 June 1906.

40. Freer to Fenollosa, 18 October 1906.

41. For a catalogue of the collection, see *Copy of a Certified Catalogue of a Collection of Ancient Korean Pottery: Purchased and Owned by Horace N. Allen, U.S. Minister, Seoul, Korea* (Nak Tong: Seoul Press, 1901).

42. Freer to Frank J. Hecker, 6 May 1907.

43. Ibid., 30 May 1907.

44. Freer to Frederick J. Flagg, 13 November 1907.

45. Ernest F. Fenollosa, "The Collection of Mr. Charles L. Freer," *Pacific Era* 1, no. 2 (November 1907): 57-66.

46. Freer to Alan Chester, Fenollosa's stepson, 7 October 1908.

47. Freer to Fenollosa, 3 January 1905.

48. Fenollosa's notebook, 98.

49. Freer to Francis W. Kelsey, 24 September 1908.

50. Freer to Arthur W. Dow, 31 January 1910.

Chapter Six

1. Freer to Dwight W. Tryon, 27 July 1893.

2. Freer to Charles F. Williams, 11 August 1893.

3. Freer to Thomas W. Dewing, 6 March 1893.

4. Freer to Tryon, 27 July 1893.

5. Freer to Dewing, 19 July 1893.

6. Abbott H. Thayer to Freer, 20 May [1893].

7. Freer to Frank J. Hecker, from Florence, 17 October 1894.

8. Freer to Charles J. Morse, 16 February 1906.

9. Freer to Beatrix Whistler, 6 May 1892, Whistler F436, Glasgow University Library, Scotland.

10. Freer to William K. Bixby, 7 February 1902.

11. Freer to Howard Mansfield, 3 March 1893.

12. See Ross Anderson, *Abbott Handerson Thayer* (Syracuse, N.Y.: Everson Museum, 1982).

13. Freer to Hecker, from Venice, 7 July 1899.

14. Freer to Newman E. Montross, 4 May 1892.

15. Thayer to the curator of the Smith College Art Gallery, [1912], typescript, Nelson C. White Papers, Archives of American Art, Smithsonian Institution, Washington, D.C.

16. Freer to Tryon, 7 July 1907, typescript, Henry C. White Papers, Archives of American Art.

17. Thayer to Freer, 20 May [1893].

18. Ibid., 26 November 1918.

19. Ibid., 28 September [1908].

20. Ibid., 17 April 1914 and 29 July 1915.

21. Ibid., 20 May [1893].

22. Ibid., 31 January [1894].

23. Ibid., 20 May [1893].

24. Thayer to Mrs. William Amory and Rev. George F. Weld, undated typescript of a draft of a letter in the Nelson C. White Papers, Archives of American Art.

25. Thayer to Freer, 24 January 1913.

26. Thayer to Gladys Thayer, undated, typescript, Nelson C. White Papers, Archives of American Art.

27. Tryon to Freer, 3 September 1896.

28. Ibid., 1 May 1913. See also Linda Merrill, *An Ideal Country: Paintings by Dwight William Tryon in the Freer Gallery of Art* (Washington, D.C.: Freer Gallery of Art and University Press of New England, 1990).

29. Freer to Bixby, 5 March 1900.

30. Freer to Tryon [September 1894], typescript, Nelson C. White Papers, Archives of American Art.

31. Tryon to Freer, 7 August 1907.

32. Freer to Tryon, 3 August 1907. Freer believed that *Waterfall,* the painting he had seen in the Chishakuin temple in Kyoto, was the work of Omakitsu (Wang Wei, A.D. 697–759); it has since been reattributed to a follower of Li Tang (A.D. 1050–1130).

33. Tryon to Freer, 7 August 1907.

34. Freer to Tryon, 10 April 1893. For more about the triptych, see Kathleen Pyne, *The Quest for Unity* (Detroit: Detroit Institute of Arts, 1983), 222–24.

35. Tryon to Freer, 22 November 1899.

36. Ibid. See also Susan Hobbs, "Thomas Wilmer Dewing: The Early Years, 1851–1885," *American Art Journal* 13 (Spring 1981): 5–35.

37. Dewing to Freer, 16 February [1901].

38. Ibid.

39. Ibid. [29 June 1894].

40. Ibid., 9 August [1894].

41. Freer to Hecker, from Paris, 16 November 1894.

42. Freer to Tryon, en route to Ceylon, 9 December 1894, typescript, Nelson C. White Papers, Archives of American Art.

43. Dewing to Freer, 4 June and 12 August [1896]. Christina Miller Cocroft first raised the possibility of Emerson's inspiration in "Thomas Wilmer Dewing: The Man and His Art" (Master's thesis, George Washington University, 1971), 151.

44. Dewing to Freer, 21 December [1893]. See also Kathleen Pyne, "*Classical Figures,* A Folding Screen by Thomas Dewing," *Bulletin of the Detroit Institute of Arts* 59 (Spring 1981): 10–11.

45. The screen (96.82), described in Freer's original list as "One six-fold screen by Sōtatsu, flowers on gold background," was purchased from Matsuki Bunkyō in December 1896.

46. Dewing to Freer, 18 July [1892].

47. Freer to Dewing, 7 June 1892.

48. Freer to William A. Coffin, 2 May 1901.

49. Freer to Harrison S. Morris, 2 October 1893.

Chapter Seven

1. Freer to Rosalind Birnie Philip, 28 January 1904.

2. Whistler to Frederick R. Leyland [ca. 30 October 1876], Whistler L109, Glasgow University Library, Scotland.

3. Freer to William Burrell, 20 August 1903.

4. Freer to Gustav Mayer, 27 January 1904; to Philip, 28 January 1904.

5. Philip to Freer, 11 February 1904; Freer to Philip, 7 March 1904.

6. Freer to Philip, 22 July 1918.

7. Freer to Richard A. Canfield, 7 September 1904.

8. Freer to Dwight W. Tryon, 7 July 1907, typescript, Henry C. White Papers, Archives of American Art, Smithsonian Institution, Washington, D.C.

9. Freer to Philip, 24 January 1905.

10. Freer to Samuel P. Langley, 27 December 1904.

11. Freer to John Caldwell, 9 November 1898.

12. Freer to James McMillan, 6 February 1900.

13. Tryon to Freer, 14 July 1900.

14. Charles Moore to Freer, 19 November 1902.

15. Freer to Moore, 19 August 1903.

16. Freer to Langley, 27 December 1904.

17. Freer to Mayer, 26 January 1904.

18. Freer to Canfield, 8 April 1904 and 19 August 1907.

19. Freer to Tryon, 10 February 1903.

20. Ernest F. Fenollosa, "The Place in History of Mr. Whistler's Art," *Lotus* (December 1903): 16.

21. Freer to John Gellatly, 30 March 1904.

22. Ernest F. Fenollosa, "The Collection of Mr. Charles L. Freer," *Pacific Era* 1, no. 2 (November 1907): 62.

23. Leila Mechlin, "The Freer Collection of Art: Mr. Charles L. Freer's Gift to the Nation, to Be Installed at Washington," *Century Magazine* 73 (January 1907): 357.

24. Freer to Langley, 27 December 1904 and 18 January 1905.

25. Freer to Tryon, 6 February 1905.

26. Freer to Langley, 18 January 1905.

27. Fenollosa, "Collection of Freer," 59.

28. Freer to Rabbi Fleischer, 3 February 1905.

29. Freer to Charles J. Morse, 28 January 1905.

30. Ibid., 7 February 1905.

31. Ibid., 8 February 1905; Charles Moore, *Washington Past and Present* (New York: Century, 1929), 224.

32. Freer to Philip, 10 March 1905.

33. Freer to Morse, 8 March 1905.

34. Freer to Fenollosa, 10 April 1905; to Thomas S. Jerome, 23 December 1905.

35. Moore to Theodore Roosevelt, 1 November 1905, copy enclosed in a letter to Freer, 2 November 1905; Roosevelt to Freer, 6 December 1905.

36. Freer to Roosevelt, 14 December 1905.

37. Freer to Jerome, 23 December 1905.

38. Freer to Truman H. Newberry, 30 December 1905.

39. Marian Bell Fairchild to Freer, 6 January 1906, and enclosed press cutting, "The Freer Collection," (Washington) *Evening Star,* 3 January 1906.

40. Roosevelt to Chief Justice Melville W. Fuller, 19 December 1906, reprinted in "President Is Earnest," *Detroit Free Press,* 30 December [1905], Freer Gallery press-cutting book 3: 10.

41. Gari Melchers to Corinne Melchers, 28 February 1908, Belmont, The Gari Melchers Memorial Gallery, Fredericksburg, Virginia.

42. Charles D. Lanier to Gari Melchers, March 1908, Belmont.

43. Freer to Gari Melchers, 19 March 1908, Belmont.

44. Freer to Frank J. Hecker, 3 February 1907.

45. Fenollosa, "Collection of Freer," 62; Mechlin, "Freer Collection," 359.

46. Freer to Hecker, 3 February 1907.

47. Freer to Maurice Nahman, 27 October 1908.

48. Mechlin, "Freer Collection," 358.

49. Freer to Willard L. Metcalf, 23 July 1917. William H. Truettner discusses the Evans gift in "William T. Evans, Collector of American Paintings," *American Art Journal* 3 (Fall 1971): 57.

50. Lloyd Goodrich, *Winslow Homer* (New York: Whitney Museum of American Art and Macmillan, 1945), 188; Freer to Roland Knoedler, 17 January 1908.

51. William Innes Homer and Lloyd Goodrich, *Albert Pinkham Ryder: Painter of Dreams* (New York: Abrams, 1989), 234.

52. Freer to Walter P. Fearon of Cottier and Company, 7 April 1908.

53. Agnes E. Meyer, "The Charles L. Freer Collection," *Arts* 12, no. 2 (August 1927): 67, 69.

54. Freer's diary, 14 June 1903. Thanks are extended to Mary Crawford Volk for verifying that Sargent registered to copy Velázquez paintings in the Prado on 12 June 1903.

55. Freer to Metcalf, 23 July 1917.

56. Metcalf to Freer, 15 July 1918.

57. Freer to Metcalf, 22 November 1918.

58. Freer to F. O. Yardley, 17 April 1909; Percy Moore Turner to Freer, 26 June 1919.

59. Freer to Philip, 25 August 1919.

60. Meyer, "Freer Collection," 81.

61. First Codicil to the Last Will and Testament of Charles Lang Freer, 4 May 1919, in *Material Papers Relating to the Freer Gift and Bequest* (Washington, D.C.: Smithsonian Institution, 1928), 14.

62. Freer to Langley, 18 January 1905.

Chapter Eight

1. Freer to Thomas S. Jerome, 12 June 1911.

2. For details of Freer's illness, see Helen Nebeker Tomlinson, "Charles Lang Freer: Pioneer Collector of Oriental Art" (Ph.D. diss., Case Western Reserve University, Cleveland, 1979), vol. 4, 587–93.

3. C. T. Loo, preface, *An Exhibition of Chinese Archaic Jades Arranged for Norton Gallery of Art, West Palm Beach, Florida* (New York: Gallery Press, 1950). The jade tiger plaque (Musée Guimet, Paris, MG. 18437) is reproduced in color in Hayashi Mínao, *Chūgoku bijutsu* (Chinese art) (Tokyo: Kodansha, 1973), pl. 103c.

4. In 1912, Berthold Laufer (1874–1934) published *Jade, A Study in Chinese Archaeology and Religion,* Publication 154, Anthropological Series, vol. 10 (Chicago: Field Museum of Natural History), one of the first serious studies of Chinese jade in a Western language. The book was widely accepted by Western specialists as the definitive statement on the subject and remained so for many years. Indicating how little was then known about early Chinese jade, Laufer devoted the first chapter of his book to his theory that China did not experience a Neolithic period.

5. For example, see *Liangzhu wenhua yuqi* (Jades of the Liangzhu culture) (Hong Kong: Wenwu chubanshe, 1989), pls. 6, 112, 115, 128–130, 237.

6. *Taozhai guyutu* (Ancient jade in the Tao Studio illustrated), *juan* 2: 84a–85a.

7. Laufer, *Jade,* pl. IX, 40–44.

8. *The Great Bronze Age of China* (New York: Metropolitan Museum of Art, 1980), 90–91, 107.

9. Seaouke Yue to Freer, 12 November 1917.

10. Freer became interested in Japanese paintings in 1892 when he saw several examples owned by Howard Mansfield. See Howard Mansfield, "Charles Lang Freer," *Parnassus* 7, no. 5 (October 1935): 16.

11. Dwight W. Tryon to Freer, 20 February 1897.

12. Freer to Mary K. Williams, 4 March 1901.

13. Freer to Richard A. Rice, 14 March 1905.

14. Freer to Julian H. Harris, 16 February 1906.

15. *Exhibition of Oriental and American Art* (Ann Arbor: Alumni Memorial Committee and Ann

Arbor Art Association, 1910).

16. Fenollosa quoted in ibid., 6.

17. Laurence Binyon, *Painting in the Far East: An Introduction to the History of Pictorial Art in Asia, Especially China and Japan* (New York: Longman's, Green, 1908), 184.

18. Ushikubō Daijirō to Freer, 4 August 1905.

19. Berthold Laufer, *Catalogue of a Selection of Art Objects from the Freer Collection Exhibited in the New Building of the National Museum* (Washington, D.C.: Smithsonian Institution, 1912).

20. Herbert A. Giles, *An Introduction to the History of Chinese Pictorial Art* (Shanghai: Kelly and Walsh, 1908); and Friedrich Hirth, *Scraps from a Collector's Note Book* (Leiden: Oriental Printing Office, 1905).

21. *Philadelphia Enquirer,* April 21, 1912.

22. *Chinese, Corean and Japanese Potteries: Descriptive Catalogue of a Loan Exhibition of Selected Examples* (New York: Japan Society, 1914).

23. Ibid., 113–14.

24. Translation by Edward Kamens in his *Word in Flower* (New Haven: Yale University Art Gallery, 1989), 31.

25. S. C. Bosch-Reitz, *Catalogue of an Exhibition of Early Chinese Pottery and Sculpture* (New York: Metropolitan Museum of Art, 1916).

26. *Kaogu tongxun* (Archaeology communication) 3 (1955): 34–44; *Gugong bowuyuan yuankan* (Palace Museum bulletin) 2 (1960): 43–60. (See illustration above.)

27. *Wenwu* (Cultural relics) 9 (1989): 72, fig. 21.

28. Freer to Dikran Kelekian, 28 November 1917.

29. Frederick William Gookin, *Catalogue of a Loan Exhibition of Ancient Chinese Paintings, Sculptures and Jade Objects from the Collection Formed by Charles Lang Freer and Given by Him to the Nation through the Smithsonian Institution* (Chicago: Art Institute, 1917). At approximately the same time, in 1915 or 1916, Gookin also prepared a descriptive catalogue of the Japanese paintings in Freer's collection. In letters to Freer, Gookin expresses his concern about questions of authenticity, recognizing the need to change some of the attributions Fenollosa had published in *Epochs of Chinese and Japanese Art,* 2 vols.

Seated Bodhisattva, China, Northern Qi dynasty, dated A.D. 575. Stone. Palace Museum, Beijing (from *Gugong bowuyuan yuankan,* fig. 43). The features of this piece are remarkably similar to those on the Seated Bodhisattva (see fig. 154), particularly in the modeling of the drapery and the bas-relief ornamentation on the base. The Bodhisattva is inscribed with a date that corresponds to A.D. 575.

(London: Heinemann, 1912). Freer was amenable to Gookin's proposed changes, but as the work progressed he decided to delay publication because of problems of authenticity, thereby avoiding any position that later might have to be given up. The manuscript was never published.

30. Quoted in Gookin, *Catalogue of a Loan Exhibition of Ancient Chinese Paintings,* 12.

31. Ishii Kikujirō was the Japanese signatory to the Ishii-Lansing Treaty, for which American Secretary of State Robert Lansing (1864–1928) represented the United States. The treaty, which recognized Japan's special interests in China, was interpreted in Japan as granting extraterritorial rights in China. The treaty was abrogated at a conference held in Washington, D.C., in 1923.

Chapter Nine

1. Gertrude Read to her uncle, Professor Richard A. Rice, ca. 23 May 1923, copy presented to the Freer Gallery in 1942, Freer Gallery of Art Central Files Records.

2. Freer to Samuel P. Langley, 27 December 1904.

3. Freer to Alfred Chapman, 6 February 1906.

4. Freer to Senator Russel A. Alger, 4 January 1906.

5. Charles D. Walcott to Freer, 13 April 1908.

6. Freer to Walcott, 21 April 1908.

7. Freer to Wilson Eyre, 10 January 1906.

8. Charles Moore to Theodore Roosevelt, 1 November 1905, copy enclosed in a letter to Freer, 2 November 1905.

9. Freer to Augustus Saint-Gaudens, 26 February 1906.

10. Freer to Charles F. McKim, telegram dated 25 June 1906 but probably sent the next day.

11. Freer to Abbott H. Thayer, 12 August 1912.

12. Ernest Fenollosa, "Notes Taken before Mr. Freer's Collection in Detroit," unpublished manuscript, Rare Book Collection, Library of the Freer Gallery of Art and Arthur M. Sackler Gallery. I am grateful to Thomas Lawton for drawing my attention to this notebook.

13. Freer to Walcott, 21 April 1908.

14. Freer to J. J. Albright, 20 October 1902; to Charles M. Kurtz, Albright Gallery, 20 October 1905.

15. Freer to Thayer, 12 August 1912.

16. Freer to Frank J. Hecker, from Berlin, 8 July 1909.

17. Freer to Charles A. Platt, 26 July 1913.

18. Freer to Hecker, from Berlin, 8 July 1909.

19. Ibid., from London, 12 and 26 June 1909.

20. Freer to Rosalind Birnie Philip, 22 July 1918, Whistler F528, Glasgow University Library, Scotland.

21. Freer to Hecker, from London, 19 June 1909.

22. Ibid., 26 June 1909.

23. Freer to Thomas S. Jerome, 17 November 1900.

24. Charles A. Platt, "Italian Gardens," *Harper's New Monthly Magazine* 87 (July 1893): 166. Keith N. Morgan is editor of a recent republication of Platt's *Italian Gardens* (New York: Saga Press, 1992).

25. See Keith N. Morgan, "Charles A. Platt's Houses and Gardens in Cornish, New Hampshire," *Antiques* 122 (July 1982): 117–29,

and John H. Dryfhout, "The Cornish Colony," in *A Circle of Friends: Art Colonies of Cornish and Dublin* (Durham, N.H.: University Art Galleries, University of New Hampshire, 1985), 33–58.

26. Freer to William Mather, 28 June 1898.

27. Keith N. Morgan, *Charles A. Platt: The Artist as Architect* (Cambridge: Architectural History Foundation and MIT Press, 1985), 242; Freer to Emory W. Clark, 25 November 1916.

28. Freer to Thayer, 15 October 1912.

29. Ibid., 12 August 1912.

30. Ibid.

31. Freer to Platt, 24 January 1913.

32. Platt to Freer, 3 November 1913.

33. Platt, notes on the Freer Gallery, 1920, typescript, Commission of Fine Arts, Washington, D.C.

34. Platt to Freer, 14 July 1915; Freer to Langley, 27 December 1904.

35. Freer to Hecker, from Venice, 9 October 1894. For a fuller discussion of Platt's design, see Keith N. Morgan, "The Patronage Matrix: Charles A. Platt, Architect, Charles L. Freer, Client," *Winterthur Portfolio* 17 (Summer/Autumn 1982): 131–34.

36. Freer to Dwight W. Tryon, 21 August 1901.

37. Royal Cortissoz, "Freer Museum Soon to Be Built in Washington, *New York Tribune,* 5 December 1915, Freer Gallery press-cutting book 3: 19.

38. Platt, notes on the Freer Gallery.

39. Platt to Freer, 14 December 1917.

40. Platt, notes on the Freer Gallery.

41. Freer to Philip, 22 July 1918, from Great Barrington, Whistler F528, Glasgow University Library. For more information on the Great Barrington commission and a photograph of Freer's bungalow, see Morgan, "Patronage Matrix," 129–31.

42. Freer to George Draper, 15 October 1917.

43. Freer's notes on a meeting with Platt at the Saint Regis Hotel, New York, 28 May 1918.

44. Freer to Agnes E. Meyer, 26 August 1917, Papers of Agnes E. Meyer (15), Manuscripts Division, Library of Congress, Washington, D.C.

45. Platt to Freer, 14 February 1918.

46. "Freer Gift Contains Superb Collection," *Commercial Appeal* (Memphis, Tennessee), 5 October 1919, Freer Gallery press-cutting book 3: 22; Brainerd Bliss Thresher, "Charles Lang Freer and His Art Collection," *Asia* 19 (December 1919): 1203.

47. Royal Cortissoz, "The Freer Gallery of Art," *New York Tribune,* 6 May 1923, Freer Gallery press-cutting book 3: 38.

48. Louisine W. Havemeyer, "The Freer Museum of Oriental Art," *Scribner's Magazine* 73 (May 1923): 529; Elizabeth K. Phelps Stokes, "Art Gems in Rich Setting at Capital," *New York Evening Post,* 7 May 1923, Freer Gallery press-cutting book 3: 33.

49. John R. M. Taylor, "The Freer Gallery," *Boston Evening Transcript,* 5 May 1923, Freer Gallery press-cutting book 3: 29; "The New Freer Gallery as a Test of Taste," *Literary Digest* 77 (2 June 1923): 32.

Atil, Esin. *Ceramics from the World of Islam.* Washington, D.C.: Freer Gallery of Art, 1973.

————. *The Brush of the Masters: Drawings from Iran and India.* Washington, D.C.: Freer Gallery of Art, 1978.

Atil, Esin, W. T. Chase, and Paul Jett. *Islamic Metalwork in the Freer Gallery of Art.* Washington, D.C.: Freer Gallery of Art, 1985.

Auth, Susan H. "Ancient Egyptian Glass from the Dattari Collection." *Apollo* 118, no. 258 (August 1983): 160–63.

Beach, Milo C. *The Imperial Image: Paintings for the Mughal Court.* Washington, D.C.: Freer Gallery of Art, 1981.

————. *The Adventures of Rama.* Washington, D.C.: Freer Gallery of Art, 1983.

————. "Colonel Hanna's Indian Paintings." *Apollo* 118, no. 258 (August 1983): 154–59.

Binyon, Laurence. *Ma Yüan's Landscape Roll in the Freer Collection.* New York: Privately printed, 1916.

Bloom, Jonathan Max. " 'Raqqa' Ceramics in the Freer Gallery of Art, Washington, D.C." Master's thesis, University of Michigan, Ann Arbor, August 1975.

Brunk, Thomas. " 'The House That Freer Built.' " *Dichotomy* (University of Detroit School of Architecture, Michigan) 3 (Spring 1981): 5–53.

Cahill, James F. *Chinese Album Leaves in the Freer Gallery of Art.* Tokyo: Benrido, 1961.

Chisolm, Lawrence W. *The Far East and American Culture.* New Haven: Yale University Press, 1963.

Clark, Nichols. "Charles Lang Freer: An American Aesthete in the Gilded Era." *American Art Journal* 11 (October 1979): 54–68.

Cort, Louise Allison. *Seto and Mino Ceramics.* Vol. 1 of *Japanese Collections in the Freer Gallery of Art.* Washington, D.C.: Freer Gallery of Art and University of Hawaii Press, 1992).

Curry, David Park. "Charles Lang Freer and American Art." *Apollo* 118, no. 258 (August 1983): 169–79.

————. *James McNeill Whistler at the Freer Gallery of Art.* New York: Norton and Freer Gallery of Art, 1984.

Dennison, Walter. *A Gold Treasure of the Late Roman Period.* New York: Macmillan, 1918.

Ettinghausen, Richard. *Ancient Glass in the Freer Gallery of Art.* Washington, D.C.: Freer Gallery of Art, 1962.

Fenollosa, Ernest F. "The Collection of Mr. Charles L. Freer." *Pacific Era* 1, no. 2 (November 1907): 57–66.

Fong, Wen. *The Lohans and a Bridge to Heaven.* Washington, D.C.: Freer Gallery of Art, 1958.

Fu, Shen, Glenn Lowry, and Ann Yonemura. *From Concept to Context: Approaches to Asian and Islamic Calligraphy.* Washington, D.C.: Freer Gallery of Art, 1986.

Guest, Grace Dunham. *Shiraz Painting in the Sixteenth Century.* Washington, D.C.: Freer Gallery of Art, 1949.

Guth, Christine. "A Tale of Two Collectors: Hara Tomitarō and Charles Freer." *Asian Art* 4, no. 4 (Fall 1991): 29–49.

Havemeyer, Louisine W. "The Freer Museum of Oriental Art." *Scribner's Magazine* 73 (May 1923): 529–40.

Hayward, Mary Ellen. "The Influence of the Classical Oriental Tradition on American Painting." *Winterthur Portfolio* 14 (Summer 1979): 107–42.

Hobbs, Susan. "A Connoisseur's Vision." *American Art Review* 4 (August 1977): 76–101.

————. "The Little Known Side of One Great American Collector." *Smithsonian* 7 (January 1977): 50–57.

————. *The Whistler Peacock Room.* Washington, D.C.: Freer Gallery of Art, 1980.

————. "Whistler at the Freer Gallery of Art." *Antiques* 120 (November 1981): 1194–1202.

Lawton, Thomas. *Chinese Figure Painting.* Washington, D.C.: Freer Gallery of Art, 1973.

————. "A Group of Early Western Chou Period Bronze Vessels." *Ars Orientalis* 9 (1975): 111–21.

————. "The Sixtieth Painting: An Ancient Theme Reidentified." *National Palace Museum Quarterly* 11, no. 1 (1976): 17–36.

————. *Chinese Art of the Warring States Period: Change and Continuity, 480–222 B.C.* Washington, D.C.: Freer Gallery of Art, 1982.

————. "China's Artistic Legacy." *Apollo* 118, no. 258 (August 1983): 127–35.

————. "The Gold Treasure." *Apollo* 118, no. 258 (August 1983): 80–82.

Lawton, Thomas, and Hin-cheung Lovell. *Eugene and Agnes E. Meyer Memorial Exhibition.* Washington, D.C.: Freer Gallery of Art, 1971.

Lippe, Aschwin. *The Freer Indian Sculptures.* Washington, D.C.: Freer Gallery of Art, 1970.

Louie, Richard. *Freer Gallery of Art.* Washington, D.C.: Freer Gallery of Art, 1983.

Mansfield, Howard. "Charles Lang Freer." *Parnassus* 7, no. 5 (October 1935): 16–18.

Mechlin, Leila. "The Freer Collection of Art: Mr. Charles L. Freer's Gift to the Nation, to Be Installed at Washington." *Century Magazine* 73 (January 1907): 357–68.

Merrill, Linda. *A Pot of Paint: Aesthetics on Trial in "Whistler v. Ruskin."* Washington, D.C.: Smithsonian Institution Press and Freer Gallery of Art, 1992.

————. *An Ideal Country: Paintings by Dwight William Tryon in the Freer Gallery of Art.* Washington, D.C.: Freer Gallery of Art and University Press of New England, 1990.

Merrill, Linda, and Sarah Ridley. *The Princess and the Peacocks; or, The Story of the Room.* New York: Hyperion Books for Children and Freer Gallery of Art, 1993.

Meyer, Agnes E. "The Charles Lang Freer Collection." *Arts* 12, no. 2 (August 1927): 65–82.

————. *Charles Lang Freer and His Gallery.* Washington, D.C.: Freer Gallery of Art, 1970.

Morey, Charles Rufus. *Early Christian Paintings in the Freer Collection.* University of Michigan Studies, Humanistic Series, vol. 12. Ann Arbor: University of Michigan, 1914.

Morgan, Keith N. "The Patronage Matrix: Charles A. Platt, Architect, Charles L. Freer, Client." *Winterthur Portfolio* 17 (Summer/Autumn 1982): 121–34.

Pope, John Alexander. *Ming Porcelains in the Freer Gallery of Art.* Washington, D.C.: Freer Gallery of Art, 1953.

Pope, John Alexander, et al. *The Freer Chinese Bronzes.* Washington, D.C.: Freer Gallery of Art, 1967.

Pope, John A., and Thomas Lawton. *The Freer Gallery of Art: China.* Vol. 1. Tokyo: Kodansha, 1972.

Rhoades, Katharine Nash. "An Appreciation of Charles Lang Freer." *Ars Orientalis* 2 (1957): 1–4.

Saarinen, Aline. *The Proud Possessors: The Lives, Times and Tastes of Some Adventurous American Art Collectors.* New York: Random House, 1958.

Sanders, Henry A. *The Old Testament Manuscripts in the Freer Collection.* Part 1, *The Washington Manuscript of Deuteronomy and Joshua.* University of Michigan Studies, Humanistic Series, vol. 8, pt. 1. New York: Macmillan, 1910.

————. *A Facsimile of the Washington Manuscript of Deuteronomy and Joshua in the Freer Collection.* Ann Arbor: University of Michigan, 1910.

————. *Facsimile of the Washington Manuscript of the Four Gospels in the Freer Collection.* Ann Arbor: University of Michigan, 1912.

————. *The New Testament Manuscripts in the Freer Collection.* Part 1, *The Washington Manuscript of the Four Gospels.* University of Michigan Studies, Humanistic Series, vol. 9, pt. 1. New York: Macmillan, 1912.

————. *The Old Testament Manuscripts in the Freer Collection.* Part 2, *The Washington Manuscript of the Psalms.* University of Michigan Studies, Humanistic Series, vol. 8, pt. 2. New York and London: Macmillan, 1917.

————. *The New Testament Manuscripts in the Freer Collection.* Part 2, *The Washington Manuscript of the Epistles of Paul.* University of Michigan Studies, Humanistic Series, vol. 9, pt. 2. New York and London: Macmillan, 1918.

Shimizu, Yoshiaki. "An Individual Taste for Japanese Painting." *Apollo* 118, no. 258 (August 1983): 136–49.

Stern, Harold P. *Hokusai: Paintings and Drawings in the Freer Gallery of Art.* Washington, D.C.: Freer Gallery of Art, 1960.

————. *Ukiyo-e Painting.* Washington, D.C.: Freer Gallery of Art, 1973.

Stern, Harold P., and Thomas Lawton. *The Freer Gallery of Art: Japan.* Vol. 2. Tokyo: Kodansha, 1972.

Stubbs, Burns A. *Paintings, Pastels, Drawings, Prints, and Copper Plates by and attributed to American and European Artists, together with a List of Original Whistleriana, in the Freer Gallery of Art.* Freer Gallery of Art Occasional Papers, vol. 1, no. 2. Washington, D.C.: Freer Gallery of Art, 1967.

Sutton, Denys. "The Lure of the Golden Bowl." *Apollo* 118, no. 258 (August 1983): 118–26.

Swain, George R. *Photographs of the Washington Manuscript of the Psalms in the Freer Collection.* Ann Arbor: University of Michigan, 1919.

Tomlinson, Helen Nebeker. "Charles Lang Freer: Pioneer Collector of Oriental Art." 4 vols. Ph.D. diss., Case Western Reserve University, Cleveland, 1979.

Vikan, Gary. "Byzantine Art as a Mirror of Its Public." *Apollo* 118, no. 258 (August 1983): 164–67.

Warner, Langdon. "The Freer Gift of Eastern Art to America." *Asia* 23, no. 8 (August 1923): 590–94, 612–13.

Wenley, Archibald G., John Ellerton Lodge, and John A. Pope. *A Descriptive and Illustrative Catalogue of Chinese Bronzes Acquired during the Administration of John Ellerton Lodge.* Washington, D.C.: Freer Gallery of Art, 1946.

Yonemura, Ann. *Japanese Lacquer.* Washington, D.C.: Freer Gallery of Art, 1979.

————. "Korean Art in the Freer Gallery of Art." Number 5 in a series of articles titled "Korean Art in Western Collections." *Korean Culture* 4, no. 2 (June 1983): 5–15.

————. "A Pioneer Collection of Korean Art." *Apollo* 118, no. 258 (August 1983): 150–53.